Supporting Staged Intimacy

Supporting Staged Intimacy: A Practical Guide for Theatre Creatives, Managers, and Crew examines the relationship between staged intimacy, intimacy direction, and those supporting the process during pre-production, rehearsal, and performance.

First, this book addresses challenges and trends in staging intimacy, helping backstage and offstage theatre artists recognize the problematic approaches and culture that led to the emerging field of intimacy direction. This text will then provide tools and recommended practices for supporting the creation and maintaining of staged intimacy, enabling team members to enact contemporary protocols concerning advocacy and agency. Finally, this book will educate and empower readers with the necessary skills to prompt change; by providing modern techniques, essential workplace protocols, and achievable action items, this book will transform the way theatre designers, managers, crew, and other creative team members engage with theatrical consent.

Supporting Staged Intimacy is written for every pre-professional and professional artist working behind the scenes who wishes to better support consensual workplaces, physically intimate stories, and the individuals telling those stories.

Alexis Black is an Assistant Professor of Acting and Movement at Michigan State University, an AEA actor, a fight director and movement specialist for regional, international and Broadway productions, and a certified intimacy director and guest lecturer with Intimacy Directors and Coordinators.

Tina M. Newhauser is a theatre professional with over 30 years' experience in theatre management, production, and design. She is Head of the BFA Stage Management program at Michigan State University and guest lecturer for Intimacy Directors and Coordinators, co-teaching workshops on notices and casting, and stage managing intimacy.

Supporting Staged Intimacy

A Practical Guide for Theatre Creatives, Managers, and Crew

Alexis Black and Tina M. Newhauser

NEW YORK AND LONDON

Cover Designed by Eloy Gómez Orfila. Theatre image by Gizmo/Getty Images; Two Men About to Kiss by Joshua Mcknight/Pexels

First published 2023
by Routledge
605 Third Avenue, New York, NY 10158

and by Routledge
4 Park Square, Milton Park, Abingdon, Oxon, OX14 4RN

Routledge is an imprint of the Taylor & Francis Group, an informa business

© 2023 Alexis Black and Tina M. Newhauser

The right of Alexis Black and Tina M. Newhauser to be identified as authors of this work has been asserted in accordance with sections 77 and 78 of the Copyright, Designs and Patents Act 1988.

All rights reserved. No part of this book may be reprinted or reproduced or utilised in any form or by any electronic, mechanical, or other means, now known or hereafter invented, including photocopying and recording, or in any information storage or retrieval system, without permission in writing from the publishers.

Trademark notice: Product or corporate names may be trademarks or registered trademarks, and are used only for identification and explanation without intent to infringe.

ISBN: 9781032072395 (hbk)
ISBN: 9781032072081 (pbk)
ISBN: 9781003206064 (ebk)

DOI: 10.4324/9781003206064

Typeset in Goudy
by KnowledgeWorks Global Ltd.

*To those bringing intention and compassion to vulnerable work.
And for all the intimacy pirates, sailing the five C's...*

Contents

	Foreword	viii
	Acknowledgments	x
	Introduction: Intentional beginnings	1
1	Fundamentals of staged intimacy	14
2	Creating a culture of consent	62
3	The pre-production process: Laying the groundwork	96
4	In rehearsal: Consensual crafting	139
5	Technical and dress rehearsals: Collaborating with care	186
6	Running the show: Continuity and closure	207
	Appendix A: Intimacy organizations	233
	Appendix B: Practice scenarios	235
	Appendix C: Partial guide to desexualized language	238
	Appendix D: Checklists for staging intimacy	240
	Appendix E: Glossary of key terms	246
	Appendix F: A partial list of pertinent resources	253
	Index	259

Foreword

What was once a niche idea, the practice of intimacy direction, has recently and quickly moved to center stage, demanding attention and change in the creative industries. The foundations of intimacy direction have revolutionized how we think about consent and body autonomy in the arts. They support creative practices that dismiss urgency in favor of advocacy and collaboration and lead us towards a more inclusive future. This future is one where all artists are invited to the table with the understanding that their boundaries and needs will be respected. While these concepts have been popularized through the development and integration of the role of the intimacy director or choreographer, when they are discussed exclusively within this context, we miss out on an opportunity to inject consensual collaboration throughout the entire creative process.

As the CEO of Intimacy Directors and Coordinators, I try to return regularly to our organization's mission: "to equip every institution with the tools and resources needed to create a culture of consent, in which intimate stories can be told with safety and artistry." To me, the most critical part of this mission is the idea that intimacy direction cannot be fully successful if it is not operating within a larger culture of consent. The role of the intimacy director is not a panacea for an industry culture that has historically denied power abuse and rewarded complicity. To create change, the inclusion of practices that encourage body autonomy and agency must become a shared responsibility, at every level of production. We all have a part to play in making this industry a safer place to work and create.

Alexis Black and Tina M. Newhauser have written a remarkable tool for the creative community that not only offers guidance for the creative team on how to work through a scene of intimacy but also provides step-by-step instructions on how to create a culture of consent in which scenes of intimacy can be told with safety and artistry. While this book focuses on the roles of the stage management and other creative and production team members, the practices outlined here are essential reading for anyone who is working on an intimate scene, regardless of whether they are a director, actor, lighting designer, or crew member. Black and Newhauser take the topic of intimacy, one that is often uncomfortable and that deeply challenges the industry's relationship to power, and offer a clear path forward to finding the tools that will serve your organization, production, and self.

As artists, we are all after the same goal: to tell amazing stories. We cannot do this if we are not first and foremost prioritizing the individuals who make this storytelling possible. As intimacy direction continues to deepen as a discipline of both practice and study, I feel confident that we will continue unearthing new and creative ways to practice consent and agency. I have seen the evidence that if our industry remains accountable to these values and new ethical standards, the foundations of intimacy work have the potential to dramatically improve the performing arts far beyond scenes of intimacy.

It takes everyone to build a culture of consent, so let's get started.

Jessica Renae Steinrock, PhD
CEO | Intimacy Directors and Coordinators, Inc.

Acknowledgments

Throughout our journey to write this book, we were lucky to become connected with a large community of outstanding professionals. In collaborating and communicating with theatre artists and professionals from the worlds of movement, direction, design, management, producing, advocating, and more aspects of the industry, we realized the importance of this work. Perhaps more importantly, we discovered that creating fundamental change truly does take an engaged community of enthusiastic collaborators and advocates. The large community that supported the writing of this book includes collaborators, interviewees, colleagues, students, friends, and family; we are grateful for the opportunity to work with and thank these many wonderful humans listed below.

First, we thank those who added their voices to this book. We had the incredible opportunity to connect, share ideas with, and receive written contributions from the following artists, advocates, professionals and educators: Jhanaë Bonnick, Elaine DiFalco Daugherty, Maya Herbsman, Deborah Hertzberg, Katharine M. Hude, Teniece Divya Johnson, Sarah Lozoff, Laurie Goldfeder, Rocio Mendez, Adam Noble, Marie C. Percy, Cristina (Cha) Ramos, Richard C. Rauscher, Siobhan Richardson, Dr. Jessica Steinrock, Matthew Aaron Stern, Darrell Wagner, Claire Warden, Claire Wilcher and Bobby Wilson. Thank you all for your wonderful contributions on choreography, specializations in theatre, advocacy, and more.

We also want to thank Robert Kaplan for his icons and images, Karen Schierhorn for beautiful artwork for our Intimacy Mapping section, Eloy Gomez Orfila for design brainstorming, Claire Wilcher for making our sentences more sensical through her editing ideas, Siobhan Richardson and Cristina (Cha) Ramos for nuanced guidance on advocating, and Kari Bentley Quinn for allowing us to use her powerful play script as an example for content notices and choreography notation.

Acknowledgments

To those who met with us and shared their stories, insights, and knowledge, such as Steve Lukens, David "dstew" Stewart, Allison Franck, Rachel Dart, Dave Landis, Brian Bogin, we can't thank you enough for your presence in our minds as we filled these pages.

We would also love to thank the stage management trailblazers whose work contributed to the writing of this book. We want to thank Narda Alcorn and Lisa Porter, whose own text *Stage Management Theory as a Guide to Practice* and their many articles, workshops, and webinars have helped to change the landscape for stage managers across this country. A special thank you to Alcorn and Porter along with Zev Steinrock, Terri Ciofalo, Cynthia Kocher, and Amber Schultz from the Department of Theatre at the University of Illinois at Urbana-Champaign who participated in collaborative workshops and roundtables with Alexis Black, Sarah Lozoff, and Dr. Jessica Steinrock, exploring the connection between anti-oppression and consent for stage management in 2022. Your research, advocacy, and empathy are inspirational and essential to a healthier future in our industry. A special thanks to D. Christian Bolender; your expertise as an AEA stage manager and as a contributor to our Stage Managing Intimacy course for IDC in 2020 was invaluable and inspirational.

In addition to many intimacy professionals who added written contributions to this text, there are several mentors from the specializations of intimacy direction and coordination who went above and beyond to collaborate, answer questions, clarify, brainstorm, and keep us honest, empathetic, and focused. To Dr. Jessica Steinrock and Marie Percy, we want to extend mountains of gratitude for your incredible work and many hours of consultation on this text, including your advice, support, creativity, warm spirits, and general awesomeness. Gratitude to Alicia Rodis, Rocio Mendez, and Claire Warden for their support, consultations, expertise, and answering late night emails and texts. A special thank you to Sarah Lozoff for her contributions to the building of the Stage Managing Intimacy course in 2020 for IDC; your compassion and intuition were indispensable.

We would be remiss to miss all of our amazing colleagues at Michigan State University, with extra appreciation to Rob Roznowski, Dr. Ann Folino White, Kirk Domer, and Dr. Deric McNish. We cherish every bit of your support and feedback in our preparation of this book, our grant proposal drafts, and so much more. We also wish to thank the MSU Humanities and Arts Research and Development Program whose grant funding helped to bring this book to production. Finally, a special thank you to our students in the 2019 advanced stage management class at MSU. To Chris Badia, Shelby Eppich, Troy Gährs, and Brianna Kubiak, and to all of our acting, design, and stage management students who have embraced the work of advocacy and consent, thank you for all you do as we integrate this work into the MSU Department of Theatre and beyond. Your ideas, curiosity and heart helped fuel our drive and passion to create this book. GO GREEN!

As this book focuses on those working behind the scenes, we want to spend a moment thanking those "behind our scenes"; our incredibly supportive family and friends.

From Tina: I want to thank my amazingly patient and loving family Mark, Zack, and Sofia. Your ability to put up with my absence, even when I'm present, has been remarkable. I promise to cook again. To all my stage management students, thank you. Your curiosity and drive give me joy and motivate me to be and do better. To Ann, thank you for quickly responding to my many texts, for always being willing to share a glass of Malbec and being a wonderful mentor and friend. To the DOT ladies, thank you for the laughter. And most importantly, to Alexis. Your passion and care for this work is everything. This book could not exist without you. Thank you for coming to my class and inspiring, leading, and joyfully taking us on this journey.

From Alexis: I want to thank my husband, Erik Trabka, for everything he does to support my work and my heart. You have filled my life with joy and laughter, reminded me to take a deep breath and snuggle Sadie, and helped me stay inspired (and fed!) during many hours of research and writing… just your love. I also want to thank my mentor and friend David Leong for guidance and collaborations over the past nine years. Without you I would not be the artist and teacher I am today. Gratitude and love for my mother Kaye, always present even from the beyond, who inspired these words by inspiring me to be the person I am. Another warm thank you to everyone in my life who puts up with my "pun-ishment" and helps me decompress, especially my ever-loving and ever-witty father Ray and (favorite) brother Ryan Black, my incredible in-laws, and my wonderful friends. And last but not least, a very special thanks to Tina; your patience, wisdom, passion, appropriate attention to chip dip and humor (alongside that wonderful twinkle in your eye!) made writing this book a true joy, and much more love than labor.

Finally, we are beyond grateful that you, the reader, are now joining the community we experienced in building this text. There truly is a wave of change occurring in the theatre industry, and whether you have been a part of the wave since its inception, joined along the way, or are now discovering it on the horizon, we are thankful. The water's lovely; let's dive in.

Introduction

Intentional beginnings

When considering how best to introduce the concepts and practices within this book, about which we are so passionate, we paused. Staging intimacy is a relatively new specialization within theatre as an industry, and those aware of these emerging practices were often introduced to them in contrasting ways. Some were introduced to this work while seeking ways to improve and empower their own practices. In this search, they learned from or collaborated with other compassionate, enthusiastic artists who have invited significant shifts industry wide by helping actors work more consensually, dynamically, and safely. Others have discovered the specialization of staged intimacy as a part of more sweeping administrative changes; many companies, universities and more are incorporating various modern practices around agency, inclusion, and consent that better their workspaces. However, some readers have encountered the need for professional staged intimacy practices due to experiencing and witnessing problematic practices. There have been abusive behaviors, unqualified personnel, a lack of support for the vulnerable, or other inappropriate actions that have sparked demand for change throughout the industry and created the need to reevaluate the way teams engage with staged intimacy and our theatrical processes in general.

Given these differing initiations to the work, we asked ourselves how to begin. Do we start with the "positive" connotations and roots of intimacy direction in personal agency, better storytelling, and consent? Do we begin with the more "negative" roots in problematic industry-wide practices, or do we start somewhere in-between? So, we took a breath and realized that to introduce this new working method, we should practice the mindfulness and authenticity encouraged within it. We then asked ourselves, What is it about this contemporary approach that speaks to us as individuals, professionals, and educators? Why do we believe so deeply in these processes and this

DOI: 10.4324/9781003206064-1

content? What actions led us to author this book, teach this work, and support our artistic team members in creative endeavors? And finally, we asked ourselves how our lens as writers impacts the information we share.

By beginning with these questions and sharing what motivates us as artists, we hope that each reader and creative team member, like you, will bring this work to your practice in your way. Your lived experiences, self-discoveries, desires, and goals that lead to artistic creation may support your process and that of those who create and collaborate alongside you as you work with staged intimacy.

Tina on her journey to staged intimacy through stage management

The reason this work is important to me stems from my time in school. I was in college in the late '80s, at a Midwest small state school. The culture was incredibly different back then, especially in our theatre department. I worked in the scene shop and was one of two female students hired; it was mostly me and a bunch of guys who were the "tech kids" at that time. I loved working behind the scenes, and I was able to do a lot. I designed, built, painted, stage managed, welded; you name it, and I did it. But I was naive. I didn't know how to respond when our department chair bragged about choosing work based on the desire to have female cast members rehearse in corsets. My naiveté blinded me to our working culture and to the ways we spoke to each other. I was oblivious to the ways we treated each other, and things didn't improve when, a few years later when working professionally, I found myself dumbfounded when a director bragged about having every male actor get naked during auditions "just to see them."

In those early years of my career, it never dawned on me that I had any ability or power to change the way we worked or how this industry functioned. I felt powerless. I have spent nearly 30 years working in this creative world, a world that I cherish, and for the first time, I am starting to feel a shift, a palpable shift in culture. I believe old behaviors are now evolving; willingly or not, they are changing. Many years later, students and professionals—young and old—have the desire, confidence, and power to want and ask for a better way to work. They are standing up and saying "No." Their strength inspires and reinforces for me that this work is important.

We can take the steps needed to change the ways in which we want to approach our work and each other. It is okay to want and ask for a more inclusive and supportive working environment. And if what we've written here can help to change the culture in just one rehearsal room or help just one individual put into place policies that create a more consensual work environment, then I'll be content knowing that we did something good and that this work has value.

Alexis on her journey to staged intimacy as an actor, choreographer and educator

My connection to this work is multifaceted; it has impacted my artistry as an actor, choreographer, and educator. Like Tina, I have experienced or witnessed a culture in all these contexts in which inappropriate actions by coworkers and those in power were common, and I felt it was "just the way it was" for years. But when it came to engaging in intimacy as an actor, my experiences were different than those I heard about or witnessed.

As an actor, I experienced many scenes with romantic and platonic intimacy and a few shows that required simulated sex acts. As a person and artist, I was very comfortable with physical touch in storytelling. Due to this natural comfort within my process, I often assumed that my partners felt the same. My ease and comfort with physical intimacy in the context of rehearsal left me in moments where later, looking back on these moments with new eyes, I saw I could have bordered on or pushed boundaries. I simply did not have the knowledge or language to support those workplace relationships, or the tools to make the movements repeatable.

Additionally, I experienced other problems, such as injuries when moments would happen unsafely due to lack of clarity or consistency. I once had a coworker change a kiss integral to the story arc into an awkward hug with no warning because his girlfriend was in the audience that day. I witnessed "showmances" or unrealistic relationships between actors engaging in intimacy, which sometimes led to antagonisms that impacted the entire ensemble. All these problematic practices created a sense of helplessness for myself as a performer as I wondered, How do I support my coworkers and the story we are telling? How do I continue to witness problematic workplace practices and be a healthy artist in a malfunctioning ensemble? I felt adrift.

As I moved away from acting and became a fight choreographer and movement director, I wondered why these moments of intimacy were left practically untouched from a choreographic perspective. When asked to choreograph scenes of sexual violence, the relief created by working through the story with communication and safety was palpable by all in the room. However, then I would sit and watch as they were told to "go for it" in other scenes of romantic intimacy in the same show, where actors were just as physically vulnerable. I witnessed discomfort, embarrassment, shame, and lots of "Let's just get this over with," while every other movement in the show would be examined, refined, supported. Frankly, I witnessed many stereotypical, awkward, and uninventive moments of intimacy as well, as this work was often left untouched in an otherwise polished production. Again, I felt adrift.

Then, through graduate school, industry connections, and colleagues, I came to find the rescue craft for these issues and questions: intimacy direction! I have been on board ever since. What excites me so much about this set of practices as an artist is all the creative possibilities that occur when using mindful, compassionate communication. Actors are hungry to make unique choices and tell stories in a way that is organic to their own experience and supports their research into the character. Intimacy need not be stereotyped, "paint by numbers," painful, dangerous emotionally, or at the mercy of a roll of the dice that the energy will be there night by night. These crucial moments of scripted passion can be made more collaboratively, dynamically, and safely by the artists crafting them. All aboard!

How we connected

Our journeys intersected when Alexis joined Tina as theatre faculty at Michigan State University in 2018. Her knowledge of this field led to faculty conversations regarding incorporating elements from intimacy direction into our teaching. We began to embrace the philosophies that supported this work and welcomed these innovative approaches and consent practices into our classes, rehearsals, and performances.

Intimacy work became a breath of fresh air sweeping through the department for many students in our program. But not only the acting students were eager for changes; we found when culture shifts are embraced with empathy and curiosity by faculty and students across all areas, new practices can soon become a welcome change to routine. This led to a discovery: we could intentionally incorporate the elements of intimacy direction into other areas of production, extending our reach beyond the performance students alone.

Our first connection was to our stage management teams. Tina was still shaping the new BFA in Stage Management program that had launched a year earlier, and she knew that the program should incorporate these practices in some way. The stage manager's role helps set the tone of rehearsal, supports the creative team, and has a significant impact when welcoming new individuals into the room. It was logical to incorporate this new practice into the program's curriculum.

Tina invited Alexis into her advanced stage management class in the spring of 2019, intending to introduce this new practice to her students. Her objective was to have them learn about and explore the foundations of this specialization, and then write a new toolkit for intimate staging to add to the BFA *Stage Manager's Handbook*. During these classes, it quickly became apparent that there was a significant synergy between these two areas; stage managers and intimacy directors could work together in many practical ways to establish a culture of consent within the creative process.

This discovery led us to connect with Alexis's contacts at Intimacy Directors and Coordinators (IDC) to consider this work on a broader scale. We suggested that the synergy between these two positions be further explored and set as a codified curriculum for pre-professional, professional stage management practitioners and those who oversee stage management programs. Their administrative team (led by Marie Percy and Dr. Jessica Steinrock) was thrilled with the idea of this new perspective. Tina and Alexis worked with Sarah Lozoff (certified intimacy director) and Chris Bolender (AEA stage manager), and later Cristina (Cha) Ramos (intimacy director) and Claire Wilcher (intimacy director) to formulate and hone course content focused on the relationship between stage management and staged intimacy. Our goal was to codify necessary protocols, vocabulary, practices, and other elements to prepare stage managers to work more cohesively and collaboratively with movement and intimacy specialists.

Expanding our objectives to theatre creatives, managers, and crew

When developing our intimacy course for stage management team members, it became clear that a wider audience of administrative and creative team members could benefit from understanding these new practices. Artistic directors, company managers, designers, technicians, and crew could all benefit from our research if we delved a little more deeply into overlaps with staged intimacy. Additionally, it was at that time that we noted changes in personnel across the industry: the HBO network (working with intimacy professional Alicia Rodis)[1] began requiring intimacy professionals to be on set for moments of intimacy, for example. And the Oregon Shakespeare Festival hired a resident intimacy professional to support their entire season (intimacy professional Sarah Lozoff)[2] for the first time. We knew that it was only a matter of time before this specialization would be introduced to more organizations and artists; it may quickly become integral for creative team members to have access to these new practices and protocols.

Given the expansion of research and awareness within the field, we discovered our purpose for this book: to reach the artists and managers who collaborate with those more directly engaged with staged intimacy. While there has been a flurry of publications surrounding intimacy for theatrical, TV, and film productions throughout the past few years, most articles focused on the skills that actors and choreographers require. Others focused on the positive impact that intimacy work has on the actors and directors during the creation and storytelling. Some articles focus on teachers and actors in a theatrical education setting, and some mention the benefits that occur company wide for theatres or network companies when embracing consent culture.

One notable publication on theatrical intimacy was penned by Chelsea Pace (with contributions by Laura Rikard) and is titled *Staging Sex*. In the introduction, Pace directs readers to use tools shared in her book to stage (choreograph and/or perform) theatrical intimacy safely and consensually and expresses a target audience of directors, actors and theatre teachers.[3] As the title suggests, Pace explores the practical process for those staging intimacy or being staged into a scene with theatrical intimacy; it is a useful set of tools for directors, teachers, students, and professional performers.

Supporting Staged Intimacy has a different focus: highlighting the concepts and practices of staged intimacy specifically from the vantage point of creative and production team members, or those outside the physical creation process looking in. This book explores broader elements of workplace culture in live performance and the nuances of this specialization before and after the staging of choreographed moments. Our goal is to provide vocabulary, points of connection, and action items that will help all members of the creative, production, and administrative teams engage in an informed, thoughtful, and harmonious manner with the specialization of staged intimacy. While many artists who stage or act within intimacy would find the tools explored in this text helpful, this publication is designed for individuals who are "behind the scenes" or who engage with live performance from beyond the fourth wall or from behind an administrative desk.

This book also highlights practices and protocols that lead to effective collaborations between intimacy professionals and creative team members. Collaboration in storytelling is key to creating moving and memorable experiences, and thrives in environments where everyone comes to their work understanding how the various roles within the process intersect and overlap.

Three action items guide our artistic research for this text: recognize, empower, and transform.[4]

Recognize

We hope readers of this book will recognize the need for change. Recognition of one's desire to learn new methods, techniques, and tools can be the first step in supporting strategies that create a healthier and more compassionate culture. We hope you recognize the value of individuality and autonomy in building live performances and recognize that a more consensual workplace supports everyone in this collaborative environment.

Empower

We hope this text will empower readers by providing new skills, vocabulary, and protocols. By engaging with these tools in written form, we hope you will feel empowered to engage with them in practice to create a culture of consent in your artistic workspaces. We hope to empower you with a desire to create with more care, produce with more purpose, and engage with more empathy.

Transform

Creating and supporting transformation takes knowledge, passion, resilience, and follow-through. We hope this text leads the reader to transform their thought processes around the building of intimate physical storytelling and discover how methods from staged intimacy can holistically inform one's practice. We hope the reader will transform their working methods and, by extension, their working environments through self-reflection, careful consideration of others, and ongoing actions. Each of us has the power to transform ourselves, our communities, and the future of this industry.

Everything within this text is designed to support these three foundational ideas with our hope that moving forward, they will be fully embraced and encouraged by you, our readers, in your artistic practice.

Structure of the text

Here we communicate some context and intentions, sharing the general layout of the book, our purpose behind this layout, and how our identities, training, and professional experiences shaped this text and the concepts held within.

Structure of the timeline

While our first chapter explores the basics of the field of intimacy direction in a foundational manner, the rest of this text parallels the timeline structure of production, starting before pre-production and continuing through the run of the show. We hope to allow exploration of how one can support intimacy direction in this familiar, step-by-step way of working through a production. This chronological approach is because each of our own brains works best this way after years of working with similar timelines during our other responsibilities and creative endeavors.

However, as you, your students, or your team traverses through our chapters, we realize that not all timelines are the same. Chapters 2 and 3 contain elements that overlap, for example. While we cover the subject of integrating understudies in Chapter 5, which focuses on the run of the show, your company may integrate practices for understudies in pre-production, or elements in Chapter 4 may surface in year two of an ongoing Broadway tour.

Other highlighted sections

As you explore the chapters you will notice special sections in outlined boxes, separated from the main text, titled *Notes from the field* and *Creative team spotlights*. *Notes from the field* are brief perspectives from a specialist in the field sharing personal experiences or advice in relation to a topic we are covering in that chapter. It is important to us that in addition to our views, we also share perspectives from industry professionals. Their input may relate to the material in practical, theoretical, or historical ways. The other section is the *Creative team spotlight*, which serves to magnify or "light up" an area of practice within the theatrical team, such as administrators, choreographers, or designers, and focus on a specific topic. These spotlights may be from a generalized perspective or written from the vantage point of an individual practitioner and will cover an important aspect of intimacy direction as it relates to that area of expertise.

At the end of each chapter, there will be another box that includes a *Chapter discussion, exercise, or activity*. In these boxes, the reflection or action included is built to solidify an element covered in the chapter or encourage the reader to expand upon one on their own.

Our last section, the *Appendices*, includes coverage of known major intimacy organizations at the time of the writing of this text, additional resources for mental health, resources for human rights, self-care, and more, an opportunity for troubleshooting scenario practice, and a glossary of terms. Also, since this book details elements of staged intimacy for those who work behind the scenes in an expanded or comprehensive manner, we have included checklists and brief guides within the appendix to provide a condensed overview of what was covered.

Context for language and perspectives within the text

Understanding context or the interrelated conditions surrounding the theatrical concepts or environment in which one is learning and working is vital to working responsibly with practices within staged intimacy. Context will be explored in relation to storytelling in later chapters, but it is just as important to understand the context in which this text was created. This includes understanding why certain vocabulary is chosen, why certain methods are included, and what is the impact of our identities as writers when reading this book.

U.S. perspective: We want to openly acknowledge that our research, interviewees, and consulted experts of these techniques are largely from a western, American background, specifically within the United States.

Intimacy Organizations: Also, important to acknowledge, many of our intimacy experts (co-author Alexis included) have worked alongside, trained with, or been certified by the intimacy organization Intimacy Directors and Coordinators,[5] or IDC. When writing this work, several references and/or resources come from working and collaborating with professionals from this group. However, there are many different organizations that have created training around staged intimacy, including Intimacy for Stage and Screen, Intimacy Coordinators of Color, Theatrical Intimacy Education, and others. Please see the appendix for a more fully realized list of organizations.

Terms for the specialization of staging intimacy and the professionals within the field of practice: Professionals within the field utilize various terms within the specialization of staging intimacy. These terms are similar, adjacent, or interchangeable, which may be because foundational terminology has been decided upon by different organizations somewhat simultaneously or based on the fact that job responsibilities differ in specific aspects of staging intimacy. One example to reference is the vocabulary covered in Chapter 1, which defines possible differences in job responsibilities between intimacy choreographers, intimacy directors, and intimacy consultants, and additional titles for intimacy professionals or specialists. Still, other professionals may designate these responsibilities slightly differently. The field itself may be called staged intimacy, intimacy choreography, intimacy direction (defined in Chapter 1), or more titles. There may always be differences in opinion about the best terminology for the field and the positions therein. Note that the same has occurred in the field of stage fighting after decades of prominence as a position: it is called stage combat, staged violence, fight direction, and more, and the professionals within are called fight choreographers, fight directors, violence designers, and more. Thus, when we use terminology in this book, consider the spirit of the term and allow for interchangeability in vocabulary when working with different professionals.

Commonalities within theatrical movement, terms, and themes: This book contains vocabulary terms that are challenging to cite effectively given commonalities in language that are based on and evolved from general theatrical movement practitioners and the field of fight direction. Over the past decade (or more) existing language has been adopted or adjusted by intimacy professionals. A good example of this can be seen with the term "container," now a common term used by many intimacy professionals. This term was utilized by Stephen Vaughn, inspired by the work of Jerzi Growtowksi and his concept of plastiques, in his book *Acrobat of the Heart* in 2000. "Container" was then adopted and defined by Daniel Kucan in his article "Coriolanus" for stage combat work in the 2010 *The Fight Master* magazine.[6] It was then adopted by intimacy professionals Tonia Sina and Chelsea Pace in reference to intimacy choreography and actor boundaries (shared in workshops starting approximately in 2010) and then published in *Staging Sex* as a term in 2020. We find it important to note that as you read key terms in this text, our use stems from our collaborations with industry professionals, our engagement in the classroom with students at Michigan State University, our experience in the professions of movement direction and stage management, and while workshopping our course "Stage Managing Intimacy" created for IDC. We acknowledge there will be ideas, terms, and themes that may have been utilized by like-minded professionals, and we have cited whenever possible, but it is important to note there is a common vernacular within the theatrical field of movement and within the study of consent practices and that this common vernacular has become interwoven into the fabric of this industry.

Live Theatre: For this book, when applying practices from staged intimacy, we have worked primarily from our main professional perspective as theatre artists: live theatrical professional and pre-professional/academic productions. We acknowledge, however, that there are many other forms of live work that engage artistic creative teams and engage with staged intimacy. We hope that this work can be more universally applied to other areas of the performative arts other than nonprofit, commercial, regional theatre, such as improv, circus, opera, dance, and more.

Author identities: We think it pertinent to acknowledge that we wrote this from our personal perspectives as cis-gendered white women working in professional theatre and academia in the United States. In an effort to balance the limitations created by working from our personal viewpoints, we conducted research and have connected with other voices for our lens to have as wide an angle as possible and will continue to expand this viewpoint as we gain new training, research and partnerships. We will continue to expand this viewpoint through research, new learning, training, and creative partnerships in future editions.

Recommended practices versus *best* practices

When working with staged intimacy, the language we choose to use is important. We began to reflect on the phrase "best practices" regarding the field of intimacy, especially since it is still actively evolving, and we consulted with other intimacy professionals. These conversations led us to acknowledge that the term "best" in the phrase "best practices" is not the language we want to use for this work.

We considered who has generally established the standards for what is determined to be "best." We then acknowledged the possibility that this may often be those granted visibility or opportunities due to structures of oppression. Additionally, in the article "Why Best Practices Don't Translate Across Cultures," Pamela Hinds shares another reason to reconsider the term "best practices," stating that "best practices are optimized for a particular place and time and don't necessarily transfer well between cultures. They're like a shoe that doesn't always fit. You can put the shoe on, and it may even look nice, but it will likely create blisters if the fit isn't exactly right. That's how it is with practices that don't quite fit another cultural context."[7] While this article is referencing different cultures within various international industries, a correlation can still be drawn to the performative arts industries. The culture, resources, customs, identities, and more found within a small community theatre in rural Texas, for example, is much different than that of a big-budget Broadway musical starring Hollywood actors. "Although some practices transfer intact, many require adaptation."[8]

Today, given the diversity of our communities and the evolving nature of the field of theatrical intimacy, we want to support each individual, ensemble, or organization as they adapt practices that fuel their vision and their values in conversation with modern research. These diverse individuals and groups can examine these recommendations and then establish for themselves their own preferred, recommended, or intentional methods based on their needs, working processes, the community they serve, and what is feasible given their resources.

Embracing the future

Questions and self-reflection are a vital part of the work of staged intimacy, as we discovered when we started this introduction. We want to ask you, a reader who is passionate or interested enough to pursue this work, to reflect on what can come from this journey we are on together. What do we want to see when looking to the future of this industry and its relation to consent? What methods of engagement, operation, and support can we all put into practice now to lay the groundwork for creating this future? What innovations and evolutions can you utilize for *Supporting Staged Intimacy*? We can do more than consider these questions by engaging with this text and other similar resources and bringing consent into all our communities and organizations. We can, together, create our own answers and support our collective future within the art of theatrical innovation.

Notes

1 Kerr, Breena. "How HBO Is Changing Sex Scenes Forever." *Rolling Stone*, Oct. 24, 2018, "https://www.rollingstone.com/tv/tv-features/the-deuce-intimacy-coordinator-hbo-sex-scenes-739087/
2 "Oregon Shakespeare Festival Hires a Resident Intimacy Director." *The New York Times*, Jan. 24, 2020, https://www.nytimes.com/2020/01/24/theater/oregon-shakespeare-festival-intimacy-director.html.
3 Pace, Chelsea. *Staging Sex: Best Practices, Tools, and Techniques for Theatrical Intimacy*. Routledge, 2020.
4 Concept developed for an Introduction to Staged Intimacy workshop at Michigan State University led by Alexis Black, and adapted through work with MSU's Advanced Stage Management class in spring 2019.

5 https://www.idcprofessionals.com/.
6 *The Fight Master*, Spring/Summer 2010, vol. 32, no. 1, https://mds.marshall.edu/cgi/viewcontent.cgi?article=1078&context=fight.
7 Hinds, Pamela. "Research: Why Best Practices Don't Translate Across Cultures." *Harvard Business Review*, June 27, 2016, https://hbr.org/2016/06/research-why-best-practices-dont-translate-across-cultures.
8 Hinds, Pamela. "Research: Why Best Practices Don't Translate Across Cultures." *Harvard Business Review*, June 27, 2016, https://hbr.org/2016/06/research-why-best-practices-dont-translate-across-cultures.

1
Fundamentals of staged intimacy

Staging moments of intimacy, formally introduced as a concept in 2006,[1] is a relatively new practice and an evolving field. Perhaps you have worked with or witnessed others working with what is now considered "staged intimacy" for many years but have not had the language, tools, and protocols to support this type of physical storytelling. This book hopes to guide members of the creative and production teams to learn how to best support these moments, whether seeing the work with new eyes, or with fresh eyes.

As mentioned in the introduction, the following chapters will include many practices advanced by practitioners within Intimacy Directors and Coordinators (IDC), a leading organization for intimacy professionals. As writers of this book, we have also researched methods from team building methodologies, the field of psychology, standard business practices, theatrical academic training, physical acting techniques, other staged intimacy organizations and unaffiliated intimacy professionals, stage management training as well as incorporating our own experiences as artists and educators. While many practical elements are needed to support staged intimacy and responsible partnering procedures, and we will expound upon these in following chapters, this chapter's focus is to set an intellectual foundation for the work.

Sections in this chapter explore the following:

- Noteworthy events surrounding staged intimacy
- The production pillars of intimacy
- Foundational vocabulary for staged intimacy
- The discomfort scale
- Methods for supporting mental health in theatrical productions
- Methods for advocating for intimacy professionals
- Specializations within the field of staged intimacy

DOI: 10.4324/9781003206064-2

Fundamentals of staged intimacy

The objectives of this chapter are to build or refresh one's fundamental knowledge around the field of staged intimacy, to explain foundational elements, and to clarify what intimacy professionals do and do not do. This knowledge may help organizations decide when this specialization is needed on a production, what to expect when working with intimacy professionals, and their impact on the creative process.

Noteworthy events surrounding staged intimacy

Practitioners within the entertainment industry have engaged with staged intimacy for centuries, although their methods have drastically changed over time. These changes have been due to many factors, including differences in culture, staging, style, and more. In her PhD dissertation titled "Intimacy Direction: A New Role in Contemporary Theatre Making," Dr. Jessica Steinrock, CEO of IDC, says that "Intimacy is at the heart of the human experience, and the dynamic portrayal of its multitudes of forms continues to captivate audiences. Whether familial intimacy, romantic intimacy, violent intimacy, or any other category—it is often the core of the stories we choose to reenact."[2]

Staged intimacy, as a theatrical specialization, gained visibility in the performance industry due to individual research practices, publications, and societal movements. These spotlighted the need for new practices and acknowledged the catalysts pushing for change. However, when identifying key points of research and societal events (for our timeline, these events will be focused mainly within the United States of America), we acknowledge that any summarization of this rise of recognition for intimacy direction in the performative arts will be incomplete. Historical documentation can be based on power imbalances resulting in those who traditionally have had privilege to be made more visible. As a result, any genealogy will not be comprehensive and will likely be more western-centered, as well as white-cis centered, due more to inequalities in what has been publicized rather than what has occurred in practice.

Many in this discipline are grappling with how to honor the genealogy of ideas found within staged intimacy, such as leaders from IDC, who in their statement on historical narratives and intimacy direction, discuss that "[w]riting a history is an inherently political statement and will always carry a specific lens and bias." They continue, saying, "[T]he discipline of intimacy direction would not have been possible without the work of Black women and trans/nonbinary activists and Global Majority intimacy practitioners, scholars, and artists, whose theories and work on power, agency, and consent built many of the foundations for the professionalization of intimacy direction/coordination. However, these voices are not proportionally reflected in the media's representation of the popularization of this field. These practitioners have and continue to contribute to this industry while experiencing more resistance and violence when challenging social and industry constructs than their white/cis counterparts and also often simultaneously being erased from any narratives surrounding the positive impact of their contributions."[3]

In The Journal of Consent-Based Performance,[4] Amy Rose Villarrel speaks to this same challenge, saying, "While some voices have become very prominent as they advocate for consent-based practices, other artists, who have been using consent-based approaches for generations prior to the emergence of 'intimacy coordinator' or 'intimacy choreographer' titles, may have gone unnamed. Many of those whose work has gone unnamed are artists of color, women, disabled individuals, trans and nonbinary individuals whose own experiences of disempowerment in society and in the performance industry forced them to forge practices to protect themselves. These people are the pioneers of consent-based practice."[5]

While recognizing that certain societal events and cultural movements had an undeniable impact on the industry-wide acknowledgment of the emerging field of staged intimacy, we want to honor that many more artists and educators have been denied their acknowledgment. This has created and continues to create erasure. We, Alexis and Tina, think this is an important conversation to consider, and grapple with as you read the following section of this book.

> ### *2006: Tarana Burke coins the phrase "#metoo"*[6]
>
> Though the #metoo movement and hashtag went globally viral as a response to highly public sexual misconduct accusations against Harvey Weinstein in 2017, the campaign truly began in 2006. Tarana Burke, the movement's originator, was working with a youth camp for marginalized communities when she found herself acting as a sounding board for a young survivor of sexual violence. Moved to support further, she launched a website dedicated to empathy and solidarity for survivors of sexual violence, especially women of color. The cause grew within Burke's activist circles, permeating social media only after widespread Weinstein accusations from Hollywood's elite. "Part of the message here is that a viral hashtag that was largely spread and amplified by white

women actually has its origins in a decade of work by a woman of color. But it is also this: It will take more than a hashtag, however meaningful it has become, to do the real work that is needed now. As Burke said, 'It's also people's lives. It's a very touchy private, deeply personal thing'" (*Chicago Tribune*, 2017). Burke's cause sets the tone for the intersectionality that is integral to and required of the field of intimacy direction.

2006: Tonia Sina presents the concept of intimacy direction as her thesis at Virginia Commonwealth University, titled "Intimate Encounters: Staging Intimacy and Sensuality"[7]

Using her skills as an actor, fight choreographer, and director at VCU, Sina often found herself acting as an unofficial consultant for staging intimate moments and using her fight techniques as touchstones for coaching sexual scenes. As a result, Sina proposed codifying the language and process of staging intimacy, to give actors agency and help them feel safe.

2011: Adam Noble publishes his "Extreme Stage Physicality" method

Movement specialist Noble presented *Practical Approaches for Dealing with Extreme Stage Physicality* in a 2011 issue of The FightMaster.[8] The approach laid out techniques actors can use to support consensual and communicative partnering between themselves when working with intense physicality. Adam Noble pointed out that actors are often left to work these moments on their own, especially while in a university setting. He wrote that his method "assumes that the actors are working without a movement coach, so it relies upon their own creativity and impulses; however, it first provides them with a foundation of safety, and a framework in which their creative partnership may flourish."

2013: Black Lives Matter Movement is created

In response to the acquittal of Trayvon Martin's murderer, George Zimmerman, three women created a website, hashtag, and subsequent movement known as Black Lives Matter. Alicia Garza, Patrisse Cullors, and Opal Tometi created a powerful and palpable example of movement-building that created a landscape where harmful power was being challenged. Cullors explains, "Alicia, Opal, and I created #BlackLivesMatter as an online community to help combat anti-Black racism across the globe. We firmly believed our movement, which would later become an organization, needed to be a contributing voice for Black folks and our allies to support changing the material conditions for Black people."[9] The BLM movement started a dynamic national conversation around power and systemic racism that may have impacted the relationship between power and consent within the theatre industry and moments of staged intimacy.

February 2015: **Not In Our House** *is created by Lori Myers and Laura T. Fisher*

Amid the high-profile accusations of Harvey Weinstein and the public emergence of #metoo, Chicago actors Lori Myers and Laura T. Fisher formed an organization that aimed to set standards for theaters and theatremakers that ensure a safe and transparent work environment. In their public document, they address everything from Day One rehearsal agendas to a chain of command for harassment complaints to the expectations of staging scenes of sexual violence. For example, "Prior to rehearsing scenes with Sexual Content/Nudity (SC/N), the actors, director, choreographer, and stage manager should discuss the content and create consent for the rehearsal. Participants should build consent and discuss boundaries before rehearsing scenes with SC/N. A safe word (such as "hold") should be established for SC/N rehearsals."[10] The concept of boundaries, safe words, and many other standards found in Not In Our House are commonly used in the field of intimacy direction.

2015: Organizations focused on staged intimacy begin to form

Multiple groups of passionate, consent-forward theatrical artists began to form organizations that focus on professional and educational applications of staged intimacy throughout the US and abroad. Examples within the United States include Intimacy Directors International (IDI) in 2015, Theatrical Intimacy Education (TIE) in 2017, Heartland Intimacy Design & Training in 2018, IDC in 2019, and Intimacy Professionals Association (IPA) in 2019. Intimacy Coordinators of Color (ICOC), the first organization "dedicated to supporting and promoting decolonized intimacy education,"[11] was also formed in 2019. Additional national and international organizations can be found in Appendix A.

June 2016: Profiles Theatre exposé in Chicago Reader[12]

Profiles Theatre, a now-defunct storefront theater in Chicago, was highly regarded among the Chicago theatre community for its edgy work. Much of the theater's reputation was driven by prominent company member Daryl Cox, whose manipulative behavior was an open secret among the theatre community. During a 2010 production of Tracy Letts's *Killer Joe*, Cox's acting often betrayed boundaries set in rehearsals, improvising moments of violence and intimacy throughout the production. Affected company members and witnesses to this repeated behavior beyond *Killer Joe* remained quiet for years. "Actors in Chicago, especially female actors, feel they're in a vulnerable position. There are only a few roles to go around to begin with, and no one wants to have a reputation as being "difficult" or a complainer. It's really hard to break in, and it is a very tight-knit community," says Sue Redman, an actress and producer who now lives in LA, "and so having someone powerful say, 'Yeah, your career is not going to happen if you say anything,' I mean it's a very real thing."[13] Profiles Theatre closed in 2016, soon after the story broke.

August 2016: Intimacy Directors International (IDI) creates the "Pillars of Intimacy"

Tonia Sina, Alicia Rodis, and Siobhan Richardson founded the not-for-profit 501c6 in 2015 to define the role of the *intimacy director* (ID) and promote its use in professional entertainment. Then in 2016, they created and codified practices for theatrical intimacy based around what they called the Five Pillars—Context, Consent, Communication, Choreography, and Closure—that "make their advocacy crystal clear." IDI indicated that the Pillars allow for the "facilitation of consent, communication with production, and comfortable choreography, as well as providing context surrounding the scene's place in the narrative and support in terms of actor closure, so that performers can separate the characters from their real lives."[14] While the Pillars are a creation of IDI, they have become a popular framework for academic and professional intimacy on a broader scale since 2016, when IDI placed the pillars online as an open resource.[15]

February 2017: Rachel Dart creates "Let Us Work" initiative

Motivated by both the exposure of behavior at the Profiles Theatre and an experience with her own harasser, New York director Rachel

Dart created a survey that gave voice to artists' experiences with sexual harassment in theatre. "Let Us Work" picked up steam as more artists used the network to share information regarding the following topics: theaters adopting harassment policies, names of harassers, navigating complaints in non-union companies, etc. "Let Us Work, Dart hopes, could catch the stories that fall through the cracks, and could even help to fill those cracks once and for all."[16]

June 2017: The New York Times *writes a story about intimacy direction for* The Bakkhai *at the Stratford Festival*

The New York Times covers Tonia Sina's intimacy direction at the Stratford Festival, sparking a national conversation about the conception of the new field of intimacy direction. The article specifies Sina's process: "Ms. Condlln, who had done only one onstage sex scene before 'Bakkhai,' said that Ms. Sina's presence allowed the company to have 'really fluid communication' about the moments of intimacy. Ms. Condlln, too, likened the practical, technical nature of the work to stage fighting, which is tightly planned even when it feels explosive to the audience. 'Inside the fight, it's like paint by numbers,' she said. 'And there's something about Tonia's building a vocabulary that she's endeavoring to make the intimacy the same. So that in the throes of onstage passion, things never wander. Nobody ever gets lost along the way, and therefore everybody is safe.'"[17]

October 2017: Accusations against Miramax Mogul Harvey Weinstein made public

A collection of accusations against Weinstein are made public in an article from *The New York Times*. A memo by Miramax employee Laura O'Connor, anonymous statements from other colleagues of Weinstein, and ultimately an account by Hollywood star Ashley Judd all revealed a common narrative of the media mogul's inappropriate behavior. "An investigation by *The New York Times* found previously undisclosed allegations against Mr. Weinstein stretching over nearly three decades, documented through interviews with current and former employees and film industry workers, as well as legal records, emails and internal documents from the businesses he has run, Miramax and the Weinstein Company."[18] Soon after the story broke, The Weinstein Company fired its co-founder.

January 2018: Time's Up Foundation is formed

Spearheaded by over 300 women in entertainment, an anti-harassment coalition known as "Time's Up"[19] is created with three goals for women in mind: Safety (insisting on workplace safety), Equity (leveling the playing field), and Power (disrupting harmful power structures). Time's Up pushed the conversation about abuse of power and harassment in Hollywood to a new level, and now works toward creating change beyond the entertainment industry as well. The organization is also known for its support of the development of intimacy coordination; the Time's Up website offers an extensive guide to working in entertainment and includes a document titled "Your Rights in Nude, Intimate, and Sex Scenes."[20]

February 2018: Alicia Rodis develops the role of intimacy coordinator for HBO's The Deuce

After actress Emily Meade found herself grappling with her level of comfort with the sexually explicit material in HBO's drama *The Deuce*, she met with the show's creators to discuss the involvement of an intimacy coordinator.[21] They agreed to add one to the team, and IDI's co-founder Alicia Rodis became the network's first intimacy coordinator. A regular addition on set, Rodis acted as advocate for all actors involved in intimate scenes, as well as an ambassador for consent practices among cast, crew, and staff of the show. "Meade describes Rodis as 'like a mother or a sister on set' who looks out for her and other actors. The job has existed in the theater world for several years, but it is relatively new to film and television."[22]

October 2018: HBO commits to using intimacy coordinators network-wide

Becoming an advocate for the field of intimacy direction after hiring Alicia Rodis for her work on *The Deuce*, showrunner David Simon vowed never to work without an intimacy coordinator again. As a result, HBO publicly committed to using an intimacy coordinator for all their shows that include nudity and/or intimacy. Rodis was hired as the Lead Intimacy Coordinator for the network. "In practical terms, Rodis is a mediator among actors, directors, producers and crew. She reviews scripts, facilitates group discussions about the sex scenes they're going to film and meets with actors individually. When new or tweaked sex scenes are added to a day's shoot, she is often the one to break the news to an actor, checking in to clarify what their personal boundaries are." Rodis adds, "I am here to give a voice to actors, especially actors who feel like they don't have one. And I'm also here for the producers, to make sure that they know they're doing their best to make sure the set is safe."[23]

May 2019: Intimacy direction moves to Broadway

Claire Warden, IDC co-founder, directed intimacy for Broadway's revival of *Frankie and Johnny in the Clair de Lune*, starring Audra McDonald and Michael Shannon. Additional Broadway productions began to include intimacy direction, including the production of Jeremy O. Harris's *Slave Play*, which was co-choreographed by Teniece Divya Johnson (Broadway's first black and non-binary ID)[24] and Warden. Says Warden, "There's a lot of talk about making actors comfortable.... I don't use the word comfortable, because most of our really exciting drama is not comfortable. My job is to make sure that my actors are confident in what is happening so they can do their work."[25]

July 2019: Stage Directors and Choreographers Society Publication SDC Journal *focuses on intimacy choreography*

The union for theatrical directors and choreographers focused an issue of the journal on staged intimacy. Laura Penn, Executive Director of SDC, wrote that as directors, movement directors, and choreographers, "one of the most acute industry shifts right now is in the discourse around staging intimacy. This issue of the *Journal* provides a glimpse into some of the wide-ranging approaches and responses to this rapidly evolving movement."[26]

January 2020: Oregon Shakespeare Festival hires a resident intimacy director

Intimacy professional Sarah Lozoff was hired as resident ID for all 11 of the Oregon Shakespeare Festival's productions in 2020. While some other companies within the United States had hired resident intimacy directors, the visible support of intimacy work from a leading regional theater highlights the importance of the role. Laura Collins-Hughes writes for *The New York Times*, "Evren Odcikin, the festival's interim associate artistic director, said in a news release on Thursday that the 'naming of intimacy direction as an essential artistic resource' would 'have long-lasting impact at our institution and nationwide.'"[27]

March 2020: Staging Sex *is published*

Intimacy Director Chelsea Pace, co-founder of the organization Theatrical Intimacy Education, published *Staging Sex: Best Practices, Tools, and Techniques for Theatrical Intimacy*[28]—the first comprehensive text on tools and techniques for crafting and staging moments of nudity, intimacy, and sexual violence for the stage.

June 8, 2020: We See You, White American Theatre *call to action document is published online*

A collective of Black, Indigenous, and People of Color (BIPOC) theatremakers formed to expose racism, white supremacy, and other abusive practices. The collective states that they are a "multi-generational, multi-disciplinary, early career, emerging and established artists, theater managers, executives, students, administrators, dramaturges and producers, [formed] to address the scope and pervasiveness of anti-Blackness and racism in the American theater. Our response was to draft a strong testimonial letter, 'DEAR WHITE AMERICAN THEATER', collectively crafted by theatremakers from across the country, exposing the indignities and racism that BIPOC, and in particular Black theatremakers, face on a day-to-day basis in the theater industry."[29] Over 50,000 signatures were added to the attached petition within the first 24 hours of being posted online. Calls for professional support of the staging of intimacy are mentioned several times in the document.

September 2020: ELLE *magazine releases article on Black intimacy coordinators*

ELLE magazine's Candice Frederick interviewed intimacy coordinators Teniece Divya Johnson and Sasha Smith concerning the lack of diversity in intimacy for stage and screen, saying that while "intimacy coordination is a new industry, only slightly predating the Harvey Weinstein story that broke in 2017, it is overwhelmingly led by white people—many of whom don't have the context to recognize deep-rooted racial stereotypes like hyper-sexualization or trauma."[30] Johnson and Smith discussed the importance of the inclusion of black professionals not only for the work itself but for the actors involved. "Thankfully, there's been a line drawn in the sand, where we're not going back to this place of exclusion and our voices not being heard. We're seeing it in theater with the We See You movement. And in Hollywood there's a push for more representation behind the camera," says Sasha Smith during the interview. "I feel I am not doing my job if I am not advocating for all voices in the space and speaking to the direct oppression and harm that has been done before."

October 2021: Intimacy direction moves to the West End

Yarit Dor was appointed as the first intimacy director for UK's West End Theatres, being dually credited as fight and intimacy director for the Young Vic's transfer production of *Death of a Salesman*. Rosemary Waugh wrote for UK publication *The Stage*, "Dor suggests that a previous lack of adequate support when directing intimacy scenes wasn't down to inherently 'malicious' behaviour from directors, but a combination of work pressures and a genuine lack of knowledge—maybe even embarrassment—around how they were meant to handle these moments. Offering a recognised intimacy director or coordinator has been met with relief."[31]

February 2021: *Saturday Night Live* includes a sketch about intimacy oordination

Due to work on the Shonda Rhimes's Netflix sensation, *Bridgerton*, intimacy coordinator Lizzy Talbot gained visibility for the specialization in the United States and abroad through multiple publications and cast interviews.[32] SNL then creates and runs a comedy sketch titled "Bridgerton Intimacy Coordinator,"[33] based on the position held by Talbot. The skit humorously acknowledges the need for well-qualified and trained professionals to be involved with intimacy choreography. Phoebe Dynevor, who plays Daphne Bridgerton in the series, told Grazia UK regarding her work with intimacy coordinator Lizzy Talbot, "It was so great, because it felt safe and fun: you choreograph it like a stunt or dance. It's crazy to me that that hasn't been there in the past."[34]

April 2021: SAG-AFTRA sets intimacy coordination accreditation program

After a 2019 announcement that committed SAG-AFTRA to standardizing the use of intimacy coordinators and their practices, the labor union for screen artists eventually established an accreditation program for professionals seeking to practice intimacy coordination. "The purpose of these standards is to assure SAG-AFTRA members that when they are on set with an intimacy coordinator, they are being protected and advocated for by a qualified professional. Qualified intimacy coordinators will not only have been trained with tools to help keep actors and production safe but also will have completed the minimum amount of days and training to be considered a professional experienced enough to handle a variety of situations during intimate and hyper-exposed scenes."[35] SAG-AFTRA also set out to create a registry for those coordinators who meet the qualifications to practice under union approval.[36]

March 2022: SAG-AFTRA accredits seven training programs for intimacy coordinators

SAG-AFTRA has accredited seven intimacy-coordinator training programs to help expand the pool of qualified intimacy coordinators, who serve as advocates and liaisons between actors and production in scenes involving nudity and simulated sex. "Having experienced, qualified intimacy coordinators on set," the union said, "helps to ensure that SAG-AFTRA members who are filming scenes with nudity or simulated sex are able to work in a manner that maintains their personal and professional dignity while realizing the director's creative vision."[37]

July 2022: SAG-AFTRA National Board approves membership path for Intimacy Coordinators

SAG-AFTRA National Board unanimously passes a resolution to create a path to SAG-AFTRA membership for intimacy coordinators. "The role of intimacy coordinators greatly improves safety and well-being on sets and in productions requiring intimate scenes," said SAG-AFTRA President Fran Drescher. "Their value is immeasurable and the National Board is committed to bringing intimacy coordinators into the SAG-AFTRA family and ensuring they have the kind of benefits and protections other members already enjoy."[38]

Moving forward: A wide variety of practitioners continue to collaborate, evolve, and innovate within this field. We have included contributions from several of these professionals throughout this text, and highlight several prominent intimacy organizations in the appendix. We recognize and celebrate the achievements of these professionals and organizations, as well as the ongoing contributions of multiple intimacy pioneers, advocates and passionate artists around the world who have yet to gain visibility or have gained visibility since this publication.

The Production Pillars of Intimacy

One of the early and most essential tools that emerged during the formation of IDI was the Pillars of Intimacy Direction. These pillars are five foundational elements that create a structure to support the healthy and safe staging of intimate storytelling: Context, Consent, Communication, Choreography, and Closure. While IDI created these pillars primarily for actors and creators most directly involved in the staging of intimacy, we have adapted these definitions to apply more broadly to the entire creative team.

While we will be exploring and defining these five pillars separately, they all intersect, interact, and have constant interplay when in practice. One pillar may take precedence in certain moments, but they often work in tandem to create an even sturdier structure.

Working relationships built upon the framework of these pillars will empower every member of the team to come to their work with understanding, confidence, and the knowledge that they are working in a values-driven environment.

Context

Context is the W's of a show: who, what, where, when, why? Who is involved? What is the story? And where, when, and why is this particular story occurring? It is an understanding of the story that leads to staged intimacy, or the purpose of the scene or scenes to the overall arch of the story. Scripted intimate moments may exist to create catharsis or conflict, or may be used to incite humor, excitement, fear, or more. Context may also refer to the community within which the intimacy is being staged; for example, are we performing for youth audiences, in an academic setting, or on a long-running tour? Another perspective of context is from the creative team involved, as in, is the team producing the work composed of first-time or long-time collaborators? Understanding context allows everyone involved on the production to start out on the same page.

Consent

Consent in the practice of building physical theatre is a willingness to participate, partnered with the ability to say "no." This means that consent takes a deep awareness of one's personal boundaries when asked to perform or receive an action and the confidence and trust in the ability to refuse or

ADAPTED FROM THE PILLARS CREATED BY
INTIMACY DIRECTION INTERNATIONAL (IDI)

Production Pillars for Intimacy

Context
UNDERSTANDING STORY & INTIMACY

The **W**'s of a show: **W**ho, **W**hat, **W**here, **W**hen, **W**hy
Understanding the story and purpose behind the intimacy and how it may relate to each department of the production

Consent
INDIVIDUAL AGENCY & AUTONOMY

Understanding expectations and context, appreciating the significance of the information and choosing to engage.

Communication
CLEAR CONTINUOUS CONNECTION

Maintaining open and continuous connections across the entire production team by understanding boundaries, sharing reporting structures, and supporting the company through continued discussion.

Choreography
PHYSICAL STORYTELLING

Established physical movements - both onstage and backstage - that are clear, specific, repeatable; built with consent, understanding of context, utilizing clear communication.

Closure
STEP OUT WITH SELF-CARE

An established mindful routine, used by members of the production, to step out of the fabricated story and back into their own everyday reality.

ORIGINAL PILLARS CREATED BY:
TONIA SINA, ALICIA RODIS, AND SIOBHAN RICHARDSON

Figure 1.1 Five boxes that contain the terms and definitions of the production pillars of intimacy. Image created by Tina M. Newhauser.

request an adjustment to the suggested action. For performers involved in the physical storytelling, consensual partnering is assisted through self-analysis (Will this work for me?), partner communication (Am I supporting what works for them?), and ongoing check-ins as necessary (Does this still work for me and them?). For leaders in the room, actors in the process of deciding whether to consent will need specificity in communication, openness to shifts in the way stories are told, and the active mitigation of social or power-based pressure that may be inhibiting the capability to say "no." We will discuss this in more detail in Chapter 2, when we dive into building a culture of consent in the theatrical workspace.

Intimacy directors are skilled at navigating consent in the rehearsal hall and are a liaison between production and performers when creating challenging content. Dr. Jessica Steinrock, CEO of IDC, supports this assertion, saying that "when seeking consent, the answer of either yes, no, or maybe can be accepted graciously into the creative process. This can be done by presenting multiple options along with the caveat that if none of those options work, another one will be found and presented. Intimacy directors are particularly skilled with this type of communication, making them an invaluable member of the team for scenes of intimacy when the risk level is generally much higher."[39]

Consent is not fixed but ongoing and should be evaluated and supported by the creative team throughout rehearsals and the entire production. According to Dr. Steinrock, "Consent is a nuanced and collaborative process. The intimacy director facilitates consent and support[s] actors through problematic and coercive power structures, but the intimacy director cannot create consent alone."[40] Establishing a creative process based on mutual respect of each individual's decision to engage on their terms should be the foundation for workplace culture. Steinrock reminds us that "consent is a core concept in all that we do as entertainers, not just for scenes of intimacy, and calls for reflection as we interrogate our responsibility in each other's health, well-being, and safety through the utilizing of active and informed consent."[41]

Communication

Throughout this book, we will be highlighting the importance of communication at every step of the process. Improving communication involves steps that range from building an intentional institutional culture that supports consensual working relationships to navigating individual productions to staging moments of intimacy. Communication for the creative team is multifaceted. We will give multiple practical tips and tools to support staged intimacy from pre-audition to performance. However, in utilizing the pillars in the rehearsal hall, communication will first be considered on the macro level by asking, "How can this particular team and these particular people best tell this story?" The answer lies in discussing the unique boundaries of that ensemble alongside the desired theatrical narrative. Considering the boundaries of actors and other creative team members will help maintain physical and emotional health while the team determines the best story to be told.

During the staging of intimacy within classes and productions, ongoing communication also prioritizes people and process over product. Discussions may impact scheduling, reinforce the utilization of mindful and affirming language throughout rehearsal, provide room to ask questions, enable check-ins between scene partners, support processes for conflict resolution or reporting if issues arise, and more. Methods of communication should always be inclusive, ongoing, and transparent.[42]

Choreography

Choreography, or sequences with choreographic parameters, should be built with consent from all involved and always be clear, specific, and repeatable. Intimacy choreography entails the physical movements involved in staged intimacy, which may be impacted by elements such as tempo, duration, intensity, and more. For our purposes in this work, we have called choreography the muscular script[43] or the body language that may go along with or exist in between moments of scripted dialogue in a show.

Choreographed moments may range from stories of breath and eye contact that contain no actual physical contact, or may contain a masked moment that tells a different story to the audience than what is physically happening to the actors (similar to a stage punch not actually landing on a stage partner). Choreography may also include simulated sex acts or shaping moments around staged nudity.

There are different methods to script intimate physical moments. Intimacy choreographers create tailored pieces of movement for each show in connection with actors and the director. However, sometimes there may be transitions between choreographed moments that allow for flexibility or improvisation by the actors. These moments of spontaneity will still be built with respect to the boundaries of the actor and have a clear container (see lists in Appendices C and E) for the actors involved. We will speak more about choreographic methods in Chapter 4.

The choreography pillar may apply to other members of the creative team in regard to consent, such as the choreographing of costume quick changes. Choreographing may also apply to how an actor safely leaves the stage after a scene of simulated sex or nudity, and this could involve lighting, scenic or stage management to protect modesty, and professionalism in the transition to a backstage space. This application of the choreography pillar usually takes place during technical rehearsals, which is discussed in Chapter 5.

Closure

Within the pillars crafted by IDI, closure is used both as a ritual to signify the ending of the work and as an active framing for self-care. Defined by the American Psychological Association as "the act, achievement, or sense of completing or resolving something,"[44] closure involves setting a repeatable, physical bookend for challenging content. Whether bookending a scene in rehearsal, an entire day of rehearsal, or the run of the show, this bookending routine will help actors release the emotional or physical stories the characters are experiencing, allowing them to actively separate actor from character, or art from life. However, this is not used only for actors. We highly recommend that stage managers, directors, run crew, or anyone witnessing or having an emotional response to the storytelling also form their own ritual for closure that supports self-care.

Closure practices vary from person to person and may include routines or elements that center the person mentally and ground them physically. Fulfilling these requirements may include moments of repeated deep breaths, feeling one's feet firmly on the floor, a quiet pause of mindfulness while listening to the sounds of the space one is in, or purposeful mental focus as one uses physical movements (such as clapping together one's hands or brushing off invisible energy from one's body). Whatever the routine, it should provide healthy methods for individuals to step out of the fabricated story and back into their everyday reality.

An additional component of closure is self-care. Self-care involves engaging with practices or strategies that promote well-being or more regulated functioning. The process of engaging in self-care may look very different from individual to individual. Ultimately, self-care should be a holistic practice that supports one's physical, mental, and emotional health.[45]

Establishing a healthy closure practice allows every creative team member to process the day's activities emotionally, mentally, and physically. A stage manager, director, designer, or any team member may not realize how much a moment of physically or emotionally charged content can affect their health in the short or long term. In their article *The Impact of Acting on Student Actors: Boundary Blurring, Growth, and Emotional Distress*,[46] Burgoyne et al. highlight the importance of agency when it comes to self-care within theatrical storytelling, as theatremakers are sometimes telling stories very close to their own emotional histories. "Our study suggests that actors' awareness of these issues may not only lead to developing strategies for preventing uncontrolled blurring, but also give them a context in which to understand problems that may arise," Burgoyne writes. Through self-reflection or processing, the act of intentional closure will allow for care of self and a release of residual energy in a positive way. For more information on this vital pillar, look to Chapter 6 to further explore closure, emotional resilience, and self-care.

Pillars in practice

Tonia Sina, founder of Intimacy Directors International, often expands the 5 C's of the Pillars with what she calls the "secret sixth Pillar: Change."[47] Change exists both externally and internally in intimacy direction. Outwardly, this work is about transforming the industry by transforming current standards, expanding individual willingness to adapt to new practices, and creating change through storytelling. Inwardly, this relatively new specialization is constantly evolving so it may better support the needs of creatives, actors, as well as support the well-being of the entire production team.

Positive communication practices found in the pillars demonstrate one clear way production teams can have a transformative effect on the creative output of both individuals and ensembles. The article *Proof that Positive Work Cultures are More Productive* concludes that "a positive workplace is more successful over time because it increases positive emotions and well-being. This, in turn, improves people's relationships with each other and amplifies their abilities and their creativity."[48] More beneficial work environments and relationships can be nurtured through the use of these pillars, not only for the actors taking part in the staging of intimacy but also for the entire creative team.

Foundational vocabulary for staged intimacy

Staged intimacy is, at its core, a movement specialization. Like stage combat, dance, or other movement techniques, there are terms and phrases that are unique and yet common. Understanding this language before an intimacy professional arrives will help with communication, notation, and maintaining of these moments. While this list contains some foundational terms, in subsequent chapters we will begin by highlighting that chapter's key terms for staged intimacy and intimacy direction to aid the reader in navigating the material. These key terms support specific content in each chapter. For a full list of vocabulary from all chapters and citations for the trainings and reference materials that informed definitions, please see "Terms & Language Acknowledgement" and the "Glossary of Key Terms" in Appendix E.

Staged intimacy

Staged intimacy can be broadly defined as scenes with intimate physical contact, such as sex scenes and kissing, as well as scenes that contain nudity. This can be expanded to include familial and platonic intimacy, sexual tension, and "chemistry" where no touching occurs. It often is an element in scenes of sexual violence.

Intimacy direction

A comprehensive approach to the creation of scenes or moments of intimacy on stage and screen. Intimacy direction may also be referred to as intimacy choreography, intimacy design, intimacy movement, intimate storytelling, or other descriptors.

Intimacy director

An intimacy director, or ID, is a choreographer, an advocate for actors, and a liaison between actors and production for scenes that involve nudity/hyper exposed work, simulated sex acts, and intense physical contact in live performance. IDs work to achieve the vision of the director while respecting the boundaries of the actors. Intimacy professionals may work under other titles, such as "Intimacy Choreographer," "Intimacy Specialist," or "Intimacy Designer."

Intimacy coordinator

Intimacy coordinators are movement specialists who choreograph scenes of intimacy and serve as an advocate for consent practices and procedures around rehearsing and performing moments of intimacy for the screen (film and television).

Intimacy consultant

An intimacy consultant is a trained intimacy specialist who is brought on for a brief conversation or workshop that provides foundational tools for the performers within the run of a live production. This position does not entail choreographing each moment of intimacy within the production.

The pillars

Created by the founders of IDI, the pillars for intimacy are five foundational elements that create a structure to support the safe staging of intimate storytelling: context, communication, consent, choreography, closure.[49]

Permission

Authorization for an action to occur. Permission may be given by those in authority or in charge of leading a scene of staged intimacy (such as a director or choreographer), while consent can only be given by those performing that action (such as the actors involved in the staging).

Consent

In intimacy direction, consent occurs when a person voluntarily agrees to a proposed action or series of actions. In order to consent, one must not be under the influence of duress or coercion, be able to revoke consent, and have a full, specific understanding of the action(s) being proposed.[50]

Boundaries

Specific, defined areas on the body that are off-limits to touch for any reason, and any other personal limitations or adjustments regarding touch that will be respected by other performers. Boundaries may include not only the location of the touch but the quality of touch. Methods for supporting boundaries will be discussed in detail in Chapter 4.

Discomfort Scale

A self-assessment tool that assists in understanding both boundaries and self-care.

The "Discomfort Scale"[51]

As a self-assessment tool for understanding artistic and personal boundaries during the staging of intimacy and beyond, the discomfort scale can be verbally discussed or displayed as a visual aid. Note that the scale emphasizes a varying relation to comfort in relation to consent. An intimacy professional might ask performers about their level of *confidence* with a proposed action versus their level of *comfort*. While comfort may occur for performers in staging intimacy, discomfort is not necessarily a negative element when connected to artistic growth. When described, printed, or drawn out, this scale can be used by actors, students, and other team members to personally gauge and subsequently communicate the difference between comfort, growth, discomfort, and trauma. For an example of the visual aid, please see the charts below.

When analyzing this scale, one may note that it may work for physical work as well as emotional work. When working to grow a new skill, it is easy to

> **From Dr. Jessica Steinrock, CEO of IDC[52]: <u>Confidence versus comfort, and identifying discomfort in the rehearsal hall</u>**
>
> Many intimacy practitioners use a scale or spectrum for measuring or classifying discomfort and how it relates to artmaking. Not all discomfort is problematic, and many times it is how one grows as an artist. However, it is vital to be clear that the discomfort scale is a tool the intimacy professional would share with actors to use for their own self-analysis. The scale is not a tool of coercion for those in directorial, management or choreographic positions to push actors beyond physical or emotional boundaries: Only the actor involved in the physical staging can determine whether they are experiencing growth or have reached a boundary.
>
> Below we have included two examples of how intimacy professionals may describe the scale to help an actor distinguish between being uncomfortable and being unsafe.

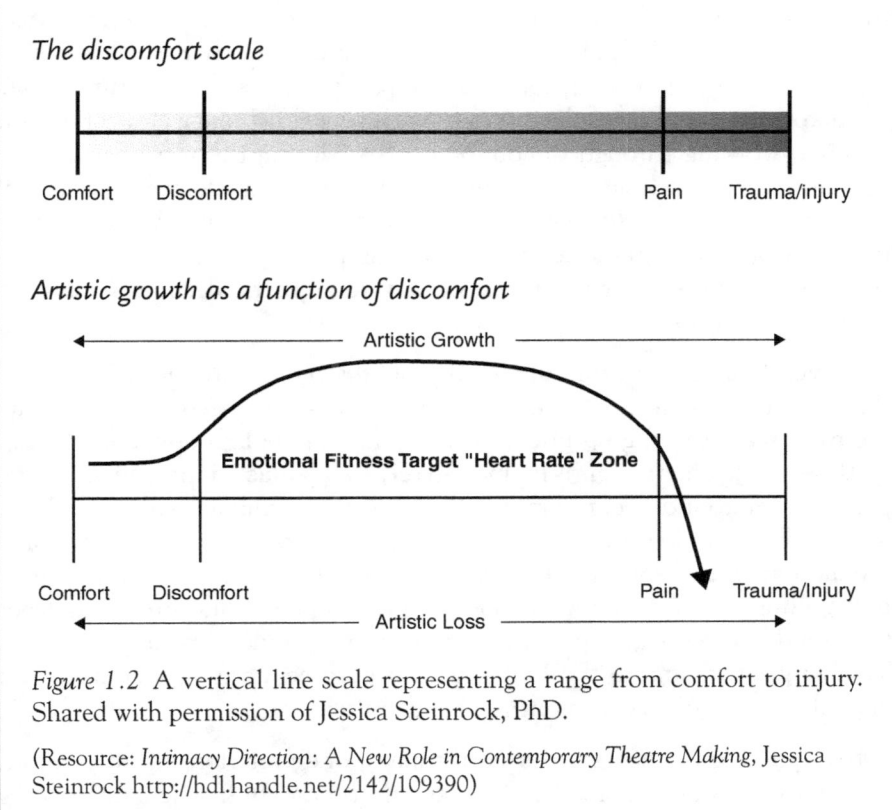

Figure 1.2 A vertical line scale representing a range from comfort to injury. Shared with permission of Jessica Steinrock, PhD.

(Resource: *Intimacy Direction: A New Role in Contemporary Theatre Making*, Jessica Steinrock http://hdl.handle.net/2142/109390)

become uncomfortable. When working physically, it may take only one or two repetitions of an exercise to experience discomfort. But this discomfort is not pain, and it may take many more repetitions of an exercise to become severely uncomfortable or to experience pain. When educating intimacy students about this scale at a training workshop,[53] instructors explained that within intimacy work, physical or emotional pain (as defined by the person experiencing it) is an indicator that something needs to change or stop. This could be noticing that one needs a knee pad to continue to repeat choreography that involves kneeling, or noticing that the emotional content is building to distress in a non-repeatable way. Overall, those engaging with theatrical intimacy should keep examining their personal relationship between discomfort and pain while building intimate choreography. Artistic growth may still exist at the first sign of pain for some, but progress may generally become stunted if one continues to ignore or push past the pain threshold.[54]

Intimacy direction's goal is not to make every moment fully comfortable, but the actor should always feel secure or confident in what they are doing. Much like training the body for a stunt as part of a physically strenuous role, the actor interested in exploring roles with staged intimacy can train their stamina, working through discomfort so that during the run of the show, they are able to work sustainably and safely. Another analogy for a practical use of the discomfort scale could be the process of gaining flexibility in a limb. While stretching, one will be moving past their comfort and experiencing the pressure or tension necessary to gain the desired increase in flexibility bit by bit.[55]

However, like physical training, emotional discomfort and growth requires that the actor is meeting their biological and safety needs, such as staying hydrated, warming up prior to the work, and cooling down afterwards. Without these practices, it is far more likely that a practitioner will cross the pain threshold and become injured or experience trauma—which will set the performer back, ultimately ending in artistic losses on an individual and production level. To again reference our flexibility analogy, one can imagine that pulling or tearing a muscle due to ignoring pain while stretching leads to extended time needed for rest, recuperation, physical therapy, or worse. That kind of trauma to the limb would stop someone from reaching their flexibility goals for weeks, months, or indefinitely.

When building moments of staged intimacy, one's relationship to comfort, discomfort and growth may change at any time. Thus, when referencing Figure 1.2, understand that this is a highly individualized scale. While drawn permanently on the page, the lines on this rendering of the scale can adjust along the scale in either direction (toward comfort or pain). This adjustment may occur due to physical or psychological changes in a performer. The catalyst for change may occur in or outside rehearsal and last for brief or extended periods. Growth in confidence or understanding of a role or physical repetition that leads to desensitization may also change one's relationship to this scale. Due to these factors, continuous check-ins on boundaries, comfort, and confidence are vital to staging these moments. For more information on the check-in process, see Chapter 4.

Artistic and production team members may also want to gauge their positioning on the discomfort scale prior to joining a rehearsal that involves a story of simulated sex, simulated sexual violence, or nudity. Team members such as stage managers, designers, and others who witness the work daily may need to examine this scale and their need to check in prior to, during, or after these rehearsals.

Methods for supporting mental health in theatrical productions

Within the extensive training one goes through to become a certified, accredited, or qualified intimacy professional, a vital layer of education relates to mental health. Mental Health First Aid[56] is one training that intimacy professionals and other creative team members may take to ensure that an individual can understand and identify signs of distress or unease. In a 2018 article for the *Huffpost*, Claire Warden referenced mental health when mentioning that fight scenes and those involving intimate, physical touch can be uniquely similar in their psychological impact on those performing them. "Our psyches have an enormously difficult time differentiating between real and staged violence, even if no contact is made. It's the same with this. It becomes real in the moment," she said, comparing intimacy direction to the precautions taken to avoid physical injury in cases of staged fighting. "You have equipment you work with so you don't get hurt," Warden said. "When you're doing a fall, you ask for a mat. We don't want to break the actor. Well, we don't want to break the actor emotionally or psychologically either."[57]

Intimacy directors may advocate for the provision of mental health resources in the production's rehearsal space. Stage management may also research and post local and national resources or request this information from upper management. Irrelevant of who does the legwork, when accessing and gathering information for the production team and performers, it is preferred to find a variety of resources[58] that provide the following:

- Options of phone-in, Zoom-in, in-person counseling services
- Providers with Global Majority and LGBTQ therapists on staff
- Federal, state, and local options
- Options with sliding scales for cost

In addition to providing resources within the rehearsal hall, members of the production team could consider supporting safety in the workplace by completing training in Mental Health First Aid. Similar to the American Red Cross's First Aid & CPR training,[59] programs offered by organizations such as National Council for Mental Wellbeing[60] discuss community health care providers and national resources, support groups, and online tools for mental health. All trainees receive a program manual to complement the course material, which includes a list of local and national mental health resources.

Mental Health First Aid training offers the following skills for members of a theatrical team:

- Steps to take if someone is in flight, fight,[61] or freeze mode.
- Ways to recognize the signs of a panic attack (in oneself or others)
- Preparation for possible scenarios that may occur
- Ways to recognize the signs of inebriation

In planning for staged intimacy, possible physical conditions of the performing actors such as reactive immobility (otherwise known as "freeze mode") as a trauma response or insobriety due to prescriptive or non-prescriptive substances can have a profound impact on communication and consent. Access to tools and training on initial signs of these conditions can allow for the rehearsal being paused or halted when necessary, and assistance or redirection to occur.

When working in academia, mental health resources and preventative training may be available for educators through human resources or departments specializing in physical and mental health. Suzanne Shawyer and Kim Shively, co-authors of *Education in Theatrical Intimacy as Ethical Practice for University Theatre*, suggest that "theatre educators should be aware of the potential for triggers and trauma responses in the acting classroom and rehearsal hall, and seek out tools to teach students how to establish physical and emotional boundaries that help distinguish self from character."[62] One can seek out

 Creative team spotlight: Upper administration

While many intimacy specialists/directors (IS/Ds) may take training in these areas, administrators hoping to provide resources around mental health should remember that IS/Ds are not a replacement for psychologists or mental health professionals in the rehearsal hall. As movement specialists who support communication, consent, and self-care, intimacy professionals will work to help actors work mindfully and consensually, which may promote a more psychologically healthy working environment. However, remember that a deep understanding of mental health, psychology, and the nuances of navigating interpersonal conflict is a job for human resources or other specialized consultants. For additional resources, reference the mental health section in Appendix F: A Partial List of Pertinent Resources.

programs at their university that offer how to identify warning signs, offer supportive language to use when speaking with students who may be in distress, and programs that provide additional health-related resources for students as needed. While it is becoming standard for most departments to provide a variety of online or in-person workshops and training that help to ensure teachers support a collaborative learning environment, these can be sought out independently when unavailable on the local level.

Methods for advocating for intimacy professionals

As we explore taking on a project with staged intimacy, the first step to take is determining if an intimacy professional is needed for the project. Making this determination will take asking a few important questions, and IDC helps us by providing several questions to get one started. Found within their resource guide, available online,[63] they ask the following:

- Does the scene require nudity and/or simulated sex of any kind?
- Does the scene involve simulated genital contact, either over or under clothing?
- Does the scene contain heightened sexually charged physicality? (e.g., intense kissing)
- Are there any power dynamics or pre-existing relationships within the company that may necessitate the use of an outside eye?

Examining the needs of the production regarding staged intimacy may begin with these technical questions regarding the physical stories being told and the dynamics of the environment in which they are being built. (See Chapter 2 for more information on power dynamics and staged intimacy).

In addition to these four factors there may be considerations regarding the content of the story being told, such as when a script contains charged language and themes. For example, stories that explore racism may require specialized care. When considering the role of an intimacy specialist in these productions, it is important to have an understanding of the area of expertise of the intimacy specialist. While some staged intimacy choreographers have multiple points of nuanced training, an intimacy specialist's skillsets are not synonymous with those of other specializations, such as cultural consultants, mental health professionals, or other workplace advisors. These areas of expertise can take years of specialized training to perform safely and responsibly. (See the following section, "Specializations Within the Field of Staged Intimacy," for more information.)

When it is determined that a project would greatly benefit from the expertise of an intimacy professional, how does one begin to encourage the inclusion of the position and its practices? The solution could be found through advocacy. "Perhaps the simplest and most well-known definition of advocacy is to defend or promote a cause. This definition clearly shows that advocacy is active, not passive. As practitioners and researchers have attempted to define advocacy, action words such as identifying, influencing, supporting, recommending, representing, defending, intervening, and changing, are often used in the definition."[64] When it comes to being active in promoting the work of an intimacy professional, there may be a definitive need to identify, influence, support, recommend, represent, defend, and intervene, all in the name of change. Realizations that there is a deep need for change in some theatrical systems have given many the inspiration to advocate (this book's authors included).

Motivation to advocate is sparked by human connection and interaction. It is fueled by listening without ego and questioning with compassion. The desire to advocate grows through a deepening respect for identities, boundaries, and vulnerabilities and invites engaged and authentic communication. Advocates understand that change doesn't often happen overnight, and it doesn't happen in a vacuum. When minds are opened and new perspectives are explored, new approaches can be considered, such as the framework of intimacy direction. Advocating for change can be a long journey, but every tiny action is one small step in the right direction.

When starting down this road, one can look to Siobhan Richardson[65] for direction. As a co-founding member of Intimacy Directors International who pioneered this practice through Canada and into Europe and helped to define the Pillars of Intimacy, Richardson offers advice on how to advocate for intimacy direction as a practice. In a workshop hosted by Humble Warrior Movement Arts, a multi-faceted movement company based in Denver, Colorado,[66] Richardson and assistant instructor Cristina (Cha) Ramos[67] formulated an astute advocacy game plan: start by identifying and sharing successes. This means sharing stories about the productive work and positive results achieved from working with intimacy professionals, instead of warning companies or individuals about consequences that could occur if they do not hire one. This creates a tone of integrating intimacy as part of an uplifting growth process, rather than an avoidance of punitive action, and it allows conversations to focus on the process, the exploration, and the journey, rather than any "what-if" scenarios. Overall, to Ramos and Richardson, advocacy is a method of creating space for the practices and people in question to speak for themselves, rather than presuming a defensive position and "speaking for" intimacy.

Using positivity as a guide is helpful at all levels, from academic to professional. Sharing articles about industry professionals who are welcoming these modern practices and experiencing the positive impacts may change perceptions of those previously ingrained in less contemporary methods. Integrating the work of an intimacy professional into the educational system introduces these modern procedures early, helping emerging professionals reinforce these theatremaking processes as new standards of practice. Rather than focusing on negative consequences, which may cause more resistance or frustration, noting positive impacts of intimacy direction could create excitement to foster an evolving practice.

At times, sharing positive stories, press, or personal experiences does not lead to the desired result of hiring an intimacy professional such as an intimacy director. If one wants to continue to advocate for the hire, those receiving the request may continue to show reluctance or pushback and cite reasons why including an intimacy director is unwanted or impractical. Siobhan Richardson and Cha Ramos have created counterpoints to this pushback, which they state many times falls into one of four categories: money/funding, time, established practice, and artistic license. Below are responses Ramos and Richardson suggest one can have at the ready for the points of resistance to the hiring of an intimacy director, although all can be related to the hiring of any intimacy professional, such as an intimacy "choreographer," "consultant," or "designer."

Money/funding

When advocating for an ID, those receiving the suggestion may frame their response around the idea of budget or funding. In this case, an opening question could be "What do you perceive to be the cost of bringing in an intimacy professional?" What may be perceived as unaffordable could stem from a lack of knowledge. Intimacy direction is a new practice, and rates charged by intimacy professionals are not currently standardized. One base rate or scale has been established by the Society of Directors and Choreographers for fight direction, which may be used for reference by some intimacy choreographers, but this is not consistently utilized industry wide. This lack of reference and comparisons may make it difficult for upper management to know if it is financially feasible to add the position to the creative team.

One factor that highly impacts possible cost is the duration of rehearsal and consultation time that may be needed by an intimacy director. ID's may not need to join the creative team for the entire rehearsal process and asking the question of a professional ID can clear up the amount of time needed. Management could reach out to professionals (such as those listed on the websites of intimacy director associations and training companies) to inquire about the details on a certain project to determine the time and estimate a cost.

To expand on this further, here is a partial list of ways an intimacy director could be brought onto the team:

- Work on a part-time capacity, establish a day rate, then identify specific days when needed in rehearsal, or work on an "as-needed" basis, agree on an hourly rate, then identify specific hours when needed in rehearsal. These options are appropriate when the choreography is needed or when power dynamics must be navigated.
- Provide a few hours' consultation or one-time workshop at the start of rehearsal to establish base practices for the actors and team in rehearsal moving forward. This is appropriate when the choreography required is of a lower complexity (such as no nudity or simulated sex acts).
- Ask certified professionals if they can consult and/or offer initial workshops, and then have an experienced apprentice who would be right for the position come in for rehearsals. Note that the number of hours would still need to be clearly negotiated.

When compensation is a consideration, there is usually flexibility in this area as well:

- Offer alternate compensation such as work in exchange for publicity materials. This may include explicit thanks and uplifting of ID work as part of promotional work; for example, ensuring that an agreed-upon number of interviews include the ID, ensure that promo video shoots include time to capture (or to stage) footage of the ID in the process of working, feature exposure on the company's social media platform.
- Offer to barter for the work. Can the company provide space to the ID for them to use in their practice? Maybe they can teach workshops in that space rent-free for a set period, for example. Can the theatre offer access to digital subscriptions, such as a set number of premium Zoom hours, or permit the ID to access the theatre's script database, or offer free access to professional development provided by the theatre?

Whatever the perceived obstacle, a solution can usually be found if compromise is an option when considering services required and compensation.

Fundamentals of staged intimacy   43

Rehearsal time

The perception of time can have a strong influence on funding decisions. An argument may be made based on the *perceived* time that would be needed during rehearsal in what is already considered to be a tight schedule. Members of the creative team may believe that adding an extra person into the rehearsal room will take away more valuable rehearsal time than necessary. This may mean their understanding of the work of an ID is based on assumptions rather than any first-hand experience.

The reality is that engaging with a specialist may very well save you time, not take from it. The following can support this claim:

- The ID will save time because their knowledge and experience with established practices help actors quickly become confident with staged intimacy, allowing these scenes to reach "performance-level readiness" with less repetition.
- The ID will save time by understanding movements that fit best within the story; they will not spend time on movements that they already know won't work.
- The ID can make this work more efficient by creating a more collaborative environment in the rehearsal hall where every team member feels a reduction of resistance caused by a lack of comfort, whether in a scene of intimacy or not.
- If approved by the director, the ID can work with actors and an assistant director or assistant stage manager in a separate space, while the director works with a different set of performers, similar to how a fight director might work with a few actors in another rehearsal space.

And lastly, scenes attempted without an ID may lead to other unexpected problems. An actor may ask for one to be brought in after the scene's been repeatedly staged without causing delays in the process. The actors may have had an unsafe or uncomfortable experience creating moments with the director, or they may be inappropriately asked to create these moments on their own, leading to unhealthy relationships that permeate the process—or worse. When rehearsing, a director might use their power (knowingly or not) to coerce the actors into choreography, and actors can likewise coerce each other. Performances crafted in this manner are inevitably less sustainable and may lead to interpersonal conflict, less satisfying performance, and time wasted as the scene gets more rehearsal time because "it's just not working." It would be unfortunate to look back at the amount of time or discomfort one could have saved in cases such as these. Hours upon hours may have been spent navigating moments of intimacy in rehearsal before giving in to the realization that the need for the specialist was legitimate.

Established practice

Another argument may fall to established practice. When a producer, artistic director, director, or actor is presented with the opportunity of working with a staged intimacy professional for the first time, their initial response may be to decline. They may express the belief that their years of experience within this industry provide sufficient understanding, and they believe there is no need to add this new member or practice to the creative team. A belief that "we have always done it this way" may be the first reaction, as when faced with a new idea or challenge, one's instinctual response may be to do what is easy and remain in one's comfort zone.

The phrase comfort zone, coined by Judith M. Bardwich, PhD,[68] states, "The comfort zone is a behavioral state within which a person operates in an anxiety-neutral condition, using a limited set of behaviors to deliver a steady level of performance, usually without a sense of risk."[69] This anxiety-neutral condition, one that is believed to be risk free, may feel comfortable at the start and take little to no effort to maintain. Easy is not always better; being firmly rooted in zones that may stifle creativity or growth is counterproductive, especially when working with challenging material.

Working through past insecurities and inexperience can be scary, and those advocating should lead with empathy and perseverance as they begin to nudge anyone resisting this change. "It takes courage to step from the comfort zone into the fear zone. Without a clear roadmap, there's no way to build on previous experiences. This can be anxiety provoking. Yet persevere long enough, and you enter the learning zone, where you gain new skills and deal with challenges resourcefully. After a learning period, a new comfort zone is created, expanding one's ability to reach even greater heights."[70] These greater heights in how we work creatively result in scaling greater heights in what we produce as artists, in what we put on stage, and that is ultimately what excites an audience and draws them in.

Psychologists have visually laid out four different zones (comfort, fear, learning, growth) that one may travel through on their way to finding purpose, realizing aspirations, or for theatre artists, creating groundbreaking work. This psychological system translates into a performance-based discipline quite naturally (Figure 1.3), and may clarify the process advocates may

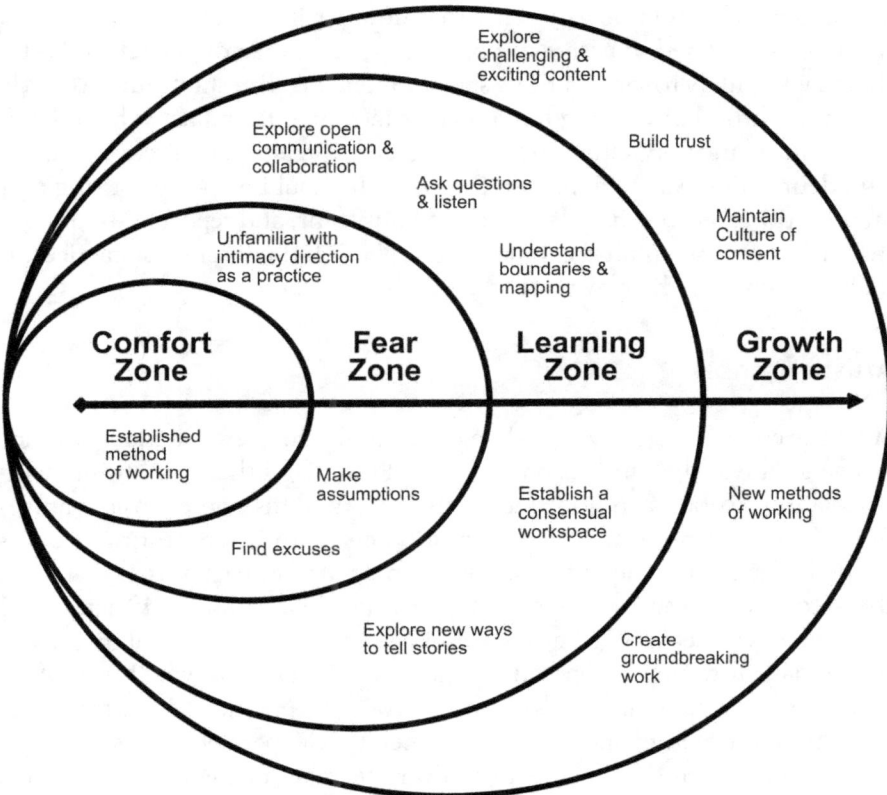

Figure 1.3 A vertical line scale representing a range from comfort to injury, adding in a line representing artistic growth.[71] Shared with permission of Jessica Steinrock, PhD.

witness in their counterparts who are transitioning from their formerly established practice.

If those feeling internal pushback toward the practices found in staged intimacy can allow the journey from comfort zone to growth zone to happen (similar to how actors work with the discomfort scale described earlier in this chapter), working with an intimacy director may become preferred. It is helpful to keep in mind that the rehearsal process included in staged intimacy is, in many ways, very similar to how the rehearsal process worked before. Intimacy directors look at the desired movement (or blocking) that supports the story being explored; emotion and intention are found to motivate these movements; and the audience is then moved by the achieved interaction. This isn't new; it's only that now we are working with someone specifically qualified to actively explore consent and actor agency and set a shared vocabulary to support these specific moments. By establishing a clearly outlined method of working for character movements and actor boundaries during intimate storytelling, the entire creative team may discover a more confident, easier way to approach the work. It should not be surprising that an intentional process based upon clear, consistent, and repeatable storytelling, character-driven physical movement, trust and consensual practices, is quickly becoming the new preferred established practice.

Artistic license

When it comes to creative freedom, one hurdle this new practice may face is a general fear that an ID's processes could hinder a theatrical team member's ability to be open and free in their work. This apprehension ranges from directors fearing the loss of artistic license to actors fearing the loss of their organic attachment to the moment. Siobhan Richardson mentions the actor's perspective in collaboration with an ID, saying that "actors will say they're worried about being over-choreographed, or that talking about it will make it weird, as opposed to what actually happens, which is it offers space for discussing all details of the story."[72] In practice, these fears may be assuaged as actors and other team members experience the collaboration involved in intimacy direction. Every member of the creative team is encouraged to bring their talents to the creation of a moment. For example, actors are encouraged to set boundaries that work for them or are asked to give input on storytelling as they work with the intimacy director. One aim of an intimacy professional is that actors have tools and agency to work creatively within a structure that supports their partners and themselves.

Needs will vary from team member to team member, but a trained ID will find agreements for the methods of working that allow for the voices of the production team members and actors to be heard and respected. Stephanie Coen looks more closely at the collaboration process with directors in the article "Staging Intimacy." Coen interviews Chelsea Pace, intimacy director and founder of Theatrical Intimacy Education (TIE), who says there are three ways directors will work. The first is that the director directly states what they personally want for each moment. The second option is that Pace and the director collaborate with the actors to find each moment together. Thirdly, Pace is brought in to choreograph moments without input from the director as it is being built. "Option two is always my preference," Pace says, "because I'm coming into the room as a collaborator. But all three of these options are responding to how the director wants to work."⁷³ Overall, the intimacy professional will support the director's work and the actor's process as well as work with the designers, dance choreographer, fight choreographer, or others. Collaboration opens the door to complete creative freedom while supporting the actors responsible for performing the movement night after night.

If the director is still unsure as to how they may work with an ID, there are a few steps that may help to guide them:

- Find a local freelance ID who may be able to meet with the director to start a conversation about this work so they may better understand the practice in general.
- Set up a meeting with the director and ID to talk through their creative process as is specific to the project at hand.
- Establish a mock rehearsal where the director and ID can explore how they would work together.

The key takeaway when bringing a staged intimacy professional into the creative process is to keep in mind that this practice is about working together, working synergistically, and allowing each artist to bring their creative self, talents, and expertise to the process. Everyone should have a voice and be open to sharing, as relationships are built upon respect, trust, and the ability to be open and vulnerable.

Advocating is open to all

Additionally, advocating is open to every member of the creative, production, and management teams. It is the right of every member of the team to inquire about or ask for an intimacy professional, either to consult or to be brought onto a project. Steps one may take to introduce the idea of an IS/D joining a project include but are not limited to the following:

- As a **director**, when reading the script and you notice there are intimate themes within the story, ask for an ID to be brought on board or to consult.
- As an **actor** who is being offered a role, after reading the script and noticing the piece has intimate staging requirements, as part of your contract negotiations, ask for an ID to be a part of the rehearsal process.
- As a **fight choreographer** who knows there is intimate staging required, whether in conjunction with your scenes or not, negotiate to have an ID brought onto the creative team when being offered the contract.

⌦ As a **designer**, after reading the script and noticing there is intimate content, inquire about any plans to bring an ID onto the project. If the intimacy does not intersect with your work, your curiosity shows interest in and offers support for this specialty and its impact on a culture of consent (discussed in Chapter 2). If the intimacy does intersect with your work, your request demonstrates how fully this specialty supports both your process and the entire production.

It is up to the entire team to advocate for the inclusion of specialists who support company-wide consent practices, collaboration, and dynamic choreography. The theatrical workplace preferably is a space where everyone feels open and supported to do their best work, from actors, to creatives to administrators. An intimacy specialist may be an integral part of the foundation needed to achieve this preferred space.

Specializations within the field of staged intimacy

Preferably, when producing a script that involves complex cultural content or themes, the goal is to create mindful, intelligent, authentic work, taking care to establish a process that does not cause harm. To achieve this goal, it is the responsibility of that creative team to bring into the rehearsal room those individuals appropriate to aid in the process. Therefore, when planning to bring in specialists, those hiring may need to ask how culture-based elements within the show will be supported and how identity-driven stories in intimate moments will be negotiated. This discussion is imperative when team members involved do not have the lived experience, research, or knowledge necessary to support narratives linked to identity in the show. Our responsibility as contemporary storytellers is now to prevent reducing characters to a cliché or propagate racist, classist, ableist, or other anti-diversity messaging.

Cultural competency

This new awareness of cultural responsibility is complex and involves careful examination, learning, and active listening. Creatives with hiring power may consider bringing one or more people into the room who have the appropriate cultural competency. Cultural competency, specifically in a theatrical setting, requires the research and specialized training (and often lived experience) to support authenticity in culturally diverse storytelling.[74] A cultural consultant, or what may be considered a cultural dramaturg, could be brought in from day one to help everyone in the room navigate the material and avoid any crisis points along the way. Artists trained in this manner allow for topics to be explored and stories to be told in respectful, non-stereotyped ways, with care for the cultural narratives shared in the theatrical arts.

Building the necessary team

When examining the intersection of cultural diversity and intimate content, the goal is to identify and navigate the material in a way that honors the themes, ideas, and characters while supporting the actors and the story. This may or may not be found in an intimacy professional. No one person can be a specialist in all nuances of storytelling; nor can any intimacy professional be a specialist in all moments of intimacy across all identities. A deep, responsible understanding of cultural competency training can take years of study and experience. So can a deep understanding of movement choreography and other elements of intimacy training. However, many intimacy directors are also specialists in areas around identity in addition to their ID training in storytelling, safety, and consent. To illuminate a few of the variety of areas related to this topic, we have reached out to several individuals on how their research or lived experiences have connected to their work as intimacy professionals.

Just because you can, doesn't mean you should— representation for Black intimacy

Black intimacy, as an empathetic and essential practice, is the unapologetic and decolonized centering and celebration of Black joy, Black dignity, Black pleasure, Black rest(oration), and Black imagination. Equal representation creates new pathways forward and allows room for shared cultural reference points. Communities of equal representation foster authentic connections and creative access into the work. These inclusive rooms simultaneously hold space and share understanding of the systemic inequities of inherited industry practices. To speak of consent without addressing the historical and present-day mistreatment of Black people, who are unable to afford the luxury of saying "no" is to sell consent as a buzzword, instead of an applicable or inclusive practice.

Lack of representation causes harm. Routinely enduring microaggressions and microinvalidations in predominantly white spaces teaches Black artists that they need to protect and preserve themselves for survival. These harms require the artist's emotional labor, time, and in some situations, a call to action from the community in addition to the already-expected workload for the occupation. In many instances these added burdens lead to feelings of isolation, mistrust, and alienation.

Understandably, quite a few Black creatives engage in this work by applying tactics of self-preservation from the onset. This perpetual splitting of focus between risk assessment based on anti-Blackness and the craft inherently limits the voice of the performer when it comes to consent work and creates high-risk situations for all involved. Consent demands the artist's full body and emotional presence as consent is not permission but a currency of the "now," and representation for Black artists is a necessary part of a holistic intimacy practice.

Intimacy work for Black performers requires vulnerability, tenderness, and the proper resources to support the artist and art. Lack of representation in the role of intimacy director or intimacy coordinator asks these creatives to compartmentalize their work and does a disservice to the health and well-being of the performer as well as to the art being created. It is our responsibility, as an industry, to ensure that Black performers are fully seen and heard, just as their white counterparts, when asked to tell dangerous stories for entertainment. Black artists must be engaged artistically without question, hesitation, or the application of mischaracterizations that limits access to their humanity. And advocates serving as intimacy professionals must recognize, continually examine, and rectify one's thoughts, language, and reactions based on anti-Blackness.

When Black intimacy is supported with resources and trained experienced Black intimacy professionals, the possibilities for collective healing and creativity are boundless. Artists deserve the opportunity to work in safe spaces with representation.

Teniece Divya Johnson
(they/them/theirs)
Movement Storyteller, MA Sociology, MFA,
Stunt Performer, Fight Director, Intimacy Coordinator,
First Black and Non-Binary Intimacy Director on Broadway

Disability justice and intimacy

Intimacy work is deeply intertwined with disability and disability justice. The first person to coin the term intimacy direction, Tonia Sina, is a person who lives with chronic illnesses—and that's no coincidence. Living with disability has so much to teach about consent and trauma-informed work, and there are so many parallels in the work we do as intimacy professionals with the fight of disability justice.

My experience with disability gives me a profound awareness of what it is to deal with the nuances and gray areas of consent, as well as what it is to have other people making decisions about one's body. When I was diagnosed with my first autoimmune disease, one of the biggest changes I faced was in how others engaged with my body. I felt as though my body had become public property, something that could be touched, examined, and monitored as doctors saw fit. While different, this is not so far from the consent issues I see in rehearsal and on set, where actors' bodies can be seen as tools, as commodities, as something to use for the vision of others.

Much of intimacy work, for me, is about helping artists obtain what they need to be safe and function to the best of their ability at work. When I do so, I'm drawing on decades of activism in many fields, but here I will highlight disability justice. Society views disability as a problem, a liability, a hassle, an expense. Disabled people have fought for decades just to be allowed to go to school, to work, to be able to use public services, to have the same basic rights as any other human. Did you know that it was legal in the United States to not hire or serve people with disabilities until 1990? There is a deep legacy and ongoing battle for accommodations not to be seen as an afterthought or something to do with extra money, but as vital to one's livelihood. The fight for accommodations informs the work we seek to do in intimacy in the performing arts, treating actors' needs and boundaries not as an extra but as necessary.

Maya Herbsman
(She/her/Maya)
Intimacy Director and Coordinator, Educator, Director,
Anti-Racism Facilitator, and Activist

Fat bodies and intimacy

My research involving marginalized bodies (specifically fat women) in theatre spaces is at the epicenter of my work as an actor, educator, and director. I am a fat woman; I embrace the word "fat" as a neutral descriptor, yet fat bodies are anything but neutral in the theatre industry. Continuously relegated to comic relief, matronly, and/or hyper-sexualized supporting roles, fat women find themselves with limited acting options and underrepresented in an art form that extols itself as a mirror to society. A true mirror would reflect the 67 percent of women who wear a size 14 or larger, yet the presence of a fat female body on stage who is not portraying a caricaturization of a fat body is rare and revolutionary. What's more, anti-fat bias that permeates our society and our stages also means those fat actresses will rarely find themselves in a scene involving staged intimacy.

In my work and study of intimacy direction, keeping the body at the root of the work is crucial to creating a sense of trust and comfort in the process. My own fat body at the helm scores points for representation, even in the absence of fat actors. If there are fat actors on stage with me, so much the better. My personal identifiers of woman, fat, actor, educator, and now intimacy director intersect naturally to ensure empathetic, progressive theatremaking where all bodies are celebrated, respected, and, most of all, worthy of representation.

Claire Wilcher, MFA
(she/her/hers)
Actor/Educator/Director/Intimacy Director

Queer identity and intimacy: Occupying the spectrum between erotic and taboo

Queer intimacy on camera becomes more three dimensional when queer directors, actors, and writers actively participate in the collaborative storytelling process. The practice of queer advocacy is the embodiment of intersectionality and all things anti-colonial.

The need for queer diversity is amplified when we consider gender identity, gender expression, and/or race within expressions of queer love. Queer representation allows for the integration of identities outside the cisgender, heteronormative experience and introduces cultural characteristics or self-identifying labels that can speak to the dynamics of queer love.

Terminology like "top," "bottom," or "switch" does not make it into a creative space with actionable intention without outspoken queer artists. This language can be instrumental in amplifying relationship dynamics between queer characters, strengthening storytelling (through specificity), and serving as an opportunity to raise the stakes in an intimate scene of connection that is physicalized by action and reaction.

If we are to inhabit the full spectrum of queer love stories between the erotic and the taboo then we need more queer advocacy within these creative spaces. We need educated decision makers who are responsible for integrating queer creatives into the process. The challenge is to grow beyond the practice of changing a character's sexuality for diversity—resulting in a flat character arch because it was penned by someone who does not understand or has not taken the time to research and potentially fall in love with a culture that exists and thrives outside of their lived experiences.

Queer intimacy demands that we empower creatives to bring more of the queer cultural experiences to the table by inviting artists to be more of their full selves with less shame, guilt, or apology. This will aid in the opportunity to exist and create with a wholeness that can occupy the spectrum of diversity within queer love stories. The goal is to increase queer representation in our narrative until the language of a love scene is not automatically assumed to be a cisgender, heteronormative cinematic experience, as love (in all its shades) is a shared human experience.

Teniece Divya Johnson
(they/them/theirs)
Movement Storyteller, MA Sociology, MFA,
Stunt Performer, Fight Director, Intimacy Coordinator,
First Black and Non-Binary Intimacy Director on Broadway

Latinidad and intimacy

When considering intimacy in conversation with Latinidad the most important thing to consider, in my opinion, is internal diversity. White American ideology (which I sometimes call the Gringo Gaze) would have us believe that Latinidad is a monolith. But the experiences, stories, and literal bodies of Latine characters and actors could not be more diverse, and that diversity inevitably affects how intimacy functions within a cultural context. It's true that there are overlaps within Latinidad due to the specific way in which Spanish and Portuguese colonialism interacted with the cultures of enslaved African people, Indigenous communities, and other groups throughout history and due to the grouping of this community within the United States. But it's important to remember that there is also a great deal of rich specificity across race, national origin, socioeconomic status, relationship to immigration, etc., within Latinidad that affects intimate storytelling and that is regularly overlooked in favor of certain narratives that Hollywood, Broadway, etc., have come to expect.

One of the most obvious places that you see this "monolith" narrative play out is in metrics about which artists are represented in our industry. You will often see Latine/Latinx/Hispanic separated from Black, Asian, Indigenous, Caucasian, etc., but the reality is that all of those other identities exist within Latinidad. How should an ethnically Chinese Cuban or an Indigenous Peruvian or a white Argentinian self-identify? What does it mean to a Black Dominican actor when the AAPAC reports that during the 2018–19 season, Black actors were represented at 29 percent of New York City stages but Latinx actors were only represented at 4.8 percent? Where is that actor represented? And how does that reinforced separation (Chinese, Indigenous, White, Black ≠ Latine) affect how we see and tell stories of intimacy within Latinidad?

Although many Latines may find connection and authenticity in some more generalized experiences of intimacy within Latinidad (e.g., abuelitos dancing in the kitchen, adult male relatives kissing hello, etc.), you can see how an Afro-Colombian love story that takes place in the recent political upheaval in Bogotá may not be fully served even by having a Latine intimacy professional if, for example, that person's

> lived and scholarly experience comes from indigenous rural Mexican culture rather than African diasporic urban Colombian culture. It is essential when working on these stories that there be highly specific cultural competencies present in multiple departments in the room to create authentic nuanced intimacy within a broader Latine context.
>
> As we work to tell stories about Latine folks with Latine bodies, we must constantly interrogate our assumptions about what Latinidad is and keep our minds open to the myriad experiences that exist within that designation.
>
> **Cristina (Cha) Ramos**
> (she/her/hers)
> Performer/Movement Designer/Dramaturg

Other specializations held by intimacy directors are not related to identity or culture but rather to established movement-based or other theatrical practices. These specializations include

- Stage combat
- Dance[75]
- Physical comedy or clowning
- Period style movement
- Circus or acrobatics
- Devising or improvisation
- Dramaturgy
- Directing, and more.

Insight from several practitioners from these areas will be included in other chapters throughout this text.

Collaboration and intimacy direction

Theatre is a cross-sectoral, collaborative art, and trained intimacy specialist/directors are enthusiastic team members along with the director, designers, and performers. When working with a story that requires specialized research, cultural competency, or lived experience in relation to specific topics, trained IDs also look to and advocate for partnership with professionals who have these skills. IDs can bring their physical storytelling techniques, safety skills, and the consent practices to the table and work synergistically with these partners to create a better working environment and story. Cohesion such as this is found across theatrical teams: just as lighting and sound designers have different but complementary skills that create better storytelling moments together, so do intimacy specialists/directors and dance choreographers, cultural consultants, or other specializations.

> **Creative team spotlight: Upper administration**
>
> As a member of upper administration, one is in a unique position to create and enact shifts of culture within their organization and possibly even their community regarding empathy-led practices, equity, and consent. As an advocate for change that moved communities in new directions, Dr. Augusto Boal, founder of the Theatre of the Oppressed, said, "Theatre is a form of knowledge; it should and can also be a means of transforming society. Theatre can help us build our future, rather than just waiting for it."[76] The art of theatre continues to change communities, and as firm believers in this new approach to the work, we no longer want to wait for change but rather encourage it. We invite theatre administrators to join us in support of and approach to producing complex, diverse material and empowering artists and collaborators to reimagine their practice so together we may change our creative communities for the better and reshape our future.

Chapter reflection

Highly trained staged intimacy professionals are passionate advocates who do essential work during the rehearsal process for all theatrical team members, providing pathways to repeatable, dynamic, and consensual storytelling. They work with fellow collaborators throughout the rehearsal process to provide techniques for mindful communication, consent, self-care, and closure, which may help support mental health for the actors and the creative team. In addition, they may have training in physical techniques such as fight choreography or dance or in specific cultural competencies concerning a nuanced approach that can assist with complex, diverse storytelling.

This chapter has been a first look at the foundations of staged intimacy and intimacy direction, including some historical landmarks, basic vocabulary, and an introduction to training, advocacy, and specializations. Intimacy direction is a nuanced field based on compassion and care. While the future and methodologies of this specialty continue to evolve, members of the creative team can grow alongside this innovative work. Whether one decides to bring in a staged intimacy professional or incorporate concepts and techniques from intimacy work into their current process, embracing these methodologies can help to change institutional culture and industry standards for the better.

Chapter discussion / exercise / activity

Advocacy Activity

Building skills around the ability to advocate for an intimacy professional to be brought onto a production team, consult on a project, lead a workshop, or encouraging implementing the pillars of intimacy during the rehearsal process takes practice and experience. Establishing these skills starts with defining and outlining key talking points to make when in conversation. Based on the makeup of your institutional audience, you may find the need to use a different approach or feature various factors when advocating for an ID (or similar professional) to be brought onto a production. To help deepen your understanding and practice when building your case, we look to the art of improv.

As an exercise, improvise the various conversations you may have when talking with different members of the creative team when advocating for the hire of an ID:

- How would you start the conversation if you were talking to an executive producer? What key points would resonate with them?
- How would these conversations be different if you were talking to an artistic director, production manager, or director? What key talking points would resonate with them?

Knowing your audience is the first step to successful advocacy work. Knowing what they need to hear and how you need to say it in order for their perspectives to be opened to change takes practice. Through improv and exploration of approach you will learn what key issues are relevant to various audiences, and slowly your workable script will be revealed.

Building a case based on relevance and specifics will help you better navigate challenging conversations, explain new approaches to the work, and hopefully end with desired outcomes.

Notes

1. Sina Campanella, Tonia. 2006. *Intimate Encounters: Staging Intimacy and Sensuality.* Virginia Commonwealth University: VCU Scholars Compass, 2006, https://scholarscompass.vcu.edu/cgi/viewcontent.cgi?article=2070&context=etd.
2. Black, Alexis, and Tina M. Newhauser. Workshop: *Stage Managing Intimacy Companion Workbook.* Intimacy Directors and Coordinators, 2020, p. 8. https://www.idcprofessionals.com/
3. Used with permission of Intimacy Directors and Coordinators. Excerpt from worksheet on intimacy direction timeline. Course materials, "Level One Intimacy Training," IDC.
4. www.journalcbp.com/
5. Villarreal, Amanda Rose, PhD. "The Evolution of Consent-Based Performance: A Literature Review." The Launchpad, vol. 1, no. 1, Jan 28, 2022, p. 7, www.journalcbp.com/lit-review
6. Ohlheiser, Abby. "Meet the Woman Who Coined 'Me Too' 10 Years Ago—to Help Women of Color." *Chicago Tribune*, June 2, 2018, https://www.chicagotribune.com/lifestyles/ct-me-too-campaign-origins-20171019-story.html.
7. Sina Campanella, Tonia. *Intimate Encounters: Staging Intimacy and Sensuality.* Virginia Commonwealth University: VCU Scholars Compass, 2006, https://scholarscompass.vcu.edu/cgi/viewcontent.cgi?article=2070&context=etd.
8. Noble, Adam. "Sex and Violence: Practical Approaches for Dealing with Extreme Stage Physicality." *The FightMaster: The Journal of the Society of American Fight Directors*, no. 13–18 (Spring 2011), pp. 15–20.
9. "About." Black Lives Matter. https://blacklivesmatter.com/about/.
10. http://www.collin.edu/department/theatre/Chicago-Theatre-Standards-12-11-17.pdf.
11. https://www.intimacycoordinatorsofcolor.com.
12. www.chicagoreader.com/chicago/profiles-theatre-theater-abuse-investigation/Content?oid=22415861.
13. www.chicagoreader.com/chicago/profiles-theatre-theater-abuse-investigation/Content?oid=22415861.
14. Song, Sandra. "How Intimacy Directors Keep Sex Scenes Safe." PAPER, Dec. 6, 2019, https://www.papermag.com/intimacy-directors-international-2641450678.html.
15. "Intimacy Directors and Coordinators." *Intimacy Directors and Coordinators,* 2021, www.idcprofessionals.com/s/IDC-Resource-Guide.pdf.
16. Sibert, Ariel. "How I harassed NYC theatre freelancer is fighting back." AMERICAN THEATRE, June 21, 2021, https://www.americantheatre.org/2017/02/09/how-1-harassed-nyc-theatre-freelancer-is-fighting-back/.
17. Collins-Hughes, Laura. "Need to Fake an Orgasm? There's an 'Intimacy Choreographer' for That." *The New York Times*, June 15, 2017, https://www.nytimes.com/2017/06/15/theater/need-to-fake-an-orgasm-theres-an-intimacy-choreographer-for-that.html.

18 Kantor, Jodi, and Megan Twohey. "Harvey Weinstein Paid off Sexual Harassment Accusers for Decades." *The New York Times*. Oct. 5, 2017, https://www.nytimes.com/2017/10/05/us/harvey-weinstein-harassment-allegations.html.
19 https://timesupnow.org/.
20 https://timesupfoundation.org/work/times-up-entertainment/entertainment-safety-initiative/.
21 Judson, Margaret. "How Do You Play a Porn Star in the #Metoo Era? with Help from an 'Intimacy Director'." *The New York Times*, Aug. 24, 2018, https://www.nytimes.com/2018/08/24/business/intimacy-director-hbo-the-deuce.html.
22 Kerr, Breena. "How HBO Is Changing Sex Scenes Forever." *Rolling Stone*, Oct. 24, 2018, https://www.rollingstone.com/tv/tv-features/the-deuce-intimacy-coordinator-hbo-sex-scenes-739087/.
23 Kerr, Breena. "How HBO Is Changing Sex Scenes Forever." *Rolling Stone*, Oct. 24, 2018, https://www.rollingstone.com/tv/tv-features/the-deuce-intimacy-coordinator-hbo-sex-scenes-739087/.
24 https://www.playbill.com/person/teniece-divya-johnson.
25 Collins-hughes, Laura. "How Audra McDonald and Michael Shannon Got Intimate." *The New York Times*, June 26, 2019, https://www.nytimes.com/2019/06/26/theater/frankie-johnny-audra-mcdonald-michael-shannon.html.
26 https://sdcweb.org/1061669-2/.
27 Collins-hughes, Laura. "Oregon Shakespeare Festival Hires a Resident Intimacy Director." *The New York Times*, Jan. 24, 2020, https://www.nytimes.com/2020/01/24/theater/oregon-shakespeare-festival-intimacy-director.html.
28 Pace, Chelsea. *Staging Sex: Best Practices, Tools, and Techniques for Theatrical Intimacy*. Routledge, 2020, https://www.amazon.com/Staging-Sex-Practices-Techniques-Theatrical/dp/1138596493.
29 https://www.weseeyouwat.com/about.
30 Frederick, Candice. "Why Hollywood Needs More Black Intimacy Coordinators." *ELLE*, Nov. 29, 2021, https://www.elle.com/culture/movies-tv/a33850492/black-intimacy-coordinators-interview/.
31 Waugh, Rosemary. "Yarit Dor: 'I Don't like to Be Boxed in – I Don't Want to Be Just a Fight Director'." *The Stage*, Oct. 28, 2019, https://www.thestage.co.uk/features/yarit-dor-i-dont-like-to-be-boxed-in--i-dont-want-to-be-just-a-fight-director.
32 One example of many publications on "Bridgerton" intimacy work: https://www.cnn.com/2021/01/05/entertainment/bridgerton-intimacy-coordinator/index.html.
33 "Watch Saturday Night Live Highlight: Bridgerton Intimacy Coordinator." *NBC*, Feb. 2021, https://www.nbc.com/saturday-night-live/video/bridgerton-intimacy-coordinator/4315668.
34 Pewsey, Guy. "Meet Phoebe Dynevor, Breakout Star of Bridgerton." *Grazia*, Jan. 11, 2021, https://graziadaily.co.uk/celebrity/news/phoebe-dynevor-bridgerton/.
35 Sagaftra.org. https://www.sagaftra.org/standards-and-protocols-use-intimacy-coordinators.

36 "Recommended Standards for Qualifications, Training & Vetting of Intimacy Coordinators."Sagaftra.org.https://www.sagaftra.org/contracts-industry-resources/workplace-harassment-prevention/intimacy-coordinator-resources-0.
37 Robb, David. "SAG_AFTRA accredits seven training programs for intimacy coordinators. Mar. 4, 2022. https://deadline.com/2022/03/sag-aftra-intimacy-coordinator-training-programs-1234971514/.
38 https://www.sagaftra.org/sag-aftra-national-board-meets-videoconference-5.
39 Steinrock, Jessica. *Intimacy Direction: A New Role in Contemporary Theatre Making*. PhD Dissertation University of Illinois at Urbana-Champaign. 2020.
40 Steinrock, Jessica. *Intimacy Direction: A New Role in Contemporary Theatre Making*. PhD Dissertation University of Illinois at Urbana-Champaign. 2020.
41 Steinrock, Jessica. *Intimacy Direction: A New Role in Contemporary Theatre Making*. PhD Dissertation University of Illinois at Urbana-Champaign. 2020.
42 Advanced Stage Management course, spring 2019. Michigan State University.
43 Advanced Stage Management course, spring 2019. Michigan State University.
44 "APA Dictionary of Psychology." American Psychological Association. https://dictionary.apa.org/closure.
45 One example of multiple references about self-care can be found at https://www.everydayhealth.com/self-care/.
46 Burgoyne, Suzanne, et al. "The Impact of Acting on Student Actors: Boundary Blurring, Growth, and Emotional Distress." *Theatre Topics*, vol. 9 no. 2, 1999, p. 157–179. *Project MUSE*, doi:10.1353/tt.1999.0011.
47 Sina, Tonia. "Intimacy Directors International O'Neill 9-day Intensive." In-person training, Waterford, CT, February, 2019.
48 Seppala, Emma, and Kim Cameron. "Proof that Positive Work Cultures are More Productive." *Harvard Business Review*. Dec. 1, 2015.
49 Sina, Tonia, Alicia Rodis, Siobhan Richardson. *The Pillars of Intimacy Direction*, https://docs.wixstatic.com/ugd/924101_2e8c624bcf394166bc0443c1f35efe1d.pdf.
50 Rodis, Alicia, and Sina Tonia. "Introduction to Staged Intimacy." In-person training. St. Pete, FL, December 2018. Instructors referenced "FRIES" acronym from planned parenthood, https://www.plannedparenthood.org/learn/relationships/sexual-consent.
51 Rodis, Alicia, and Tonia Sina. "Intimacy Directors International O'Neill 9-day Intensive." In-person training on the "Discomfort Scale," Waterford, CT, Feb. 2019.
52 www.jessicasteinrock.com
53 Rodis, Alicia, and Tonia Sina. "Introduction to Staged Intimacy." In-person training. St. Pete, FL, Dec. 2018.
54 Rodis, Alicia, and Tonia Sina. "Introduction to Staged Intimacy." In-person training. St. Pete, FL, Dec. 2018.
55 Analogy adapted from conversations and educational sessions about the Discomfort Scale with Alicia Rodis, Dr. Jessica Steinrock, and other intimacy professionals.

56 "Mental Health First Aid USA." Feb. 2, 2022, https://www.mentalhealthfirstaid.org/.
57 Duberman, Amanda. "Meet the 'Intimacy Directors' Who Choreograph Sex Scenes." *HuffPost*, May 31, 2018, https://www.huffpost.com/entry/intimacy-directors-choreograph-sex-scenes_n_5b0d87dae4b0fdb2aa574564.
58 This list was inspired by a variety of resources provided by Redtwist Theatre in Chicago in Fall 2020 under Artistic Director Charlie McGrath (in collaboration with intimacy director Alexis Black).
59 https://www.redcross.org/.
60 https://www.thenationalcouncil.org.
61 Cannon, W.B. "The James-Lange theory of emotions: a critical examination and an alternative theory." *Am J Psychol*. Fall–Winter 1987, 100(3-4): pp. 567–86. PMID: 3322057.
62 Shawyer, Suzanne, and Kim Shively. "Education in Theatrical Intimacy as Ethical Practice for University Theatre." *Journal of Dramatic Theory and Criticism*, vol. 34 no. 1, 2019, pp. 87–104. Project MUSE, doi:10.1353/dtc.2019.0025.
63 "Intimacy Directors and Coordinators." 2021, www.idcprofessionals.com/s/IDC-Resource-Guide.pdf.
64 Mellinger, Marcela Sarmiento. "What Is Advocacy?" *Philanthropy Journal*. June 19, 2017, https://philanthropyjournal.com/what-is-advocacy/.
65 Richardson, Siobhan, www.siobhanrichardson.com.
66 www.humblewarriormovement.com/intimacy.
67 www.callmecha.com.
68 https://judithmbardwick.wordpress.com/about/
69 Bardwick, Judith M. *Danger in the Comfort Zone: From Boardroom to Mailroom*. Amazon, 1995.
70 Page, Oliver. "How to Leave Your Comfort Zone and Enter Your 'Growth Zone'." *PositivePsychology.com*, Dec. 7, 2021, https://positivepsychology.com/comfort-zone/.
71 PositivePsychology.com "Leaving The Comfort Zone" Toolkit.
72 During consultation for this book, Ms. Richardson shared this comment July 13, 2021.
73 Coen, Stephanie. "Staging Intimacy," *SDC Journal*. Summer 2019.
74 While it is impossible to know of or mention every artist who has worked to greatly advance inclusion in this field, we wish to acknowledge several leaders in bringing their work with cultural competency, inclusion, anti-racist and anti-oppression practices to staged intimacy within the performative arts industries. Please see Appendix A1 for this list of acknowledgments.
75 See article https://www.dancemagazine.com/intimacy-directing/ for a discussion of the intersections of dance choreography and intimacy direction.
76 Boal, Augusto. *Games for Actors and Non-Actors*. Routledge.

2
Creating a culture of consent

Many theatre practitioners and employees of theatre companies understand that work on a staged production commences long before the first read-through with cast and company. First and foremost is the successful running of the theatrical institution, which includes strategic planning, managing budgets, forming protocols, facilitating venue concerns, production needs, etc. The creative concerns of productions include assembling the design team and production staff, confirming designs and vendors, then finalizing contracts. In general, there could be months or even years of work that will need to be accomplished before you come close to choosing scripts, announcing the season, or confirming the cast. This process is multifaceted, intensive, and ongoing.

This chapter will explore this early part of this process, with an aim to name contemporary "big picture" practices that could effectively support a healthier workplace overall and staged intimacy within specific projects. These modern practices will introduce or reinforce the necessity for change in institutional culture around consent, from the boardroom to the stage, and will provide an opportunity for organizations to look inward. Through creating this culture of consent,[1] theatre organizations can establish a firm foundation of inclusive and intentional workplace behaviors that will support all departments as they explore new works and more complex physical storytelling.

Over the following pages, we will take a comprehensive look at what constitutes a culture of consent and detail the recommended techniques and groundwork essential to establishing one. This culture will be built upon conscientious communication, consensual preferred practices, and careful consideration of all collaborators and is an ongoing evolving process that includes the following:

- Thoughtful leadership
- Understanding institutional structure

- Power dynamics in the hierarchy
- Types of power
- Defining sexual harassment and creating policy
- Methods for reporting harassment
- Communication techniques for moments bordering harassment
- Incorporating resources for mental and emotional health
- Questions to ask when choosing a production

Using these elements to foster a more consensual workplace will be vital to development processes when considering productions that include staged intimacy. Consent within intimate and vulnerable workspaces can be supported only by the honoring of consent in all workspaces. By putting these into practice while in board, area, and staff meetings, organizations can create the infrastructure to uphold these practices in hallways, shops, and green rooms, especially during high-pressure situations, such as the rehearsal and staging of intimacy.

> **Key terms in Chapter 2**[*]
>
> ### Audition disclosures (for actors)
>
> Disclosures are written or verbalized notices that include stage directions or language from the script that indicates a moment of staged intimacy. Disclosures will also include directorial-based decisions about staged intimacy (from concept or vision rather than stage directions) whenever possible. Also known as content notices, intimacy moment lists, or other terminology, they may be included within casting notices, posted in the audition space *in a written format, or verbalized to auditioning performers. The overall goal of these disclosures is to ensure that those auditioning are aware of expectations in regard to intimate content in the production.
>
> ### Culture of consent
>
> A workplace culture built upon conscientious communication, consensual preferred practices, mindful leadership, clear policies, and other elements further discussed in this chapter.
>
> [*] *See Terms & Language Acknowledgement and Glossary of Key Terms in Appendix E for citations, trainings, and reference materials that informed definitions.*

> **Harassment**
>
> Any pressure or intimidation used to coerce someone into behaving a certain way, or behaviors that create a hostile work environment.
>
> **Mandatory reporter[2]**
>
> An individual who, because of their position, is obligated to report incidents of harassment and/or violence to their relevant authorities (typically found in academia, social work, law enforcement, or religious institutions).
>
> **Power Dynamics**
>
> Real or perceived differences in power, hierarchy, authority, or knowledge in interpersonal and/or societal relationships that influence the ability for performers, crew, stage managers, etc., to consent fully.[3]

Thoughtful leadership

What does it take for institutions to establish a thoughtful theatrical process or a process built upon behaviors that are conscientious, consensual, and considerate of others? Leaders committed to building a culture of consent can explore behaviors and beliefs rooted in mindfulness as a first step toward answering this question. In theatre organizations, one may define thoughtful leadership as value-driven actions that do not induce harm and work to create a conscientious and inclusive state of engagement. It supports a level of awareness and empathy within leaders that encourages moral behaviors and does so in a non-judgmental way. Embracing a reflective practice, as defined here, may allow one to be mindful of one's behavior and behaviors within the organization. Preferably, this "mindfulness gives us both the insight to recognize that we are accountable and the tools for shifting into a new way of being, behaving and seeing the world that reduces our suffering and that of others."[4]

When the goal is to do production work in a more responsible and informed way, preferably both the creative team and their accountability practices will come into play. When thoughtful and mindful leaders examine the internal behaviors of their organization, they should ask themselves questions about company culture. Such as "Are we operating within a culture that will empower our entire community to take on challenges with modern, healthful work practices in a safe, supportive, and consensual way?"

These healthy work practices go beyond just leadership positions. Production on Deck (PoD),[5] a talent and consulting firm for theatrical production roles that identifies talent from marginalized communities, speaks to leadership in the article "Production on Deck: Eliminating Excuses," saying that "while it starts at the top, leadership is a quality that extends through every level of an organization. The responsibility to change a culture must be shared throughout the whole."[6] Everyone on creative, production, and administrative teams must work mindfully and collaboratively when dealing with staged intimacy. Taking time to reflect honestly upon internal relationships and institutional culture will help to indicate if the company, as a unified entity, can support necessary consensual characteristics and the recommended practices required when producing this work.

Understanding institutional structure

Leaders and participants in a production, particularly one that contains staged intimacy, need to understand that organizational structure, methods for reporting, and power dynamics are key components to ensuring the pillars of consent, communication, and context (see Chapter 1) are fully embraced. Building a culture of consent requires proper foundational support based upon understanding of the hierarchy within a theatrical organization.

This "Theatre Hierarchy Chart"[7] shows standard organizational structures found within a typical theatrical system, now with the incorporation of the intimacy choreographer and captain.

Whether oversight of this system is maintained by an executive producer, as noted in this image, or by a nonprofit's board of directors, there is a universal structure to the system. Commercial productions, nonprofit regional theaters, community theaters, and theatre departments living within academic programs all function because of the collaborative relationships within the system and may be positively or negatively affected by the system's internal power dynamics. Each theatrical company or producing organization has its own internal culture and distribution of power. Honest examination and understanding of both internal culture and where power truly resides is the first step to creating a holistic, supportive production process for the company, which is particularly important when producing challenging work.

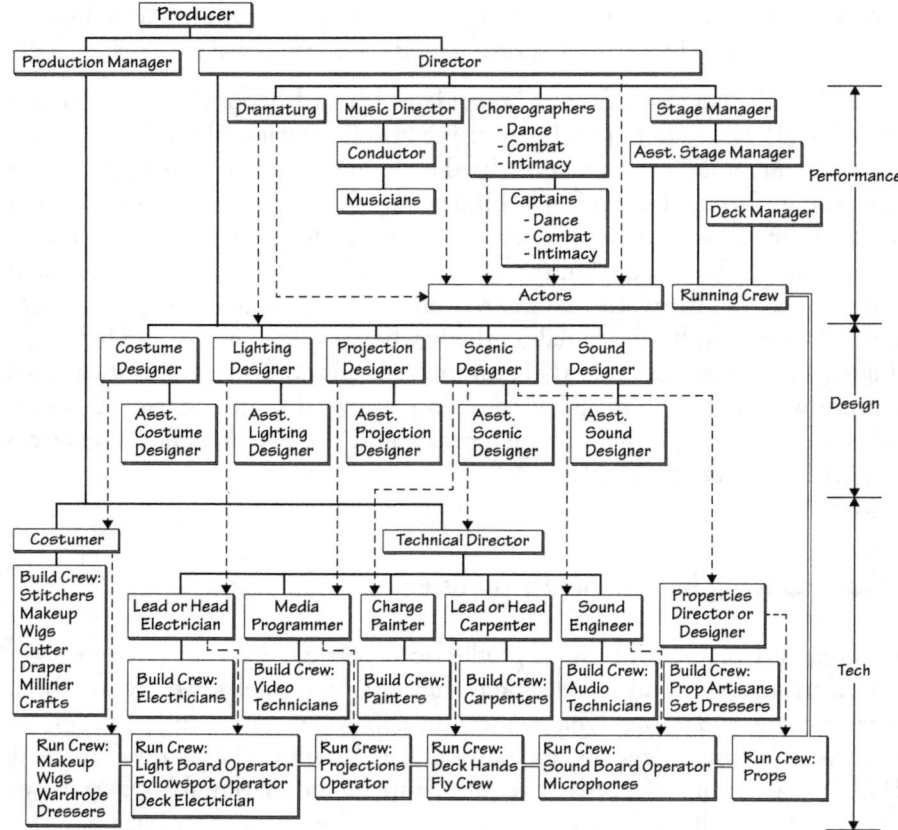

Figure 2.1 A line chart that represents roles within an organizational structure and hierarchical relationships between those roles. Image credit: Kizer, Matt. "Theatre Hierarchy Chart 2021." Matt Kizer Scenic Lighting Design, 14 Apr. 2021, scenicandlighting.com/article/theatre-hiearchy-chart-2021/.

Power dynamics in the hierarchy

To understand and examine the types of social and systemic power inherent to many theatrical hierarchies will illuminate the impact these dynamics may have on company culture. When considering power dynamics in the arts, what may unfortunately come to mind first is the abuse of power. Within the creative arenas of film and theatre, the wielding of one's capacity to control and dominate is often considered an inherent part of the culture. In a 2021 article for the Deutsche Welle Press titled "Hollywood Confronts Its Culture of Bullying," Scott Roxborough wrote, "The idea that bullying and abuse are linked to Hollywood success has become ingrained in showbiz culture."[8] The confrontation of these abuses includes the We See You, White American Theatre collective, the trial of Harvey Weinstein, #Metoo, the Let Us Work initiative (all mentioned in Chapter 1), and more. These and more movements and events have uncovered inherent problems caused by the manipulation of power within the creative industries and highlighted the need to address these dynamics head-on. By and large, power is not inherently "good" or "bad." A proverb spoken by Voltaire and repeated by comic book character Peter Parker states, "With great power comes responsibility." It is not the power itself but how the power is wielded that might lead to its corruption.

In discussing the types of social power and highlighting some of their common misuses, the creative arts industry has an opportunity to use power to improve workplace culture. This section aims not to villainize power itself but to create awareness that the creative arts industries are currently built so that the effects of power have fewer checks and balances than almost any other industry. As writer Diep Tran articulated in *American Theatre* magazine, "How do we make a theatre field that is truly safe, where everyone can do their best creative work? First, we need to confront how the field has failed its artists."[9] This failure is a systematic problem and a highly complex one. Even more impactful when staging intimacy, the unchecked or misunderstood dynamics of power can lead to unchecked abuses. Our ability to mitigate and confront these abuses starts with awareness of these dynamics on the personal and on the institutional levels.

Fortunately, on the national level in the United States, the theatre industry is beginning to gain an awareness imperative to improving work conditions. A formal joint statement on April 12, 2021, from unions representing performers, stage managers, and musicians, stated that "every worker deserves to do their job in an environment free of harassment of any kind, whether that harassment creates a toxic workplace or, certainly in the case of sexual harassment, when that behavior is also against the law."[10] Even without the direct support of unions, individual performers are working to improve work conditions. We cite the "We See You, White American Theatre Collective and Demands"[11] as a powerful example (discussed in Chapter 1's timeline).

Media attention is one way in which artists have been creating these checks and balances. One oft-noted context for their efforts is the aforementioned #MeToo movement. Signaling the call for more industry-wide change, Roxborough stated, "Emboldened by the success of #MeToo, a movement is gathering strength in Hollywood that is making workplace abuse of any kind unacceptable."[12] Although Hollywood's infractions are often publicized more widely, the abuse of power in the theatre industry is also creating toxic workplace conditions, as illustrated in Chicago's Profiles Theatre situation (mentioned in Chapter 1), specifically with Daryl Cox. However, these specified reports often redirect attention away from the industry as a whole and, as in the Profiles case, toward a specific perpetrator. On the institutional level, focusing on one individual's actions without taking a more comprehensive look at the repetitive systemic issues surrounding these incidents is harmful and may create a deflection of responsibility. Calling out individual behavior is an important step, but the problem abides in our relationship to power in the workplace and the structures creating the opportunity for abuse. As Abby Clark stated in the *Detroit Free Press*, "It's easy to fixate on the salacious details.... But that misses the point: if you don't examine the dynamics that allow this to occur—the role of power, money, connections—it will just happen again and again, only the details will change."[13]

Types of power

Before the industry can erase these "salacious details" and better address power dynamics and structures, all theatrical team members need to understand the types of social power. As they are described briefly in this section, we encourage using these as a springboard to further studies and explore power structures and dynamics relating to creating a culture of consent. These types of power can be either actual or perceived and still influence communication and the ability to consent. By remaining mindful of their possible effects, individuals and organizations will be able to engage with power in ways that benefit their own theatrical communities and others.

Systemic power

While understanding all types of power within theatrical communities is essential, there is an overarching element of power to all social structures and cultures: systemic power and oppression. The Minnesota Collaborative Anti-Racism Initiative (MCARI) defines systemic power as "the legitimate/legal ability to access and control those institutions sanctioned by the state."[14] In America, many of our critical systems and institutions were (and are) built to uphold white supremacy and to serve white society exclusively. This fact profoundly impacts today's common discourse and understanding, especially regarding how institutions should be structured, where resources are held and allocated, and who is perceived to have power in certain spaces.[15]

Intersectionality

Spaces and systems of power are greatly affected by the intersectional identities of those within them. Coined by Kimberlé Crenshaw, intersectionality is "a lens, a prism, for seeing the way in which various forms of inequality often operate together and exacerbate each other."[16] The effects of systemic oppression are nonlinear. Crenshaw argues that "we tend to talk about race inequality as separate from inequality based on gender, class, sexuality or immigrant status. What's often missing is how some people are subject to all of these, and the experience is not just the sum of its parts."

The image below helps create a visual representation of a collage of identities that reside in relationship to a line of domination. One side of the line is privilege, and on the other is oppression. A binary system discounts complexities within identity, and this image does not provide a holistic list of identities. However, this can help to visually illustrate the impact of identity on someone's real or perceived power that may be seen within a rehearsal process.

This image, while a much-simplified look at a complex topic, helps to spotlight the multiple inequities, privileges, and oppressive practices that can occur regarding one's multiple identities. Additionally, due to intersectionality, an individual may be experiencing both privilege and oppression simultaneously, as illustrated by the image below.

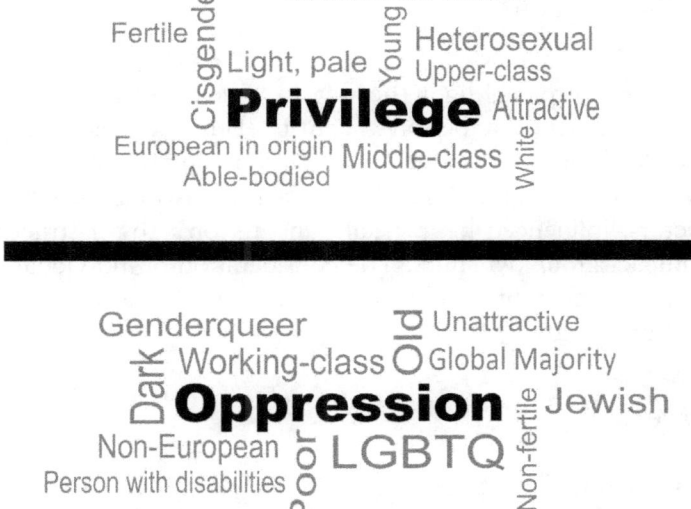

Figure 2.2 Word clouds for privilege and oppression. Artwork by Robert Kaplan.

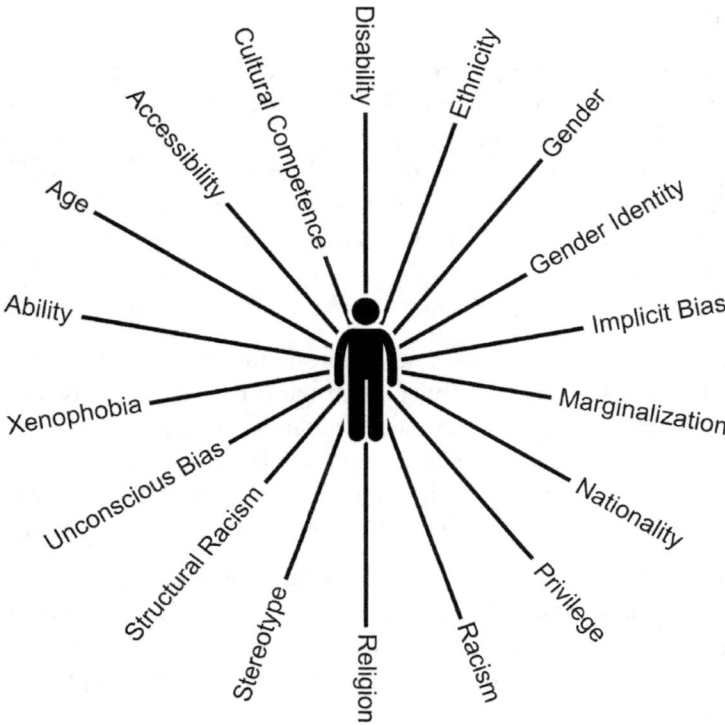

Figure 2.3 A representation of multiple identities radiating from a human figure. Artwork by Robert Kaplan.

These images help to highlight the way in which societal structures may intersect and influence a person's identity. Perceived, actual, personal, and institutional factors weigh differently given situational circumstances. Additionally, as with the individual, a theatrical ensemble may have intersecting factors, influenced by a specific institution's power structure, that may also impact group dynamics. The consideration of individual or group dynamics, intersectionality, and types of power are crucial when navigating the concept of identity.[17]

Social power

To understand transformations of power, one may reflect upon what has already been defined by various practitioners as the bases of power. As defined by IDC, the list below[18] was adapted from the early work of social psychologists John R. P. French and Bertram Raven.[19] In the late 1950s, they outlined five bases of social power and established them as "pervasive, complex, and often disguised in our society."[20] These bases of social power—in time, they added a sixth—offer an accessible vocabulary for the initial examination of power structures. However, they are limited in their ability to account for the influences of intersectionality and systemic power described in the previous section.

In looking at each of these social power structures through the lens of the creative theatrical process, we hope to clarify that these bases of social power are not inherently wrong. To reinforce this, we provide an example of a problematic or abusive use of these bases and a healthy one after each type of power is defined.[21]

Title power is the authority/influence a person has based on a specific title or role in an organization. The legitimate authority of these individuals enables them to make changes for the positive or negative based solely on their hierarchical position.
- Problematic use of power: An executive producer demands significant design changes during final preview performances.
- Productive use of power: A producer requires all incoming artists to take anti-harassment training.

Punitive power is wielded through the use of threats and force or the implication of punishment for noncompliance. Often, receivers are threatened with the loss of future or current work unless they do as ordered by an individual who holds such power.
- Problematic use: An actress is directed to perform specific staged intimate actions that violate her personal boundaries or else be threatened with abusive comments/retribution.
- Productive use: Administration establishes clear warnings of disciplinary punishments for those who engage in abusive behavior.

Reward power is the ability to offer rewards for compliance and is expressed through motivation for others by offering raises, promotions, and rewards.
- Problematic use: A stage manager is guaranteed their next contract if they look the other way when a director purposefully contradicts current contracted union rules.
- Productive use: A shop manager is offered additional compensation by a member of upper administration when asked to help draft new staff policies regarding workplace safety.

Expert power is the authority/influence a person has because of their educational background, knowledge base or expertise, or the perception of those things by others.
- Problematic use: A well-known director uses intimidation to influence an actor's willingness to work beyond boundaries, causing mental and emotional harm.
- Productive use: A certified intimacy professional/director uses expertise to support healthy consensual workplace conditions.

Referent power is the authority/influence a person has due to an impression of their social or professional connections. This type of power can arise from perceived attractiveness, charisma, likability, worthiness, and right to others' respect.
- Problematic use: A charming leading man uses smiles and affection to take advantage of hierarchical systems and individuals.
- Productive use: An anti-racist advocate, such as Nicole Brewer, gains respect through their research and dissemination of inclusive theatre practices.

Informational power is the authority/influence a person has due to their holding of information that others may want or need, and often this individual holds onto knowledge to protect their job or reputation.
- Problematic use: An artistic director withholds information about a designer's prior abusive behaviors so they may hire them without resistance.
- Productive use: A director knows and discloses the Pillars of Intimacy in the rehearsal room to encourage consensual crafting.

Every member of a project's creative team should understand and reflect upon social power structures to better comprehend how they impact consent, agency, and empowerment of the actors and other production members. IDC stresses the importance of naming power to prevent gaslighting, coercion, and abuse and foster collaborative efforts for mitigating the adverse effects of power. When developing our "Stage Managing Intimacy" course for IDC, we looked to the above exercise as a valuable tool for leading discussion when introducing power dynamics to students.[22] The sooner in one's career or education one can start to learn how to initiate and negotiate conversations about power and consent, the more confidence team members will have to navigate them successfully in the professional world.

Change needs to happen at both ends of the power dynamic. Team members should take a step back, move beyond themselves and the current situation

Creative team spotlight: Artistic director

According to a survey conducted by the National Bureau of Economic Research, 85 percent of CEOs and CFOs believe that an unhealthy culture leads to unethical behavior.[23]

Corporate culture around consent, harassment, and systems of power are being reexamined across all industries. Many are seeking training and specialists to create change, with varied success. The performative arts, however, through movements such as intimacy direction, have access to formulated practices that codify and examine contemporary, actionable items that can help to shift culture.

Artistic directors and producers have the power to bring these practices to their communities through the hiring of specialists and consciously focusing on the type of culture they wish to build in a transforming industry. This access leaves artistic directors in a unique position to manifest and uplift positive change. They can move beyond research to action, leading their company to embrace more inclusive, supportive, and respectful ways of engaging with the work.

to see, identify, and preferably call out any abusive use of power, whether they are receiving it or possibly wielding it. The goal is to empower everyone in the room to prevent harm and join in unison to call out unacceptable behavior if it occurs. As a community, theatrical institutions have the power to work together to diminish abusive power and end offensive actions.

Defining sexual harassment and creating policy

Having defined these various types of power, industry professionals must find ways to mitigate abuses and promote responsible usage. Success in this endeavor will entail understanding and identifying types of abuse that may occur and defining them clearly for the entire company. The following focus will be on the kind of abuse that may most often become directly relevant to the process of staging intimacy: sexual harassment. By examining healthy practices utilized when mitigating this type of harassment, those with status and influence will preferably use their power to create positive change in this area and beyond.

Sexual harassment is one of the more common abuses of power found in the theatre industry. Stefanie Maiya Lehmann, Associate General Manager for Lincoln Center, addressed this head-on in 2018, writing, "In the last year, stories of sexual harassment and abuse have taken center stage across the U.S.... These reports of sexual harassment in the theatre, coming from those who work onstage, backstage, in management and in creative areas, have caused shock waves across the industry, from university theatres to small professional theatres to community theatres to LORT theatres to Broadway. At theaters across the country, a wake-up call is being sounded and changes are being proposed as the reverberations from the #MeToo movement continues to be felt."[24] Specifically with regard to staging intimacy, it is important to define what constitutes sexual harassment well before building these moments on stage. In their article "Sexual Harassment in the Creative Industries: Tolerance, Culture and the Need for Change," authors Bennet and Hennekam state that "intensely physical work can obscure the line between work and sexual harassment, and ambiguities between institutional policy and practice may leave workers unsure of which behaviours should be considered sexual harassment."[25] Thus, clarity on this definition is pivotal not only for the actors but also for every theatrical team member. The entire cast, creative, administrative and production team should work to understand and adopt the institution's definition before or during the first day of employment when joining a new production.

Discussions focused on creating policies that support a culture of consent are essential. In most cases, upper administrators will be charged with formulating policies and creating reporting structures for the organization. Stage managers, designers, performers, and other theatrical team members can then fully support consent and a safe workplace through open communication and the upholding of these policies and structures to the fullest of their ability.

Posting organizational policy

One way to accomplish clarity of behavioral expectations for the entire production is for individuals to ask employers for their institution's handbook on harassment and organizational policies. Preferably, this information will include the institution's definition of sexual harassment. Employers should format this information in a way that makes it easy for members to post and share throughout the company.

Visibility of company policies is imperative when establishing a culture of consent and is not only recommended by staged intimacy organizations and independent contractors but may also be a requirement of unions. Actors Equity Association, in an effort to help change the culture within the professional theatre industry, established the President's Committee to Prevent Harassment[26] in 2018. "This new committee will help the organization develop additional forward-looking strategies to eradicate harassment and bullying in the theatre." As part of this effort, "Equity has requested that all Equity employers provide a copy of their own harassment policies to the union, as well as make those policies available to Equity members at the first rehearsal and throughout their employment under an Equity contract."[27] Additional information on this subject is available to AEA members through their union's members-only website portal.

Not only is it important for company members such as directors, intimacy choreographers, and stage managers to request this information when beginning work, but every individual signing a theatrical contract should make the same request. The hope for the field of intimacy direction is that requesting these policies will become standard practice for everyone contracted to work on any theatrical production, whether union, nonunion, community, or academic.

Definitions of what constitutes sexual harassment will vary and may be adjusted based on the type of institution crafting them. According to the Equal Employment Opportunity Commission (EEOC),[28] a federal agency, sexual harassment includes "unwelcome sexual advances, requests for sexual favors, and other verbal or physical harassment of a sexual nature" in the workplace or learning environment.[29]

An example of a definition of sexual harassment could read as follows:

Defining sexual harassment

Sexual harassment includes but is not limited to:[30]

- Unwelcome remarks, jokes, innuendos, or taunting about a person's body, attire, gender, appearance or sexual activities.
- Unwanted touching or any unwanted or inappropriate physical contact.
- Unwelcome inquiries of comments about a person's sex life or sexual preference.
- Leering, whistling, or other suggestive or insulting sounds.
- Inappropriate comments about clothing, physical characteristics, or activities.

> Transmitting by text, email, or any other delivery method offensive sexual remarks, jokes, stories, pictures, or materials that are sexually oriented.
> Requests or demands for sexual favors which include or strongly imply the promises of rewards for complying (e.g., job advancement opportunities and/or threats of punishment for refusal).
> Sexual solicitation or advance made by a person in a position to confer, grant, or deny a benefit or advancement.
> Reprisal or threat of reprisal for the rejection of solicitation of advance where the reprisal is made by a person to grant, confer, or deny advancement.

> **Rape, Abuse & Incest National Network (RAINN),** is the largest anti-sexual violence organization in the United States. RAINN also provides other important information about sexual harassment alongside their definition (based closely on the EEOC's), including possible mental and emotional side effects a victim may exhibit, and access to resources.
>
> Find out more here:
>
> www.rainn.org/

Impact versus intent

Before building policy around sexual harassment, it is important to understand the difference between impact versus intent. *Intent* is what the initiator of a behavior may have aspired to achieve from that behavior, whereas the *impact* is the experience a behavior creates for the recipient of the action or words. In other words, the impact of an interaction is determined by the receiver, no matter the intent of the giver.

When relating this concept to workplace interactions involving staged intimacy, always remember that the recipient will determine whether a behavior constitutes as harassment or sexual harassment. "It's the impact, not the intent, of his or her words or actions that has to be considered when a harasser is being held accountable."[31] Management, directors, and other members of the creative team involved in the reporting process must regard impact as the predominant factor when deciding how to address any reported incident.

Understanding impact and intent can be complex, as the impact a receiver experiences may change due to various social, personal, and institutional histories; intersectional identities; and the multi-faceted relationships of participants in theatrical ensembles. Additionally, one must consider the power dynamics woven into every interaction that affect impact for the receiver.

> **Example scenario for impact versus intent**
>
> *Low on time in a put-in rehearsal for understudy actors, an assistant director steps into a moment of intimacy to model a piece of choreography that one of the understudies has not been executing correctly. This assistant director starts to physically model the desired movement, suddenly initiating a grab to the buttocks of an actor in the rehearsal without conversation, notice, or consent.*
>
> <u>Possible outcome A</u>
>
> While the intention was to quickly move through a rehearsal in what the assistant may have believed was the most efficient manner, and the movement intended to be a clinical demonstration, the impact is still a moment of nonconsent for the actor within a challenging power dynamic. In this version of the story, the relationship between the actor and the assistant director has been communicative and trust-filled throughout the process until this point. Thus, the actor is able to use a resolution in the moment technique called "Oops and Ouch" (discussed later in this chapter). They can use the "Ouch" part of the practice to say, "Hey, that was not appropriate behavior. I need to be asked about being touched there." The assistant director uses the "Oops" method by immediately taking accountability, apologizing, and changing their methods of working moving forward.
>
> <u>Possible outcome B</u>
>
> In this version of the relationship and workplace environment, the assistant director has initiated touch that borders on boundaries for a couple of the actors without asking for consent, even when reminded to ask. They have also made a couple of objectifying comments to members of the cast. After this nonconsensual interaction, the actor informs the deputy that they have experienced sexual harassment. The deputy connects with the stage manager who then engages with the established reporting structure.

Creating or Modifying Sexual Harassment Policy

The specific definition of sexual harassment used by a theatre company or institution will be central to the creation of policy for that particular institution. When it is time to create or modify the institution's sexual harassment policy, there are many resources for theatre companies to reference. One robust resource for theatre companies, as well as for individual practitioners, is available through the League of Independent Theater,[32] which worked with the Let Us Work project, led by founder Rachel Dart, to "develop a toolkit to help guide independent theaters to work safely, without fear of abuse or harassment."[33] This free, 15-page toolkit is available online.[34]

Theatre companies may also hire consultants from established intimacy companies (see Appendix A) to build catered policies alongside theatrical or academic administrators, especially if there has been a history of complaints. The hiring of consultants allows for space and time with an experienced "outside eye" to help create an appropriate structure of protocols and support. Such a consultant can be helpful either when restructuring a current framework or when putting an entirely new system into place.

Putting a Stop to "Retaliation" in the Reporting Process

When speaking of policy concerning harassment, the fear of retaliation is both a primary concern and a frequent experience by many victims of harassment. While experienced by all gender identities, research into the experience of women who have been harassed "consistently has shown that women do not report (or delay reporting) harassment because they fear retaliation, they believe no one will believe them, or they think that reporting will make the situation at work worse."[35] This fear of damaging working relationships is especially concerning when working in collaborative and creative environments within the theatrical industry. The industry must work to change this dynamic from the inside.

A clear commitment to anti-retaliation practices can help establish a workspace that exists to eliminate harm and ensure the safety of individuals bringing forward a concern. This commitment will also establish trust and confidence that an institution's structure of power will support and protect them rather than expose them to further harm while seeking help. Preferably, these anti-retaliation policies would be among the written policies employers adopt, providing a vital first step toward changing harmful statistics and supporting healthy workplace culture.

One straightforward way to support change and model honest, open communication is to create a direct, equitable reporting path. In the next section, we discuss creating transparent pathways for reporting incidents of harassment as a method for supporting trust and assuaging fears in a culture of consent.

> **TIME'S UP** "insists upon a world where work is safe, fair, and dignified for women of all kinds." Their legal defense fund provides assistance to "survivors of sexual harassment and retaliation."
>
> Find out more here:
>
> www.timesupfoundation.org
>
> **The Actors Fund**, founded in 1882, "fosters stability and resiliency, and provides a safety net for performing arts and entertainment professionals."
>
> Find out more here:
>
> www.actorsfund.org/resources

Methods for reporting harassment

Establishing a clearly defined structure for reporting incidents of harassment and sexual harassment will help to foster a communicative and retaliation-free space. However, a reimagining of the shape of this structure is needed. Reporting paths are often organized as a rigid hierarchical structure that may not always provide a safe and flexible place for individuals to engage. For example, the stage manager may be experiencing sexual harassment from the director; yet the director may be the person to whom the stage manager would report; this scenario provides no alternate link for communication. However, a reorganization of the system may offer more positive outcomes than previous modes of reporting.

Imagining this reporting structure as more malleable, like a "web" rather than a chain, ladder, or other rigid linear system, and organizing it as such, will help to establish a more diverse and inclusive system. Instead of negotiating an implied vertical path, creating the reporting structure in a web-like design provides a more balanced set of entry points. A company member can more easily engage, report, or inquire about harassment. When built to create a culture of consent, this structure should be established with transparency and care.

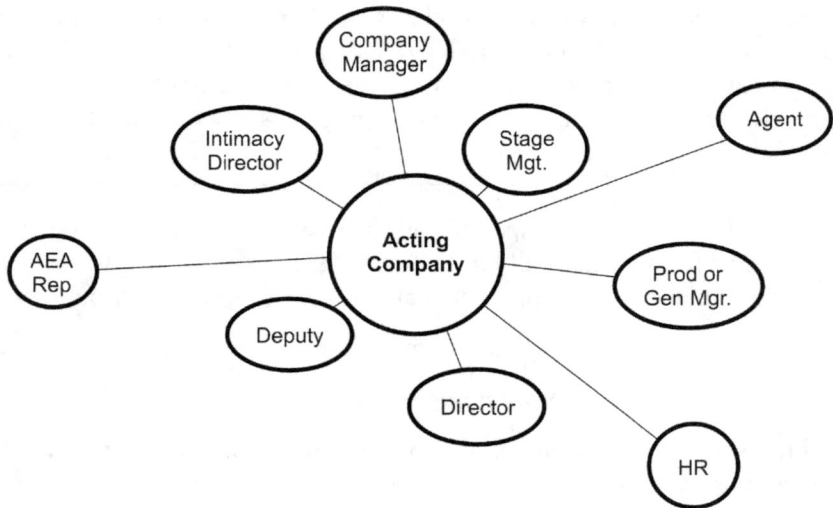

Figure 2.4 A web-like structure as a sample method for a theatrical reporting structure. Designed by the authors.

The center circle could be designed for any individual, group, area, or department within a theatre organization. Each of them would have their own web of individuals that they could reach out should the need arise. For the purposes of this example, we have designed the web structure around the acting company.

The radiating circles that surround the center "acting company," represent various individuals or groups that the acting company could reach out should there be the need. The closer to the center, the more likely they are to assist in a more immediate nature.

Providing many options for connection helps those represented in the center see the various avenues that exist and allows them to choose where to go based upon personal preference or level of comfort given the situation.

Each theatrical organization could have a variety of these reporting webs based upon the size and scope of their company.

Inclusivity within the reporting structure

Organizations should create a diverse and inclusive structure that allows for any member to easily come forward whenever they feel uncomfortable. Diversity within the webbed reporting structure will establish a more approachable and supportive process, diversity including gender identity, ethnic identity, age, class, physical ability, as well as other identities and abilities when possible. Establishing equal and balanced representation helps to create a more approachable and maneuverable reporting structural framework.

Availability of the structure

To build upon this approachable, maneuverable web-like network, especially when starting out on new projects and bringing on new company members, upper management should work to provide their reporting structure outlined in a handbook and visible through posting in common workspaces. The process of sharing this information when working on AEA union contracted productions has already been formalized through the union's President's Committee to Prevent Harassment.[36] But establishing these web-like networks should also be formalized when working on non-union, academic, or community productions.

Suppose a formalized reporting structure is not already clearly identified, documented, and easily accessible to all creative team members. In that case, a recommendation would be to ask upper administration to determine and outline their preferred method for reporting given current structures and staffing within the organization. The relevant production's creative and production teams should also be considered in relation to this larger structure. The newly outlined reporting structure should then be distributed widely through all departments, and especially with stage management, who could post the information on callboards or add it to the packets of paperwork typically shared with the company on the first day of rehearsal. The stage manager would then request any standard reporting forms or information required by the theatre company's human resource department should an incident need to be reported and documented.

Whatever position on the creative team one may hold, whether director, actor deputy, costume designer, or other, asking for access to company harassment policies and reporting structures will help to create an open and supportive environment that fosters accountability and communication and values consensual practices that build respectful workspaces.

> **Theatre Communications Group**, usually referred to as "TCG," is committed to "creat[ing] healthy organizational cultures" and to helping provide resources to those affected by harassment in the workplace.
>
> Find out more here:
>
> www.tcg.org

Communication techniques for moments bordering harassment

Communication regarding harassment sometimes has "gray areas" in the theatrical world. Theatre spaces, when built as respectful workspaces, can often have a jovial atmosphere. This atmosphere may feel welcoming to theatre artists and fuel their daily activity, but it can also create confusion around personal boundaries when clear expectations for professional and social behavior are not fully established or recognized. The "Code of Conduct" of New York's Public Theater addresses this head on by stating that "because the spaces in which we work are broad—encompassing administration, auditions, rehearsals, technical work, late nights, parties, public-facing frontline work, and more—we must acknowledge, and not exploit, the blurred boundaries between work and social spaces."[37] Due to these blurred boundaries between work and life, there may be moments or incidents that border on harassment and have clearly occurred accidentally or without malice. These incidents can occur anywhere from the watercooler in the main office to the rehearsal hall while building choreography. Thus, the time before pre-production begins is a prime opportunity to encourage healthy practices for moments of miscommunication in the workplace.

Resolution in the moment

In such instances of blurred lines or confusion about the words or actions of others, "resolution in the moment" is a technique that may be used to voice concerns and start conversations. This tool for healthy, open communication can only be used in a room that supports positive and respectful discourse and is built on a foundation of trust.

When deciding to employ resolution in the moment, it should also be made very clear that this should not be utilized as a replacement for or deterrent from reporting sexual harassment if it occurs. This tool is genuinely for moments that near "crossing the line" into abusive behavior but have not crossed it as of yet. Examples of behavior bordering on harassment may include times when a comment is made as an attempt at a joke that goes badly, or someone genuinely does not understand a direction given by a choreographer and accidentally crosses a physical boundary, or some other genuine misstep or mistake. Theatre practitioners, whose jobs are to tell stories about human conflict, may understand even more deeply that humans are fallible, make mistakes, or not fully understand the way their actions will be perceived. However, the choice to report an action or communicate in the moment will be a judgment call for those involved. Remember, sexual harassment is always judged by impact, not the intent.

If resolution in the moment feels like the preferred solution for a particular comment or action, a four-step process, adapted from multiple common conflict resolution resources,[38] could be followed:

- Voice the concern simply and clearly. An example of this could be stating, "I'm not OK with this," or "That comment made me uncomfortable."
- The recipient of this comment would take a moment to acknowledge and respond with an apology as needed.
- The parties involved decide in the moment if a further conversation is needed or if they can continue forward with work, the social situation or rehearsal.
- If continuing, the indicated behavior must shift or be changed.

Calling in or out

Calling in or out is another communication technique authority figures or co-workers may use to stop inappropriate behavior before it escalates to an incident of harassment. The concept behind "Calling out" and "Calling in" is based on confronting bias and discrimination and is applicable to consent and respect during physical storytelling as well. Multiple examples of calling in versus calling out in relation to equity and inclusion can be found online on a worksheet created by Seed the Way: Education for Justice and Equity.[39] Here we have related the concepts to incidents that could occur during the staging of intimacy.

Calling out is used when harm needs to be halted or interrupted and when it needs to be made immediately clear in the moment that specific behaviors or types of communication are not acceptable. An example in intimacy direction may be an actor attempting a touch to another actor's genitals without previous conversation or consent. This behavior would immediately be called out and stopped, as well as exploring the need for a rebuilding of trust and communication before moving forward with additional staging.

Calling in is utilized when there is space for reflection, and a deeper understanding of the motivations behind a set of words or actions can be explored. According to writer Ashley Astrew in a 2019 article, "*calling in* refers to 'the act of checking your peers and getting them to change problematic behavior by explaining their misstep with compassion and patience.'"[40] As opposed to clear statements about harm, calling in involves more questions and opportunities for clarification. An example in staged intimacy may be a stage manager writing down a slang term for a body part in a rehearsal report instead of using a term that is more clinical in tone and the intimacy specialist/director or other management having a call-in discussion regarding reasons for changing that practice.

Whether the situation necessitates calling in or out, this practice preferably is utilized positively to elicit respectful communication moving forward from all parties, and relies on all individuals being committed to providing a safe and supportive space in which these conversations may take place.

Community accountability

One way to reinforce resolution in the moment is to create a community pledge that is agreed upon by the group before the staging of intimate content begins. One example of this verbal commitment could be, "We pledge to create a positive and respectful work environment where everyone feels empowered to speak up." With a pledge such as this, all confirm a desire for and commitment to a positive and respectful working space.

The community may need to return to open discussion later if issues arise. Sometimes there may be a group realization that a particular way of working or use of language is inappropriate, and this should be addressed as an ensemble to support a healthy workplace. Preferably, resolution in the moment can be a thoughtful response for all community members working on the problematic practices that border harassment. By building a culture of consent, the company would hopefully build this mindfulness practice into all their work.

Modeling healthy workplace communication

When it comes to healthy communication practices around stopping sexual harassment, supporting boundaries, and reinforcing a culture of consent, adjustments should occur throughout the entire structure of an organization. Especially with new visibility of consent and social justice concerns, it is more important now than ever that senior level employees are making a conscious effort to examine day-to-day communication styles and practices. Company members at the top must work with an eye toward actively incorporating intentional and consensual behaviors at every level within their institution. Modeling healthful communication practices within administrative or staff-led spaces is key to honoring consent throughout a production process, even if one never enters the rehearsal hall. Culture is inclusive, and new employees quickly experience company values displayed at all levels within an organization.

Incorporating resources for mental and emotional health

During preparation for pre-production, it is recommended that a holistic approach be taken when a show contains intimacy. This approach may mean having mental health training or resources at the ready. In Chapter 1, we discussed practices for finding mental health resources and the benefits of basic training in this area, such as Mental Health First Aid, and suggest referencing this information again at this point in the process. Mental and emotional health support is important for any theatre community, but especially if the production involves a story of sexual violence or any non-consensual intimacy. Mental health resources would first and foremost be provided for the actors engaged in the storytelling. Still, they could be just as crucial for all of the performers, stage management teams, crew members, and others who are in proximity to the action, watching this story unfold time and time again through rehearsal and performance.

Notes from the field ... protocols in process

A stage manager expressed extreme gratitude for having the content communicated to them and having mental health be acknowledged in the room before the staging of a scene depicting sexual violence. They expressed a past experience in another show where a piece of graphic movement was suddenly being choreographed without notice, and they

> felt unable to call for a break, even though sensing they were nearing a state of acute anxiety. This time, in contrast, when given access to resources and being acknowledged as a participant in the room, they felt much more prepared and healthy.[41] Being considered alongside the performers and given options for support avoided a lot of tension that may have otherwise occurred and allowed them to remain fully present as the movement was staged.
>
>
>
> **An early-career stage manager**
> Anonymous by request
>

A more generalized list of resources (such as described in Chapter 1) could be researched and posted as useful material throughout an entire season. It may also be necessary to obtain additional resources based on specific content in the script. For example, the script content could prompt finding resources for domestic abuse counseling or grief counseling. Finding access to mental resources in specific areas will create a community of support in the rehearsal hall and encourage the entire creative team to practice self-care.

Questions to ask when choosing a production

Once a strong foundation of policy, reporting, and resources has been set, choosing a season can begin. A critical first step when bringing a production to the stage is choosing the right work to be performed. Whether slotting a show into a complete season or producing a one-time event or fundraiser, deciding on the script involves multiple factors. Filtered through the lens of the theatre's mission, choosing scripts may be subject to myriad considerations, like thematic connection to the overall season or a reflection of current events or trends. Certain constraints may exist, like limitations on budget, technology, or staffing. Creative personnel may also be a factor, like an actress in the company who is particularly suited to a specific role, an ensemble suited to devised physical theatre, or a designer who has particular expertise. Contrarily, the absence of certain attributes may also be considered, leading to questions such as "Do we have access to designers, directors, or actors who have the lived experience and/or cultural competency to tell this story responsibly?"

Within this plethora of considerations, careful attention should always be given to the welfare of the acting and production staff. This attention should regard both the mental and physical health of the performers and the entire theatre company. Things can go very wrong without full consideration of actor safety; searching the Occupational Safety and Health Administration (OSHA)[42] website will explain in detail theatrical productions in the United States that have been plagued by serious injuries. Injuries occurred due to everything from repetition in dance-based movements, raked stages, staged violence, aerial work, rigging, to other physical stunts. However, the likelihood of injuries occurring is greatly reduced when companies choose the right creative team for the job and have the proper safety protocols in place. These protocols need not deter a theater company from selecting a piece that includes demanding and challenging feats of physicality. Physical risk and feats of strength are part of the human experience; audiences love to watch physical feats, and artists love to perform in and tell these stories when they are confident appropriate safety and support systems are in place.

Staged intimacy, while not quickly identified as physically dangerous as aerial stunts, intense staged violence, or complex choreography, has caused both psychological and physical injury to actors over the years when mismanaged. As mentioned in Chapter 1, problematic practices have led to actors experiencing the nonconsensual building of intimate physical moments in many productions. Just as with dangerous physical stunts that harm the actors, incidents of abuse and sexual harassment can damage the health of the actors as well as the institution's reputation and financial health. The implosion of the Profiles Theatre in Chicago due to harassment allegations[43] is one example of many in the "reckoning of #MeToo." This incident was one catalyst in a series of many that helped formulate official demands for change, one being the "Chicago Theatre Standards" document (also called "Not In Our House"), an initiative to move Chicago theatres "toward a cultural paradigm shift away from turning a blind eye to sexual harassment, discrimination, violence, intimidation and bullying in our theatres and towards mentoring, prevention, and accountability."[44]

Like stories of physical prowess and aggression, stories of intimate touch, sex, and nudity are also part of the human experience. Actors understand the importance of telling these stories, and both cast and creatives are beginning to realize all of the factors that are involved but just may not know where to begin. Now more than ever, it is clear this begins before pre-production, with choosing the right creative team and establishing preferred practices to support the production of shows containing intimacy.

To help you or your organization determine if you have the right team and the right protocols in place to responsibly stage more complex staged intimacy, simulated sex acts, or nudity, we suggest asking some specific questions early on in decision-making. When choosing a script or project that includes intimate elements, upper administrative team should consider the following:

Who are our leaders? Do our creative, design, and administrative teams have a willingness to embrace modern recommended practices in consensual devising? For example, will our guest director support and respect the boundaries of the actors as they build these moments of intimacy and allow the necessary rehearsal time for these moments to be staged conscientiously?

What is our budget? Do we have the budget to hire a qualified intimacy professional for the show? If not, could our budget afford an intimacy workshop or an intimacy consultant to come in for a few hours and set our preferred practices? Is there the ability or plan in place to recover either financially or reputationally if an intimacy professional or consultant is not hired and something goes very wrong?

Can we tell this story safely? Do we have in place the resources, healthful modes of communication, company policies and established path of reporting? For example, do we have a reporting structure in place in case an incident of harassment occurs?

Can we tell this story responsibly, authentically, and without harm? If the staged intimacy involves stories related to intersectionality[45] or underrepresented identities, will we have artists with education, training, and/or lived experience to help us tell this story with cultural competency?

Utilizing open and honest self-analysis from the moment the work is chosen will establish the conditions for space where staged intimacy can be explored responsibly and give the creative team more confidence and freedom to engage in challenging work.

Chapter reflection

Through points made in this chapter, we invite you, through honest self-reflection and further education, to interrogate your own assumptions about power, agency, and body autonomy. Modifying the ways theatrical organizations support their team members is only the beginning of possible tectonic shifts in how theatre is built and performed. One significant change is how we tell stories that involve staged intimacy, and it is time for theatrical institutions to welcome and champion this progress. Championing begins when examining leadership and institutional culture to foster or support a culture of consent. The entire creative team must understand internal power dynamics and structure, company policies on harassment, resolution, reporting, methods for supporting self-care and mental health, and healthy communication practices when choosing productions.

There is a need in the performative arts industries to address inequities and better understand the coercive and oppressive practices inherent to theatrical processes. It will take openness, work, study, and long-term commitment to begin to create an inclusive, healthy work environment for all. Thus, it is highly recommended to seek out and keep up with this training over time as part of institutional and personal practice. Suggestions include anti-racist theatre, anti-oppression, and implicit bias training. Additionally, studying documents such as "We See You, White American Theatre,"[46] a list of demands created by Black, indigenous, and people of color theatre workers, is another necessary step in supporting a culture of consent.

Theater companies should not shy away from telling intimate stories as long as they have the recommended support staff and protocols in place. Establishing responsible practices does not mean limiting creativity or avoiding challenging stories but will instead allow for a confident dive into challenging and cutting-edge work. As Peter Hinton-Davis, Canadian director, playwright, and educator said, workspaces must be "safe spaces so dangerous things can happen."[47] When companies strive to create a workplace where creative individuals feel open and free to explore uncharted territories and navigate new stories, artists feel confident diving into what may be perceived as perilous waters. By following intentional practices and protocols, such as those promoted by IDC and other companies who have done extensive research and set standards, collectively we will create an environment where stories containing staged intimacy can be told confidently, responsibly, and ethically.

Chapter discussion / exercise / activity

1. **Power Dynamics Activity**

    The only way to fully understand the effects that power has on a group or individual is to examine and discuss its effects on behavior. Avoidance can be dangerous and may allow inequities to continue. For this chapter discussion, we encourage you to examine each type of power described in the power dynamics section and then consider discussing the activity below with the appropriate members of your creative team. We say "to consider," given that the confronting of power dynamics within a company structure or ensemble may not be possible for everyone based on the stability or safety they feel within an organization or ensemble. If you are unable to work on this activity as a group, it is also helpful for individual practice.

- Identify a situation where you felt you held a specific type of power. Do you feel the power had a positive or negative effect on your behavior and the situation?
- Identify when another person held a specific type of power. Do you feel the power had a positive or negative effect on their behavior and the situation?

Next, reflect upon the following:

- What actions or characteristics did you observe that helped you to identify which type of power you were experiencing or witnessing in those moments?
- Did you feel this sense of power in your body, and if so, what did it feel like?
- Did you identify this type of power in the moment, or later when thinking back?

Finally, consider the following:

- When in a group activity, observe the dynamics of the group.
- Is one individual taking the lead and making decisions for others?
- Is there a natural camaraderie that forms creating a more equal distribution of power?
- Is any single individual pulling back from fear or intimidation?

The examination of group behavior may help one to identify the dynamics of power more easily. If you are in a position of power, can you use these observations and your power in productive ways to better the workspace? Observation is key, and open discussion regarding these observations is the first step to knowing how to create a more equitable working environment.

2. **Impact vs Intent Activity:**

    Earlier in this chapter, we discussed the concept of impact versus intent and its relationship to harassment and reporting. This activity offers another opportunity to explore a few scenarios along with two possible outcomes to help further illuminate the complexities of impact when related to harassment. We hope this activity will lead to valuable discussions concerning mindfulness, communication practices, and reporting in your own ensembles.

    Read the example scenarios A and B below, then muse on how these situations would feel from these three different perspectives:

    - an outside bystander witnessing the interaction between others
    - the recipient of the behavior(s) in that scenario
    - the person in the reporting structure who is first told about the incident

    Consider the two possible outcomes for each incident and reflect. How do these two possible outcomes

    - Influence your perception of the incident?
    - Affect your relationship to the responsibilities of a bystander?
    - Affect your understanding of the responsibilities of a reporter on the structure?

Example scenario A

Actors A and B are rehearsing a scene that includes simulated sex acts. After working this scene they overhear two other actors talking about the content in the hallway outside the rehearsal hall. Actors C and D, believing they are in a private conversation, are commenting about how they hope to perform a sex act with their own partners the next time they are together.

Possible outcome A1

Everyone in the rehearsal hall has been respectful until this moment, and community agreements had been set. Thus, Actor A has the language to "call out" actors C and D, informing them that it is inappropriate to discuss the choreography off stage, and that behavior needs to stop immediately. Actors C and D take accountability and apologize. Actor B informs the deputy about the incident, saying it is resolved as of now, and check-ins are made throughout the rest of the process with Actors A and B.

Possible outcome A2

Actors A and B's ability to feel trust within the ensemble as they perform the vulnerable scene is severely damaged, as Actors C and D have been overheard making comments like these before and have already been asked to stop. Actor B decides to submit a report of harassment, and requests the staged intimacy professional be called into rehearsal as soon as possible. Punitive action is put into action for Actors C and D.

Example scenario B

A student actor enters the space wearing a tight corset at the first dress rehearsal. Their teacher/director immediately and loudly comments, "Wow, that corset looks amazing on you." Other students erupt in celebratory hollers, applause, and "cat-calls."

Possible outcome B1

The student turns beet red, laughs, and awkwardly says, "I know. Didn't the costume designer do a wonderful job?" and heads to the side of the rehearsal hall. They end up wearing a scarf to cover up until rehearsal begins. A graduate student later checks in with that actor, and afterward reaches out to their faculty mentor to communicate the possible harassment. A report is submitted to the Title IX office on campus, and later productions at the university include a workshop on harassment in the workplace during the first rehearsal.

Possible outcome B2

The student actor takes a big dramatic bow, fine with what they experience as playful attention from their peers. However, the director and stage manager both immediately quiet the room down, and use this as a moment for a reflective "calling in" activity. The director takes accountability for the comment they made, followed by a group discussion acknowledging a necessary etiquette shift; the workplace is not an appropriate environment for anyone to comment or joke, whether verbally or nonverbally, on the physical aesthetics of their coworkers. The meeting ends with a group breath and presence, with eye-contact around the circle. In the rehearsal report, the stage management team reminds all of the reporting structure should they decide to use it at a later date.

Notes

1 Concept discussed in relationship to intimacy direction during February 2019 "Intimacy Directors International O'Neill 9-day Intensive" in-person training attended by Alexis Black. Training held at Eugene O'Neill Theatre Center, Waterford, CT. Concept is also discussed in multiple publications, including 2020's *Staging Sex* by Chelsea Pace.
2 US Department of Education. "Know Your Rights: Title IX Prohibits Sexual Harassment and Sexual Violence Where You Go to School." Dec. 4, 2020, https://www2.ed.gov/about/offices/list/ocr/docs/title-ix-rights-201104.html.
3 Rodis, Alicia, and Tonia Sina. "Intimacy Directors International O'Neill 9-day Intensive." In-person training on "Power Dynamics." Waterford, CT, February 2019.
4 Bunting, Michael. *The Mindful Leader: 7 Practices for Transforming Your Leadership, Your Organization, and Your Life*. Milton, Queensland: Wiley, 2016, p. 29.
5 https://www.productionondeck.com.
6 Bellinger, Bear. "Production on Deck: Eliminating Excuses." *PLSN*, Feb. 4, 2022, https://plsn.com/articles/stage-directions-articles/production-on-deck-eliminating-excuses-2/?fbclid=IwAR0KsmaP0kEUe48H5vv_ajmB6275oldjTsj-FONuUvu3Kcn2reKAbY4V0pmE.
7 Chart updated to include intimacy choreographer and intimacy captain at the request of the authors, and used with permission by Matt Kizer. "Theatre Hierarchy Chart 2021," Matt Kizer: Scenic & Lighting Design. Accessed April 14, 2021. scenicandlighting.com/article/theatre-hiearchy-chart-2021/.
8 Roxborough, Scott. "Hollywood Confronts Its Culture of Bullying." *Deutsche Welle Press*. April 19 (updated April 21), 2021. https://www.dw.com/en/hollywood-confronts-its-culture-of-bullying/a-57247680.
9 Tran, Diep. "Unmuffling a Culture of Silence," *American Theatre*. December 6, 2017, https://www.americantheatre.org/2017/12/06/unmuffling-a-culture-of-silence/. Accessed June, 2021.
10 Shindle, Kate, Gabrielle Carteris, and Adam Krauthamer. "Joint Statement on the Need for Harassment-Free Workplaces in the ARTS." Actors' Equity press release. April 12, 2021, https://actorsequity.org/news/PR/JointHarassmentStatement/. accessed June, 2021.
11 https://www.weseeyouwat.com/demands.
12 Roxborough, Scott. "Hollywood Confronts Its Culture of Bullying." *Deutsche Welle Press*. April 19 (updated April 21), 2021. https://www.dw.com/en/hollywood-confronts-its-culture-of-bullying/a-57247680. Accessed April 2021.
13 Clark, Abby. "My Ex-Boss Is Accused of Sexual Harassment: The Problem Is Bigger than He Is." *Detroit Free Press*, March 28, 2021, https://www.freep.com/story/opinion/contributors/2021/03/28/metoo-lansing-political-consultant-harassment/7012833002/. Accessed July, 2021.
14 "Systemic Power and Race." Handout from Understanding and Dismantling Racism: MCARI Anti-Racism Workshop. 2013, https://www.ramseycounty.us/sites/default/files/Assistance and Support/Systemic Power Race.pdf. Accessed July, 2021.

15 From Intimacy Directors and Coordinators handout on power dynamics, Level One certification training, 2021. Used with permission of IDC.
16 Steinmetz, Katy. "She Coined the Term 'Intersectionality' Over 30 Years Ago: Here's What It Means to Her Today." *Time.com*. February 20, 2020, https://time.com/5786710/kimberle-crenshaw-intersectionality/. Accessed June, 2021.
17 From Intimacy Directors and Coordinators handout on power dynamics, Level One certification training, 2021. Used with permission of IDC.
18 Used with the permission of Intimacy Directors and Coordinators.
19 French, John R. P. Jr., and Bertram Raven, "The Bases of Social Power," in *Studies in Social Power*, ed. Dorwin Cartwright (Ann Arbor: University of Michigan, 1959), pp. 150–67. Reprinted in *Group Dynamics: Research and Theory*, 3rd ed., ed. Dorwin Cartwright (New York: Harper & Row, 1968), pp. 259–69, http://www.communicationcache.com/uploads/1/0/8/8/10887248/the_bases_of_social_power_-_chapter_20_-_1959.pdf. Accessed February 2019.
20 French, John R. P. Jr., and Bertram Raven, "The Bases of Social Power," in *Studies in Social Power*, ed. Dorwin Cartwright (Ann Arbor: University of Michigan, 1959), pp. 150–67. Reprinted in *Group Dynamics: Research and Theory*, 3rd ed., ed. Dorwin Cartwright (New York: Harper & Row, 1968), p. 150, http://www.communicationcache.com/uploads/1/0/8/8/10887248/the_bases_of_social_power_-_chapter_20_-_1959.pdf. Accessed February 2019.
21 Developed through consultation with the MSU Adv. SM class (Spring 2019), IDC representatives, and Claire Wilcher.
22 Classroom discussion exercise on power dynamics developed through consultation with the MSU Adv. SM class (Spring 2019), IDC representatives, and Claire Wilcher.
23 Graham, John R., Campbell R. Harvey, Jillian Popadak, and Shivaram Rajgopal. "Corporate Culture: Evidence from the Field." *National Bureau of Economic Research*. March 2017 www.nber.org/papers/w23255.
24 Lehmann, Stehanie Maiya, with Celeste Morris. "Facing (and Fixing) the Problem of Sexual Harassment in Theatre." *Sothern Theatre Magazine* 59(4). 2018, p. 9.
25 Bennet, Dawn, and Sophie Hennekam. "Sexual Harassment in the Creative Industries: Tolerance, Culture and the Need for Change." *Gender Work and Organization* 24(3). March 2017, https://www.researchgate.net/publication/312024564_Sexual_Harassment_in_the_Creative_Industries_Tolerance_Culture_and_the_Need_for_Change.
26 Shindle, Kate. "From the President: Taking Proactive Steps to Prevent Harassment." *Equity News* 103.2 (Spring 2018). https://www.actorsequity.org/news/EquityNews/Spring2018/Spring2018.pdf. Accessed April 29, 2021
27 "Actors' Equity Announces New 'President's Committee to Prevent Harassment,'" https://www.actorsequity.org/news/PR/PresidentsCommittee/. Accessed March, 2020.
28 https://www.eeoc.gov/.
29 "Sexual Harassment." U.S. Equal Employment Opportunity Commission, https://www.eeoc.gov/sexual-harassment. Accessed April 29, 2021.

30 Rodis, Alicia, and Tonia Sina. "Intimacy Directors International O'Neill 9-day Intensive." In-person training on harassment and intimacy direction. Waterford, CT, February 2019.
31 Piro Zinna Cifelli Paris & Genitempo LLC. "Do Intentions Matter When You're Being Harassed at Work?" https://www.pirozinnalaw.com/blog/2017/05/do-intentions-matter-when-youre-being-harassed-at-work/. Accessed February, 2021.
32 https://www.litny.org.
33 "Anti Sexual Harassment Toolkit," www.litny.org/antisexual-harassment-toolkit. Accessed June, 2021.
34 Todoroff, Aimee et al., "Communication and Consent for a Harassment Free Workspace." *Let Us Work*, 2018, https://docs.google.com/document/d/1t_iwus-BCR_qTT-khMQ9X2t4VeoscMz-bX_UWqADU4sg/edit. Accessed June, 2021.
35 Lawton, Anne. "Between Scylla and Charybdis: The Perils of Reporting Sexual Harassment." *Journal of Business Law* 9(3). 2007, p. 603, https://scholarship.law.upenn.edu/jbl/vol9/iss3/4.
36 https://www.actorsequity.org/news/PR/PresidentsCommittee/.
37 "Public Theater Code of Conduct," https://publictheater.org/about/code-of-conduct2/. Accessed June, 2021.
38 Pulling from personal experiences and a number of different online conflict resolution resources, we crafted this four-step process. Here is a sample of one referenced site: https://www.mindtools.com/pages/article/newLDR_81.htm.
39 Haslam, Dr. Rebecca Eunmi. *Interrupting Bias: Calling out vs. Calling In.* http://racialequityvtnea.org/wp-content/uploads/2018/09/Interrupting-Bias_-Calling-Out-vs.-Calling-In-REVISED-Aug-2018-1.pdf.
40 Astrew, Ashley. "Is There A Difference Between 'Calling In' And 'Calling Out'?" *Dictionary.com*. March 22, 2019, https://www.dictionary.com/e/calling-in-vs-calling-out/.
41 Conversation held privately with intimacy director Alexis Black during a 2019 production at an SPT theatre.
42 https://www.osha.gov.
43 Levitt, Aimee, and Christopher Piatt. "At Profiles Theatre the Drama—and Abuse—Is Real." Chicago Reader, June 8, 2016, https://www.chicagoreader.com/chicago/profiles-theatre-theater-abuse-investigation/Content?oid=22415861. Accessed July, 2021.
44 Fisher, Laura T., and Lori Myers. "Chicago Theatre Standards Pilot Project," https://www.notinourhouse.org/chicago-theatre-standards-pilot-project/. Accessed July, 2021.
45 Steinmetz, Katy. "She Coined the Term 'Intersectionality' Over 30 Years Ago: Here's What It Means to Her Today." *Time.com*. February 20, 2020, https://time.com/5786710/kimberle-crenshaw-intersectionality/. Accessed June, 2021.
46 https://www.weseeyouwat.com.
47 Hinton-Davis, Peter. "Intimacy in Theatre Education: A Roundtable Conversation." York University, Department of Theatre. April 21, 2021, https://www.eventbrite.ca/e/intimacy-in-theatre-education-a-roundtable-conversation-tickets-146801038859. Accessed April 21, 2021.

3
The pre-production process

Laying the groundwork

With the tools to build a consensual culture and the drive to support shifts in standards of operation at the foundational level, theatrical companies and teams can now launch into a like-minded pre-production process. When teams support staged intimacy early on, some of the most impactful, dependable practices for the creative team can form. For the creatives (designers, directors, choreographers, and more) pre-production is the time to establish methods of communication and protocols that work best for the entire team. In preparation for actors, this is the time to set intentional practices for auditions and expectations for first rehearsals to opening night and beyond. When considering the script, this is the time to analyze needs around staged intimacy, nudity, or other complex physical storytelling specific to the production.

This chapter details terminology, recommended practices, and protocols for supporting the responsible staging of intimacy to be undertaken during the pre-production process and will discuss the following:

- Methods for analyzing a script that contains intimacy
- Recommended practices for auditions and callbacks
- Contracts and riders
- Accessories and safety equipment
- Building rehearsal schedules
- Closed rehearsal protocols
- Effective communication within the production's creative team

Key terms in Chapter 3[*]

Acknowledgment forms

Primarily used for pre-professional theatre or academia, these written acknowledgment forms confirm in writing that performers are aware of the intimate storytelling involved in a role prior to their acceptance or declination of that role.

Contract riders

Amendments or additions to an existing contract. For staged intimacy, riders may involve expectations and protocols in regard to staged nudity, or other requests from performers or production in regard to physical storytelling.

Intimacy content notices

Verbal or written notices of intimacy movement contained within a script. These notices should be shared as early as possible during the audition process of required or potential intimacy. Intimacy content notices are key in allowing potential performers to make informed decisions about their confidence with expected physical storytelling prior to accepting a role.

Intimacy moment list

A list of moments in a production that clearly or potentially will contain staged intimacy. This list should be built using stage directions, written dialogue as well as considering the interpretations or artistic vision of the director, with input from the intimacy director when possible.

Modesty garments

Robes, body stockings, or other garments that provide coverage for actors during breaks or pauses in rehearsals that involve staged nudity or scenes that are scantily clad.

---

[*] See *Terms & Language Acknowledgement* and *Glossary of Key Terms* in Appendix E for citations, trainings and reference materials that informed definitions.

Desexualized language

Language that is more innocuous, clinical or neutral in tone regarding staged intimate content or scenes. This may include using anatomical terms for body parts instead of colloquialisms or adjusting the way scenes of intimacy are described verbally and in rehearsal reports. Examples include using a word such as "glutes" instead of "butt" or calling a scene "the reunion scene" or other neutral term instead of "the sex scene." This may also be referenced as "deloaded"[1], purposeful or mindful language.

Personal barriers

These are hygienic coverings, support, and/or padding for genitals and other sensitive areas that may be impacted during the staging and performing of more complex staged intimacy or nudity. These may be used as an extra safeguard to modesty, to maintain hygiene or physical safety, or protect and desensitize areas as needed. Examples include padded bike shorts, athletic cups, or moleskin-like adhesive barriers.

Placeholder

Substituted or "marked" actions used in place of intimate actions such as kissing, simulated sexual movements, etc. All actors involved in the action must agree and feel confident with the substitution.

Placeholder removal date

If placeholders are being used (see definition above) this is a day agreed upon to end the substituting of movements and begin performing the fully realized movements choreographed in the staged intimacy. This may mean changing from a slow speed to performance speed, adding the lip-to-lip contact in a stage kiss, or fully engaging in other more physically or emotionally challenging content. This date is to be agreed upon by the cast involved as well as necessary creative team members.

Methods for analyzing a script that contains intimacy

Once the theatre company has committed to a culture of consent, chosen a script, and hired the creative team, the next step is taking a deep dive into the words of the play. No matter the position, individual team members will immerse themselves into the playwright's world to begin their creative process. This analysis will serve many purposes and provide much insight, especially when working on a production that contains intimate content.

While every member of a design team has a different creative process, there is one individual who will play an integral role as collaboration begins: the stage manager. The stage manager has an eye on every part of the production process from design, choreography, scheduling, and actor needs to creative interpretation, director's motivation, and scripted requirements. For the stage manager, immersion into the words of the play is a vital first step to understanding the world they will soon manage, nurture, and cultivate. Acknowledging their central positioning within the creative team, this section on script analysis is written mainly from that vantage point. The additional perspectives of a director or a staged intimacy professional are considered at specific points, given there are significant creative considerations beyond those that fall solely under the responsibility of stage management. We invite the reader to apply their own perspective to these approaches and practices, as many positions on the team could interact with the script in similar ways.

The stage manager and a script containing intimacy

Before the first rehearsal and prior to meeting with the director, intimacy director, and other members of the team, the stage manager will read through the script several times. These reads are to gather and organize all pertinent information. Hopefully, their first pass through the script can be done with no other goal than to allow themselves the joy of stepping into a new world, to experience this particular story, freely experiencing the journey the playwright has crafted. Additional passes will have more structure and specific objectives as they begin an inspection of the written dialogue. During their second step of examination, a stage manager will look past the story's emotion and focus on technical and logistical details within the story's action. This step will be the time to dissect the show scene by scene, tracking through character actions, dialogue, and stage directions and to take detailed notes on every prop, cue, costume, and transition.

While looking at the script with this eye for detail, stage managers may discover moments they believe require special attention or the eye of trained specialists during the rehearsal process. These movements or actions may be related to combat, dance, vocal or physical flexibility, staged intimacy, and more, and should be tracked in the same meticulous nature as other more concrete details. There may be implied movements or actions in addition to those explicitly written. These implied moments should also be noted within the script analysis tracking sheet (see Figure 3.1). For any member of the directing, choreographic, design, and management teams, the entire picture is filled out through this deep analysis, which includes critical tracking of technical requirements and a thorough analysis of written and implied character movements.

If questioning what moments might require the assistance of an ID, communication with the specialist will help. While staged intimacy can be broadly defined as scenes that contain kissing, stories of intimate physical contact, or nudity, the team could also include familial and platonic stories, sexual tension and "chemistry" where no touching occurs, and scenes of sexual violence within that definition. An intimacy professional, such as the ID, will work with the director (and then stage manager) to determine what moments will be looked at collaboratively. As mentioned in the section on specializations in Chapter 1, there may be scenes that contain both elements of intimacy and culturally diverse storytelling. If necessary, cultural consultants who have access to the research and specialized training (and sometimes lived experience) may also be a key collaborator and should be considered as a way to support the actors and the story in these moments.

Finding consultants for theatrical productions during pre-production

Consultants for theatrical productions may include individuals or representatives from a multitude of organizations, programs, or training backgrounds with specific knowledge, training, and research practices that support a distinct need within the storytelling. For example, a story may contain a character experiencing PTSD or characters working through the aftermath of an assault, or there may be racist language or themes. In these instances, a consultant may be requested or desired to ensure responsible storytelling and provide ensemble support. While it can be helpful to work with consultants who have partnered with live performance before, this is not always necessary. For example, when working with stories that contain the story of a psychological health crisis or a character that suffers from substance abuse, a mental health professional, social worker, or addiction specialist may be the appropriate consultant. When seeking consultants specializing in cultural competency, consultants should have research and training to support the production's specific stories, themes, and character identities. In addition to research practices, some cultural consultants may have lived experiences related to the identities within the script.

As this role in theatre gains visibility, directors, actors, intimacy professionals, or other team members may inquire about the hiring of these cultural specialists or other consultants. Administrative team members may seek out these professionals or the appropriate organizations online by using an online search engine. Also, Appendix F: A Partial List of Pertinent Resources, at the end of this text, includes a list of organizations that offer mental health support, diversity, equity and inclusion training, and more, which may be a helpful place to start. If affiliated with a university or institution of higher learning, one could reach out to faculty whose research focuses on the themes or stories wished to be explored or told. Another option is social services providers or human resource departments for recommendations of individuals who have the proper education and training to support the production.

Some intimacy professionals have the training to work with specialized care when stories that require specific cultural competencies are intertwined with the stories of staged intimacy. See the "Specializations Within the Field of Staged Intimacy" section in Chapter 1 for narratives from several intimacy professionals with specific cultural competency training and experience.

Stage management will also formulate a comprehensive list of questions or notes based on specific logistical or technical elements discovered during their script analysis. Preferably, these would be explored with the director and the intimacy director in early joint pre-production meetings. An example of a tracking sheet is below, showing an organized layout used to track technical details, movements written into stage directions or implied through character dialogue, as well as to track notes and/or questions that grow out of this in-depth analysis. Directors and intimacy professionals may have their own versions of these tracking sheets, but for stage management, this type of tracking will create confidence in comprehension of the needs of the script. This will also prepare them to spearhead conversations with the creative team in order to build and maintain a culture of consent and care.

(Insert Production title)
Pre-Production Script Analysis

Act	Scene	Pg. #	Stage direction	Actor line references (who / what)	Movement Intimacy / Fight / Dance	Set Requirements	Prop Requirements	Costume Requirements	Lighting Requirements	Sound Requirements	EFX Requirements	General Notes & Questions:
ACT I	Scene 1											
	Scene 2											
	Scene 3											

Figure 3.1 A sample excel template listing components of script analysis. Created by Tina M. Newhauser.

Script analysis for directors and intimacy professionals

When analyzing a script that contains intimacy, the director may look for more than the specified actions written into the stage directions, or implied from the dialogue. They may discover that there are moments of intimacy that may not be written into the dialogue or stated in the script but rather are based upon their interpretation of story and emotional arc of the characters. This director may also find that they would like to adjust the intimacy from what is written on the page, either through stylistic choices or through a wish to make it more intricate or less complex, to better serve their vision. Sharing this information with the team and casting prior to auditions (when possible) is an effective tool for fostering a culture of consent.

Intimacy directors will likely look at technical needs such as any accessories the actors will require for privacy, hygienic practices, or safety (this is discussed later in this chapter). They will assess scheduling needs based on the intricacy of the moments. They may discover multiple questions for costuming, scenery, lighting, or sound involving staged intimate moments.

While staged intimacy professionals are focused on the physical storytelling and protocols around movement, they may also look at the script to identify possible additional resources that would be useful to the performers and the creative team. As discussed in Chapter 1, this may include mental health resources. They may also look at whether additional consultation could be suggested for charged themes or content around race, gender, disability, or more, and may examine the storytelling elements that could benefit from specific, trained eyes outside of their expertise or lived experience.

The triumvirate of consent

For script analysis, we explore the connective nature of three specific team members a little more deeply: that of the director, intimacy director (or professional under a similar title), and stage manager. During a February 2021 multi-week online course, taught by the authors, titled "Stage Managing Intimacy for Intimacy Directors and Coordinators," the class of approximately 36 stage managers came up with the term "triumvirate of consent." This was meant to lightheartedly describe what we discovered: the stage manager, director, and intimacy director can be a triad of collaborators in the room with informational or expert power and support each other in fostering consent-based practices. These three may be uniquely positioned to collaborate and use their varied and balanced power to support communication and agency during the entire rehearsal process.

Each of their roles plays an important part: the director oversees the entire story with a strong vision and a final stamp of approval on storytelling. The intimacy director supports their vision through specialized training to enhance the story and safety of these moments and serves as a liaison for actors when staging intimacy. The stage manager's role is the connective tissue for communication within the entire ensemble through notating and supporting moments of intimacy throughout the process. Additionally, the stage manager is responsible for maintaining stories of intimacy after the production has opened and the director and the ID have moved on. This switchover can be hugely impactful to a culture of consent if the SM team is not on the same page. The stage manager must have a full and clear understanding of the director's and ID's vision and established protocols involved in staged intimacy in order to maintain the storytelling and support consent throughout the run of the production.

While communication is an integral part of the process for the entire creative team, building an interconnected relationship is one of the strongest ways to cultivate a culture of consent throughout the entire process. To this end, we have created a Venn diagram to visually depict the cohesion between these three positions in regard to staged intimacy as a whole (see Figure 3.2). While the list of responsibilities around storytelling and intimacy is more

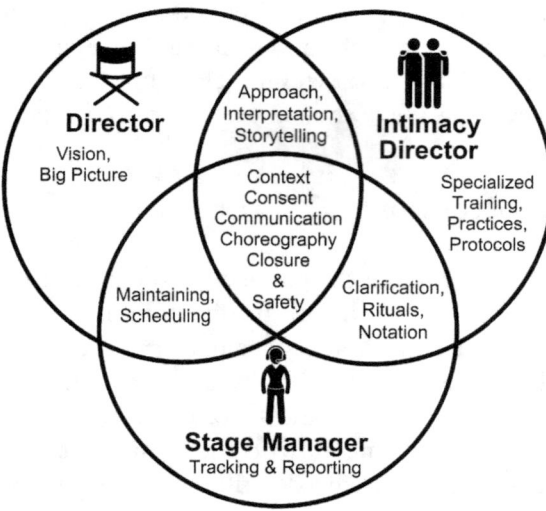

Figure 3.2 Three interlocking circles that show the overlapping relationship between the director, intimacy director, and stage manager. Created by the authors.

extensive than this diagram can contain, this version depicts the importance of a cohesive relationship between this triad of power, and when intentionally united it can be used positively and holistically.

The triumvirate during script analysis

Communications between director, intimacy director (or other professional titles), and stage manager should start as early in the pre-production process as possible, and their initial meeting should be scheduled with an agenda to specifically discuss the analysis of the script and its possible complex, intimate content. In unified support of the pillars, especially context, communication, and consent, three minds (or more, if including assistants) are definitely better than one. When each member of this team brings to the table their own analysis from their specialized perspectives, together they may begin to form a more detailed and complete picture.

When initiating pre-production communications and meetings between director, stage manager, and intimacy director, any one member of this team can start this ball rolling. It may naturally fall to the stage manager to reach out and get something scheduled, but whoever takes the first step, what is important is to start conversations early in the process. As discussed earlier, each member of this team will have their own lens regarding script analysis and what is considered intimate content. The director has a vision; the intimacy director has specialized training; and the stage manager looks at it through a more logistical lens. Separate viewpoints may allow for the highlighting of different unique portions of the script, or many ideas may overlap.

During these early conversations, the team's three different versions of the script analysis can be compared, discussed, and finally formulated into their preliminary intimacy list for the production. This list will likely change over time, so more detail is better than less. Deleting items from the list will be far easier than realizing long into rehearsals that moments were overlooked. After the team has compared information and agreed upon and finalized this list, the list will become a living document that will provide much-needed guidance during the entire production process.

Recommended practices for auditions and callbacks

The audition process is the recommended time to establish how community agreements and communication practices will work for every performer who will potentially engage in the show, and where performers may first experience the positive impact of clearly set standards supporting consensual practices. For auditioners, these early actions can define their part in a culture of consent or impact their decision to accept a role if they sense the environment may be unhealthy. Auditions are a time to clarify intentions and launch a mindful, positive work environment.

Prior to auditions, team members must first understand the director's vision or concept for the production. Concept and the pillar of context go hand in hand; it is one of the delights of theatre to see how a concept can change the production as it leaps off the page. A director's interpretation of the playwright's work will greatly impact the journey of the characters, and thus the actors. Especially when exploring heightened physical and emotional content, such as simulated sex acts or nudity, outlining the vision behind these body-based expectations is needed. Within one version a director may extend the scene with additional unscripted movements, in another they may want the lights to fade to black as the characters lean toward each other. Whatever their vision entails, it is recommended to explore the director's approach as early as possible. In fact, preparations for auditions, such as the crafting of casting notices, are where the first seeds of this new mindful approach may be planted.

Notices for communicating intimate content in the audition process

An intentional and mindful approach to audition notices is key when establishing or maintaining a culture of consent for those auditioning. Since preliminary auditions, callbacks, and contract phases look very different for different producing organizations, we present a variety of notices that could be used to communicate intimacy. Institutions could use any combination of these notices to allow for the clearest communication possible. These examples reference both professional and academic or pre-professional productions.

Notices serve several purposes for cast and creatives; creative and design teams will have more complete information about staged intimacy for design and storytelling purposes earlier in the process. Creatives involved in casting will be confident that actors who accept a role are fully aware of the intimacy involved. Actors will have information needed to opt in to auditioning for a particular role by analyzing their boundaries around the specific needs of the story and their ability to confidently consent.

Creative team spotlight: Casting directors

Using terms such as notices, lists, or acknowledgments, instead of the standard use of "warning," is done intentionally. The use of the word "warning" may imply or encourage the belief that the explored subject matter will cause harm. Assuming that harm will always be the result is not unhelpful, but acknowledging the possibility is mindful in practice. While some subjects may be complex and challenging when explored as a stand-alone topic outside of the realm of theatre, productions are working with them within a very different context: storytelling. For this reason, more neutral labels are recommended.

Types of notices include the following:

- **Casting/Audition Notices**—shared with casting agents, departments, or services for the purpose of advance casting or arranging auditions; then shared with actors for auditions and open calls for a specific production or season. Consist of more generalized information about movement needs.
- **Intimacy Moments List**—shared at second auditions or callbacks and with production or administrative staff as needed. Consists of a more detailed breakdown of intimate moments that will/may be staged within a specific production.
- **Acknowledgement Forms**—shared with students auditioning for productions in high school, college, or university theatre programs. May also be used by community or professional companies if deemed necessary.

For all these lists and notices, the goal is to support communication, provide context and specificity, and of course, ensure consent. Publicizing this information during casting calls, auditions, or callbacks allows agency for the individual actors auditioning. Being fully informed lets actors make decisions regarding autonomy long before the process of rehearsing begins. These notices also allow for time and space for inquiry should a performer need additional information regarding specifics.

Specific wording of these documents will vary from project to project. Should an ID be on the staff of an organization, they could assist in crafting the messaging of these notices with the director or provide wordsmithing of content. If there is not an ID on staff, another possibility to create these forms with surety would be to reach out to a local intimacy specialist/director as a consultant or connect with an organization that specializes in this work. Their expertise and specialized training can assist casting teams and upper administration with this work.

For additional examples of vocabulary that may be used when crafting notices, please reference the glossary of terms and information on desexualized or clinical language that can be found in the Appendix E.

Sample Content for notices: *Wendy and the Neckbeards* by Kari Bentley-Quinn.

Shared with the permission of the playwright, we use the play *Wendy and the Neckbeards* by Kari Bentley-Quinn as our sample content for these notices. As of spring 2022, this script is available on the New Play Exchange,[2] and the synopsis is as follows:

> Wendy, a 17-year-old plus sized, body positive makeup artist with her own YouTube channel, is having her life exploded by internet trolls—represented by a Chorus of Neckbeards. Jess discovers that her long-term boyfriend Chad spends his time harassing young women on the internet to "blow off steam". From here, the two stories converge in an examination of the current era of internet harassment, toxic masculinity, and the cycle of abuse towards women in America.[3]

While this synopsis is thorough, additional context regarding the script's content may be helpful. This show contains charged language around gender, race, and assault; it tells the story of both consensual and nonconsensual intimacy; and, depending upon the director's interpretation, it allows for possible nudity or moments of being scantily clad, as well as having the potential for staged violence. With this additional information regarding the contents of the chosen sample script, we are ready to dive in.

Casting and audition notices

Casting and audition notices provide a general overview of the future production, and notices sent to casting agents or services may include an overview description of the production, location and performance dates, listing of the creative team, the type of contract that has been negotiated, as well as physical requirements for each role. We suggest adding intimacy as one of these physical requirements included in this part of the notice.

At this early point in the process, notices may contain basic intimacy descriptions, such as "Role contains staged intimacy and nudity." These are similar to phrases used on notices regarding dance or stage violence, like "Role contains sword fighting," or "Actor must tap dance" and, while brief, may contain sufficient information. Additionally, only a brief amount of detail may be what is available to share with agents and services when in the early stages of casting. For some theatre companies, preliminary casting for an entire season may have to occur before directors have been chosen and contracted.

Below is an example of a casting notice that includes basic information about staged intimacy.

> WENDY—(F, 17)—Spunky, just short of plus sized, blond, All-American Texas gal. Possible nudity, intimacy, violence.
>
> BREE (F, late 20s)—Sarcastic, sassy, world weary, bartender. Staged intimacy.
>
> CHAD (M*, late 20s)—Alpha male type, rugged good looks, blue collar. White. Definitely white. Staged intimacy, derogatory sexual language, possible violence.
>
> SHIH (M*, 30s)—Chinese American "stoner guy." Affable, unmotivated. Staged intimacy, violence.
>
> JESS (F, mid 20s)—Fed up girlfriend of Chad. Hard-working, industrious, exhausted. Staged intimacy, violence.
>
> MAMA (F, late 30s/early 40s)—Big Texas mom of Wendy. A little trashy.
>
> KARI (F, 30s)—Playwright. Redhead.
>
> NECKBEARDS 1–4 (M*, 20s to 40s) Derogatory sexual language.

Expanding intimacy notices

Preferably, communication regarding staged intimacy needs to be as straightforward as possible and begin as early as possible. Thus, it may be prudent to move beyond the sample casting notice above that simply lists "Role includes staged intimacy." Utilizing an expanded intimacy notice can provide more information directly from the script regarding its needs around physical and intimate storytelling. This expansion is an appropriate choice to make, especially during the contracting stage when the script cannot be made available to those auditioning, thereby preventing them from reading the script and making a more informed decision.

Including more descriptive information around physical expectations for actors who decide to audition is already standard practice when informing them of more standard required physical abilities such as acrobatics, dance, or stage fighting. For example, these types of expanded notices may specify "Actor must be able to fight with broadsword and shield" rather than the more general notice of "Role contains stage fighting," which in this context could refer to any number of armed or unarmed disciplines. This clarity and specificity should also be applied to descriptions of staged intimacy.

When more descriptive notices of intimacy need to be included in character breakdowns, notices should include

- Basics of intimacy described in the script
- Indication of any staged intimacy not written into the script that appears to be implied
- Moments desired to be added due to director interpretation/concept
- The overall extent of expectations currently known, even if general (such as if it will be a devised piece)[4]

If the director is not currently hired, much can be gleaned from analyzing the stage directions and dialogue. If the director is on board and can help to build this list, simple language should indicate whether staged intimacy is required or potential. This wording indicates differentiation between movements or storytelling imperative to the script or director's vision and those that are more negotiable. The level of detail would be at the discretion of the director, ID, or casting director, but we suggest being as thorough as possible.

Sample language can be seen in the content below. In addition to indicating charged physical content, this notice also informs the actor about charged and derogatory language.

Wendy and the Neckbeards - (sample casting notice with expanded details)

WENDY—(F, 17)—Spunky, just short of plus sized, blond, All-American Texas gal. Role contains required moments of being scantily clad, potential nudity, potential violence.

BREE (F, late 20s)—Sarcastic, sassy, world weary, bartender. Intimacy involving the characters of Shih and Jess required. Simulated sex acts potential with the character of Jess. Potential moment of being scantily clad.

CHAD (M*, late 20s)—Alpha male type, rugged good looks, blue collar. White. Definitely white. Sexually derogatory gestures, aggressive, charged and misogynistic language required. Staged intimacy potential. The story of staged violence/attempted assault potential.

SHIH (M*, 30s)—Chinese American "stoner guy." Affable, unmotivated. Intimacy in the form of the story of a non-consensual kiss with the character of Bree required. Also potentially includes the indication of a sex act (manual stimulation).

JESS (F, mid 20s)—Fed up girlfriend of Chad. Hard-working, industrious, exhausted. Staged intimacy with the character of Bree required. Simulated sex acts potential with the character of Bree.

MAMA (F, late 30s/early 40s)—Big Texas mom of Wendy. A little trashy.

KARI (F, 30s)—Playwright. Redhead.

NECKBEARDS 1–4 (M*, 20s to 40s) Roles include sexually derogatory gestures, references to sexual assault and other aggressive, charged and misogynistic language.

Notes from the field ... intentional phrasing in audition notices

Alexis Black (certified intimacy director) was asked to consult on the phrasing of an intimacy notice from a theatre. They had written the following:

Characters (A and B) must be comfortable with same-sex sex scenes.

Alexis had three main thoughts about the notice:

- As characters A and B's gender identities were stated by the playwright as male identifying in the character descriptions, the term "same-sex" was not necessary in naming who would be involved in the stories of intimacy. Additionally, it is possible an actor with a different gender identity could be cast to play one of the roles if the

director chose to do so. In considering actor consent, the identity of the actors is likely more impactful than the identity of the characters.
- It is not recommended to use words like "must" and "comfortable" in relation to consent. Also, as discussed in Chapter 2, discomfort may be a part of the process, and confidence and security in their consent to perform the story are the necessary elements.
- The phrase "sex scenes" can be reworded to be even more specific and story-based.

Alexis first suggested that the theatre provide a perusal copy of the script at auditions. This way those needing more information about the stories being told could read about these prior to consenting to a callback or the role. She then suggested that the following notices of intimacy be added to the existing character descriptions:

Character (A): Role contains staged intimacy: simulated sex acts/the story of simulated sex will be portrayed with the character of (B). Please see the script for more details.

Character (B): Role contains staged intimacy: simulated sex acts/the story of simulated sex will be portrayed with the character of (A). Please see the script for more details.

The artistic director loved the new wording and agreed to both the perusal script and the new notice.

It is encouraging to experience more and more theaters putting thought and care into their notices, and consulting or including an intimacy professional in your process could lead to some important insights that assist the process at auditions and beyond.

Wording desired will shift from director to director and among intimacy professionals, but the goal is the same: setting the stage for a culture of consent before the process is underway.

Film and TV standards lead the way

While the samples above are a theoretical approach to notices for theatrical staged intimacy, and the language used may vary, this process of communication has not been fully codified for theatre. However, it has become more standardized in film and television. To better support consent in the audition process for live performance when working on a project that contains intimacy, one need only look to the standards pioneered by intimacy coordinator Alicia Rodis, co-founder of Intimacy Directors International as well as creative director and co-founder of IDC, and her colleagues. Their established standards can be found on SAG-AFTRA's Intimacy Coordinator Resources[5] website and more specifically, SAG-AFTRA's[6] casting guidelines page.

Recommended practices for notices in theatre continue to evolve, but a useful and current resource can be found in the Chicago Theatre Standards.[7] In this guide for self-regulation in theatrical spaces, their coverage of audition notices and invitations states the following should be communicated to those auditioning: "Any potential stage combat, feats of physical daring, nudity, partial nudity, sexual content, or other reasonably understood high-risk activities," as well as "an assertion that prospective participants can decline auditions without fear of losing future audition invitations," and "disclosure if the audition will be recorded" must be communicated in order to allow for consent from the actors. Also within the standard is the request that "[a]ny physical contact required for an audition should be disclosed and choreographed. Actors should not be asked to improvise violent or sexual contact" as well as "We will not ask prospective participants to disrobe at an audition."[8]

Devised work and notices

When a piece of theatre is unscripted, clear communication within audition notices becomes essential. After all, when given a script (such as our example of *Wendy and the Neckbeards*) details about intimacy come from the words, while storytelling and vision come from the director or intimacy director. When devising theatre, however, actors are working from only a director's concept or theme as they work to create the script; details key to consent regarding intimacy and movement may be more difficult to articulate or outline. When that is the case, it is recommended that the following be considered in order to be as informative as possible and to foster consensual practices when developing casting notices and at during auditions:

- Outline the director's "must haves" regarding physical, challenging, or intimate movement. Notate the range of movement that may be required, such as wanting actors who can backflip or are willing to do a scene with simulated sex acts or nudity.
- Include plans to include or the potential to include the story of sexual violence.

- Include the possibility of themes involving emotionally heightened content, such as the loss of a child, physical assault, racism, or other charged themes.
- Include whether an intimacy professional and/or other cultural consultants will be involved.
- Include whether there will be consent-building practices and/or other foundational elements of consent used, such as the pillars, while exploring physical content.

For directors of devised theatre with intimacy, flexibility is key. Creative team members will need to be open-minded about storytelling and move forward with mutual agreement. Just like a moment of fighting would be built with the physical and emotional safety, boundaries, and strengths of the actors in mind, so too should moments of intimacy that arise during brainstorming and story creation.

For more information about the process of devising theatre along with intimacy, the "Devised Theatre and Intimacy Checklist" included in Appendix D will be a place to start.

Intimacy moment lists

Once casting and audition notices have gone out, crafting more finely detailed lists of staged intimacy may be a next step the team chooses to take. Providing clear information for each moment of intimacy helps to keep the entire creative team informed and on the same page, as well as providing more details to potential performers. The "intimacy moments list" can also be utilized in place of the expanded casting notice described in the previous section.

Regardless of who this list may end up reaching, it should include not only the basic scripted and unscripted moments of written and potential intimacy as notated in the casting notice, but it should go more deeply into the extent of intimacy within the show, moment by moment. The overall goal is to provide specificity that will help actors (and the entire theatrical team) take a deeper look at what the audition notice's brief descriptions could mean in practice. This could be distributed to the creative team prior to auditions or shared and posted at the preliminary auditions.

The example included below is a partial write up of a more fully detailed notice. For the purposes of this example, this notates only staged intimacy, not violence, but both may be necessary for a complete list, if your team so chooses. We suggest including the scene, page, character names, and a brief description to start. Then clarify whether the movements are in the stage directions or part of the director's interpretation of the work. This can also be indicated as "Written" or "Potential"[9] movements. It also is important to include any intimacy indicated in the dialogue itself; if one character says "You kissed me!" a kiss has likely occurred.

Excerpt from an "intimacy moments list" from *Wendy and the Neckbeards*, by Kari Bentley-Quinn

Act I, Scene 9, p. 46

Characters: Bree, Jess

Stage directions: Jess, emboldened, pulls Bree to her and kisses her. They kiss for a long minute—and it's hot. There are sparks. They pull away, surprised, out of breath.

Act II, Scene 11, p. 56–58

Characters: Bree, Jess

Stage directions: Jess and Bree are on Jess's couch, making out furiously.... They kiss again.... Bree kisses Jess again.

Potential (director vision): Either Bree or Jess may remove or indicate the imminent removal of their costume's top (appearing in bra or exposed midriff).

Act II, Scene 3, p. 81

Characters: Bree, Shih

Stage Directions: Shih leaps on this rare moment of physical contact and kisses Bree. She doesn't fight him at first, then she struggles. He holds her tighter and doesn't let her go. She fights a bit, then bites his lip. Hard.

Acknowledgment forms[10]

When producing work in an educational setting, such as for a high school drama club, college or university theatre program, providing clear information regarding all scripted and potential intimate staging to the students prior to first audition is a recommended requirement. In academia, student actors may be experiencing complex power dynamics such as their professors also serving as their directors, or they may lack confidence in advocating for or fully understanding their boundaries due to the newness of the process. Their internal struggles, lack of confidence, and inexperience may result in their inability to properly prepare. When in these educational situations, those invited to callbacks should be asked to fill out an *Acknowledgement Form for Staged Intimacy* prior to their final audition or acceptance of the role. The use of these forms serves the following purposes:

- Ensures students have an opportunity to read the script, ask questions and more fully understand the content and what will be expected of them should they be cast.
- Ensures teachers and faculty begin early preparations, planning, and making decisions regarding staged intimacy and complex storytelling.
- Ensures there is documentation of communication of content with students should department protocols require.
- Ensures safety and consent are top priority during the entire production process.

And finally, with the hope this is not the case, these forms may be necessary to meet administration requirements if previous allegations of harassment have been documented within the institution in the past.

Important context for these forms

It is important to consider context when looking at the form example below (or other forms that may be created) in connection with consent in casting. In the circumstances involving the example acknowledgement form below, actors auditioning already knew the basics of working with intimacy direction: students were aware of basic consent practices and had worked with the Pillars of Intimacy in the classroom setting. If actors are unaware of these foundational elements, additional information or links to online resources may be helpful.

Creating space for questions with acknowledgment forms

It is important to support communication at this early point of the process, as actors may have questions or concerns that they need to express before accepting the role. For the academic production utilized in the above example, student actors not only received this acknowledgment form in advance,

Acknowledgment Form for Staged Intimacy

- ☐ I understand and acknowledge the proposed staged intimacy involved in the storytelling of this/these character(s). If cast, I am willing to tell these stories of intimacy, with the understanding they will be built and supported by collaborative, consensual, and mindful staging.
- ☐ I do not currently understand the extent of the staged intimacy/intimate storytelling involved with this/these character(s). I request more information before acknowledging and/or indicating my willingness to perform said intimate storytelling.
- ☐ I am unwilling or unable to engage in the stories of staged intimacy as noted for the role for which I am called back.

Name: _____

Date: _____

but they were also given email addresses of several people with whom they could connect if they had questions or concerns. These addresses included those of the director, assistant director, production manager, stage manager and intimacy director.

Flexibility in storytelling with acknowledgement forms

It is important to understand there is flexibility in staging when working with the choreography pillar. The example acknowledgment form indicates that actors are agreeing to perform intimate storytelling, not specific physical acts. This distinction is essential. The story of a kiss can be told in a wide variety of ways, whether lip-to-lip contact, masking techniques with no contact, or the dimming of lights to black as faces nearly touch. Whatever the method, working with the story rather than a physical act allows for collaboration with student actors to ensure consent.

Lastly, it is important to understand that consent culture is not censorship culture, and there are times when a certain story calls for staged nudity, specific action, or series of actions to communicate the vision of the director and/or playwright. When this is the case, and the hired actor has consented to perform those specific acts, then those movements can be consensually staged.

However, in academia, this can be problematic; student actors may be required to accept roles offered because of requirements dictated by their degree program. Or, even if not officially required, student actors may feel they would face retaliation or retribution if they do not accept a role, even if they do not consent to the included actions required for the script and the director's vision. For these reasons, an academic environment necessitates tangible and proven flexibility on the side of directors, whether faculty, student, or guest artist, when telling intimate stories.

Giving students future agency

In academic theater, it is encouraged to let students know that the use of these forms or availability of this information may differ when auditioning for established professional theaters. It is the professional actor's own responsibility to acknowledge and understand intimate content and other information provided prior to attending callbacks. But should this information not be provided it is their duty to request such information so they may go into callbacks fully informed. Agency and advocacy are a community responsibility, and while receiving content information from casting is preferred but not always possible, actors always have the power of asking questions regarding expectations for any role.

Worth the work

Once casting is complete and rehearsals have begun, and as the director's version of their story starts to come to life, everyone should strive to create a space that welcomes exploration with understanding of boundaries. This is worth the work that occurs in this stage of casting and auditions. Taking a look at consequences that occurred from poor communication during the audition phase may help to highlight the importance of these notices.

> ### Notes from the field ... a cautionary tale
>
> When conducting an interview for this book, a professional casting agent shared how they had had to recast a role because a female actor was not informed during auditions, or when signing the contract, that the director's vision for the storytelling included her character being

> nude from the waist up during a scene. This request was not presented to her until after rehearsals had begun and the director had already staged a significant portion of the script. The intimate staging was beyond her personal boundaries and comfort level due to both personal and religious beliefs and resulted in her being unable to perform this movement. Failure to communicate eventually led to this actor leaving the production and the director having to recast the role, as this moment was key to their artistic vision for the piece. This unfortunate scenario could have easily been avoided if a content notice with this intimate movement had been clearly communicated to this casting agent prior to the start of the audition process.

In this example, a failure to communicate had significant consequences for both production and performer. Drastic changes like recasting can greatly impact both time and budget, placing an unnecessary burden upon the entire production. This burden may include costumes having to be altered or redesigned, marketing materials having to be altered, programs reprinted, and possibly adding hours of rehearsal to the schedule. Additionally, there may be additional personal ramifications for the performer. What happens when this performer auditions for this director in the future? Will they be held responsible for a situation that was completely out of their control, resulting in the lack of consideration for future roles? Will other casting agents learn of this incident and think twice before submitting this performer for roles? Will the director or theatre company refuse to see this individual at future auditions due to this incident? It is altogether possible that this incident will now have a lasting and long-term negative impact on this performer's ability to confidently audition and accept roles. One must consider how much damage this specific situation may cause and how many similar situations have happened that were avoidable if proper communication had taken place during the early stages of the creative process.

The goal of auditions, other than finding the ideal cast for your production, is to avoid unwanted scenarios from occurring; such situations can be averted through careful and concise crafting of notices. This relatively simple step, while a bit laborious at the front end of the process, could potentially prevent a much more burdensome situation down the road. This step also empowers those cast to confidently walk in the room knowing what to expect from the role they will perform as well as the production they will help to create. They know they will not encounter unwanted or hidden surprises that may lead to the derailment of their performance, their reputation, or the production.

Creative team spotlight: Directors

One element directors could reexamine during the audition process is the utilization of chemistry reads or chemistry tests. According to the article "Everything you need to know to nail a chemistry read" by Caroline Liem, a chemistry read is "is an opportunity to read with actors being considered for a role opposite yours, usually lead roles. The main purpose is to see how you instinctively connect and work with the other actor."[11] While the purpose behind this part of the audition process is not inherently problematic, and sometimes a chemistry test might have to do with superficial decisions such as the relative heights of the partnered actors, chemistry reads, or chemistry tests, have a darker past in the mind of many actors. Casting directors and directors have utilized these auditions to see if the two lead actors, usually in a romantic story line, seemed to have a palpable attraction to each other. This often has included requests to become physical with a fellow performer, including kissing, fondling, or even a request for partial nudity, often without prior notice. Film and TV actress Ingrid Haas described this experience for *VICE* magazine in 2015, saying, "the experience of testing is not a whole lot of fun for the female actor. I can't speak for the male actors' experience, but I'll go out on a limb here and say: it's probably less traumatic an experience for men because of, well, a patriarchal society...."[12] While power dynamics may have made chemistry reads more taxing for female-identifying performers at times, this practice has likely left many aspiring performers of all genders and identities in a position that leaves them feeling powerless, as they may have felt it unavoidable to do whatever is asked of them in the moment to "get the role."

In training sessions to become an intimacy director for Intimacy Directors International in 2018, founder Tonia Sina spoke of the practice of chemistry tests as problematic. She not only stated the possible issues with consent and power dynamics mentioned by Ms. Haas in *VICE* but also remarked that it could be considered a strange and unbalanced trust in the craft of the performers. She mentioned that in her experience as a fight director, actors hired for a show containing a lot of staged violence were never asked to do "rage or anger" readings with the other actor in the fight. The director or casting director trusted from the actor's audition that they could act these moments of emotional and physical violence or be directed to perform it truthfully with the help of an experienced fight director. Sina left the class reconsidering the validity of chemistry tests, as it was unclear why casting directors or directors would automatically trust actors to perform heighted violent moments in connection with another performer but not trust actors to act the seductive, loving, or flirtatious storytelling without a test.

Contracts and riders

Once auditions and casting are complete, the next step is initiating contracts. Whether working for union, nonunion, or community organizations the same care and attention to detail should be made. Actor contracts can be standardized, and depending upon the inner workings of a theatre company, specifics other than dates and pay scale may not change from production to production. For this reason, and especially when roles may require the actor to perform intimate staging (for example, nudity, kissing, simulated sex, and more), additional negotiations may need to be made. These additional agreements would be noted within an attachment to the contract, or what is known as a rider. Legally, a rider is defined as "an attachment to a document which adds to or amends it."[13]

Actors Equity Association requires that nudity riders be agreed upon and attached to standard contracts when nudity is required. The AEA business representative for the production will usually assist with that process. Performers should explore additional needs or accommodations when other expectations are being placed upon them, not just when nudity is required. Additional accommodations or considerations may be needed with other extreme physical contact such as simulated sex or sexual violence. Acknowledgments or accommodations may need to be requested and outlined in a rider if the performer has any concerns requiring possibly unknown expectations and they want their concerns, requirements, or physical limitations to be known, acknowledged, and working parameters agreed upon in collaboration with the producing company prior to committing to the role.

The film industry utilizes contract riders that can be a model for theatre. SAG-AFTRA has outlined clear expectations[14] concerning the negotiation of riders when intimate staging is required. As in the film industry, one should consider and outline a general description of expectations of the performer and more specifically expectations of what is to be performed on stage.

At any time during this negotiation process, an ID may be invited into the conversation to assist with exploration of content, as well as crafting of language in order to facilitate mutually agreed upon expectations that will be noted within the rider.

> **Screen Actors Guild and the American Federation of Television and Radio Artists'** formal improvements regarding nudity and simulated sex
>
> The improvements to nudity and simulated sex are historic and include principal performers and background actors. Never in the history of SAG-AFTRA or either predecessor union has so much been achieved in this area.
>
> Find out more here:
>
> www.sagaftra.org/faq-results

A rider is intended to represent mutual agreement between performer and producing company given that both parties have needs and expectations regarding what is required for the production. The rider spells out those needs and expectations and can be as detailed or minimal as either party determines necessary but may contain the following:

Production company: details regarding who will be producing the work

Artist: details regarding who is contracted to perform in this produced work

Employment agreement: details regarding type of contract, title of the piece to be produced, details on role(s) to be performed, dates of production

Staging expectations: details regarding what the intimate staging expectations will be as a part of the role to be performed. These may include details regarding level of nudity (full, partial), simulated sex acts required to be performed, as well as details regarding additional intimate staging such as acts of sexual violence, kissing, etc. This section should explain the extent to which the performer will go and how it will be performed.

Acknowledged dates: details on dates that may include "nudity date" "removal of placeholders" etc.

Acknowledged accommodations: details outlining accommodations the producing company will provide for the performer during rehearsal and performance of the production. Accommodations may include but are not limited to providing privacy screens and robes during rehearsals and performance, requiring closed rehearsals during the staging process, prohibiting photos or video recordings to be taken during scenes of intimate staging, lighting limitations during staged scenes of intimacy, etc.

Ability to amend: the parties to the contract should give themselves the ability to further amend the rider to allow for flexibility during the artistic process (for example, the rider calls for partial nudity, but during rehearsals, the performer and the production company mutually agree that full nudity is warranted for the artistic benefit of the production; therefore, the parties state in the rider that modifications and amendments to the rider are enforceable only if in writing and signed by all parties to the contract).

Signature page: provides a space for signatures from both parties accepting and agreeing to the details outlined within this document.

When exploring what power a performer has when negotiating contracts (union and non-union) one must use that power to establish open communication and understanding of expectations. Artists should determine what they are willing to do as part of their acceptance to perform the role and what they are not willing to do. Then, through respectful negotiations, both parties will explore options and then meet in the middle where both sides feel heard and understood and then come to an agreement that both sides are willing and eager to accept. Early stages of communication, whether initiated through an actor's agent or by the performer themselves, should be open to exploration and most importantly not feel coerced by either party. Respectful communication and freedom to ask for what you want, with the expectation that the producing agent will do the same, are essential elements for fair and balanced negotiations.

Archival video taping

When negotiating contracts for a production that contains nudity, the actors who will be engaging in this movement should inquire regarding plans for possible archival videotaping. If working under a union contract, the union's business representative should be included in these conversations. Open communication at this early stage encourages decision makers to work together and explore every option available when it comes to recording sensitive material. (See Chapter 6 for more on archival videotaping.)

> **Notes from the field ... a lawyer's perspective**
>
> A contract is when two or more parties come to an agreement and that agreement is manifested in writing by a legally binding set of terms. A contract should always represent "a meeting of the minds"—it should not be a set of coerced, one-sided terms. Don't be hesitant to negotiate, artistic professionals! While you may find that the parties to a contract initially have different ideas on what terms the agreement should contain, generally you can find a way to settle those differences by adjusting or modifying your respective ideas until you arrive at mutual concessions. It is recommended that you keep records of ongoing negotiations; get all offers, counteroffers, and final agreements in writing—even if you have a verbal discussion, send an email that says "per our conversation" and/or jot down notes for yourself. If you ultimately find yourself in a position where you cannot accomplish that meeting of the minds, then you may want to ask yourself "Is this really a person or organization I want to do business with?" Look out for yourself, but keep in mind that every party to a contract comes to the table with their own goals. A contract should be a reflection of each individual party's goals that are agreed upon by the rest of the parties, and should also take into account each party's responsibilities in achieving these collective goals.
>
> Katharine M. Hude
Attorney at Law
Hude Legal Services, PLLC
Lansing, Michigan

Accessories and safety equipment

When starting work on a production whose script calls for extreme physical movement, dance, or combat, one of the first things the stage manager and choreographers may do is reach out to various production departments to inquire about safety protocols for the actors during rehearsals. These protocols usually begin with the acquiring of safety equipment to have at the ready, such as floor mats, knee pads, ace bandages, or braces. When we add physical movement in the form of intimacy staging, those same safety protocols apply, but the equipment acquired may be a bit different. Staged intimacy professionals may inquire about the use of floor mats, knee pads, or other common movement safety equipment. At times, depending on the type of intimate staging required, more personal items may also be helpful to have ready. These items range based on production needs but may include

- Hygiene products (see Appendix D for more information)
- Personal barriers (such as a dance belt, padded bike shorts, or more)
- Double-stick tape
- Individual coverings, modesty garments, robes
- Portable screens

Based on the type of items required in consideration of the actor and their safety, stage management may need to reach out to production, wardrobe, scenic, or property departments for assistance.

When determining what items would be suitable to have at the ready, the stage manager should consult with the intimacy professional during early pre-production meetings. These meetings are a launching pad not only for script analysis and tracking but also for preparations regarding rehearsal equipment and supplies. Each production will have its own needs and requirements. It is only through early conversation and creative exploration with the director and the ID that the stage manager can begin to get a better understanding of their visions for the show and thereby gain the insight to anticipate needs and requirements. Once the rest of the company joins the process, and the creative exploration begins, adding accessories and safety equipment will then be on an as needed basis. Early conversations are key, thorough preparations are a necessity, and attention to physical care will set the stage for a safe and consensual rehearsal room.

Building rehearsal schedules

Intentional scheduling is an important step in establishing clear parameters for rehearsals that will involve staged intimacy. Schedules are structured to be as efficient as possible to make the most of the entire rehearsal workday, those making the schedule should connect with all necessary team members for input on what to rehearse and when. Reflecting on the script analysis, the stage manager and director will collaborate and use the information from that document to effectively build the production's rehearsal schedule. This schedule typically includes an overview with weekly breakdowns, day-to-day breakdowns, and finally specific hourly breakdowns. It is also through the review of this information that the stage manager and director can work with the intimacy director to further breakdown the workday and highlight times when moments from the intimacy list will be staged and approximately how much time each of these moments may need.

Trained intimacy professionals are choreography specialists who will have a general idea of how much time certain physical stories may require, but flexibility should be built into the rehearsal whenever possible as the unexpected is expected in building theatre. Also, it should be determined at the scheduling stage if the director wants to work alongside the intimacy director, or if actors from one scene can work with the director while intimacy is being staged in an alternate space. If working in more than one space, an assistant stage manager or assistant director should be scheduled to be present in the rehearsal space being used for the staging of the intimacy, in order to support documentation of the choreography, call for breaks when necessary, and help to mitigate power dynamics if needed.

Closed rehearsal protocols

Once the team has completed a breakdown of their rehearsal schedule, the stage manager will identify when script pages that contain staged intimacy will be rehearsed. These scheduled rehearsals will not only include specific script pages and characters but may also be identified as a closed rehearsal. When staging intimacy, one major consideration is the possible need to limit those who will be in the room when these moments are being rehearsed. Limiting the number of individuals who can sit in on rehearsals establishes what is defined as a closed rehearsal. These rehearsals are closed to anyone not specifically required for the staging of intimate moments and may involve limiting attendance to only the actors in the scene, director, intimacy director, and the stage management team. Who is needed in the room during closed rehearsals will vary from production to production and should be determined through careful consultation with the director, intimacy director, stage manager, and the actors involved. Careful consultation should also include the evaluation of power dynamics and the balance of this power. Mindful consideration of who will be needed in the room when rehearsals require sincere vulnerability will allow for intentional distribution of power that will fuel actor agency and support a consensual culture.

After determining who will be needed in the room during closed rehearsals and developing the schedule, it is up to the stage manager to communicate this information to the entire production team. By highlighting for everyone when the rehearsal room will be closed due to the rehearsing of moments of intimacy, the stage manager will establish a transparent scheduling process that is respectful of the team and personal schedules of the entire company.

Often, a preliminary schedule cannot be as detailed from the beginning of the process as one would like, details are evolving on a weekly or even daily basis, and the stage manager may find it impossible to communicate in advance specific daily rehearsal calls let alone when those calls will be closed rehearsals. When that is the case, the stage manager will need to work with the director and intimacy director far enough in advance so they may provide no less than 24 hours' notice to the company, and when possible, 48 or 72 hours is recommended. Early notice is helpful not only for the actors so they may prepare as needed but is also helpful for the entire creative team who may be planning to make impromptu visits to rehearsal. Production schedules are complex, so planning ahead is key. Whatever the timeline, once detailed schedules have been confirmed, immediately sharing this information will help to keep the entire team informed.

Re-opening the room

Eventually the rehearsal of intimate moments will have to be opened to the rest of the production team. In consultation with the director, intimacy director, and the actors involved, the stage manager will have the knowledge needed to incorporate into the rehearsal schedule the gradual reopening. This plan will vary from production to production but should be worked through based on the comfort level of the actors and may take several days as they become more confident in the movement and become ready to invite others into their process. Whatever the timeline, the stage manager will need to effectively communicate this gradual reopening timeline out to the entire creative team so that others may align their schedules accordingly. Designer visits usually align to when run-throughs will take place, so once closed rehearsals are no longer needed, highlighting when scene or act run-throughs are scheduled to take place will help keep the team informed and engaged.

Notes from the field ... a child guardian's perspective

We spoke with veteran IATSE child guardian Bobby Wilson regarding the subject of young professional performers and challenging content. With over 30 years' experience working as child guardian, and caring for over 500 young performers, he brings more than just experience to exploring this topic; he brings compassion and care for the safety and well-being of young artists.

Grappling with the idea of underage performers engaging in or witnessing strong challenging content is a struggle like no other. The first thing that may come to mind is the physically violent battle-of-wills scene in The Miracle Worker, when Helen Keller and Anne Sullivan fight over how young Helen behaves at the dinner table, which sets up the water pump scene. The violence illuminates Helen's vibrant sense of self, locked inside a dark, silent world. It's essential to the story and it would be a tremendous loss if it were cut.

No one wants to inhibit a writer from telling whatever story they feel compelled to tell, but one can't imagine how extremely sensitive themes involving young performers can be portrayed on stage in a way that wouldn't be very difficult to watch. We also can't imagine what parents would want their young child to participate in when telling those stories. What may be considered, instead of shutting it down with a "No, never," is making sure that if the situation ever does come up, and it is a vital part of the storytelling, that there is always an intimacy director involved from the very beginning, especially during casting. An ID could use their specialized training to work alongside the director, child guardian, parents, SM and/or other specialists as needed in pre-production. This team could work together to establish what content is occurring and set in place an appropriate action plan to ensure that each step in the process proceeds in a way that doesn't negatively impact the child.

It's also my experience that everything the child hears or observes at the theater finds its way home to the parents, usually without the context in which it happened. So, it would be important for the parents to be fully debriefed by the ID and/or SM at the end of each day, so that they are thoroughly informed as to what the child was exposed to at rehearsal that day. That would also be an opportune moment to get the child's feedback on what they saw or did at rehearsal, so you have a sense of how they are processing everything that is transpiring to determine if you need to adjust course in how you proceed.

Additionally, if a child is in a production in which there are scenes of sexual intimacy occurring while they are offstage, it is recommended that they not be made available for press interviews, so they are not put on the spot and asked questions that may make them uncomfortable. If that is not possible, then there should be a sit-down with the child, the director, the ID, the guardian, and the production's press staff to explain to the child that there are questions they do not have to answer and that it is the responsibility of the production's press staff to shut down any inappropriate questions.

As artists, we don't want to be self-defeating and lock ourselves out of groundbreaking work by censoring our ability to tell certain stories. We want to find ways to support the telling in a healthful way. If there were a scene in which a child recounts details of an abusive situation to a police detective, there would not be the physical depiction of abuse. However, the child actor, writer and other relevant company members could work alongside the ID and other specialists to accommodate the child's sensitivities as they navigate rehearsing and staging the scene. It is important in those situations to be mindful of the child's age, as a twelve-year-old will have a more mature sense of some topics than a seven-year-old. It may be helpful to consult with the parents to determine the child's starting point in discussing sensitive material, so you know exactly when you are building on the child's existing knowledge and when you are introducing new, difficult concepts into the child's world.

Finally, just like the need for consultants in other situations, the ID's qualifications for working with kids should be considered. Maybe you would also need a child psychologist on board along with the ID.

Overall, special care and consideration must always be given when working with young performers. Child artists cast in these productions are entering an adult world that can be chaotic, creative, scary, and intimidating. It can be difficult for young minds to really comprehend what is going on around them, and it is the job of the adults in the room to care for and help them navigate this new landscape. Whatever the situation or story being told, we must always put the health and safety of our young artists above all else. If that cannot be done, then that story cannot be told.

Bobby Wilson
(he/him/his)
IATSE member
Retired Child Guardian

Effective communication within the production's creative team

Consent takes an open and trusting atmosphere, and leaders in the room should be encouraged to practice communication tools to support that environment. When navigating and staging complex physical content, healthy communication practices (or the lack thereof) will impact every member of a team and affect their ability to feel confident as they explore and express ideas, concerns, or fears. A team can work together to establish methods of discourse that serve both the creatives in the room and the story being told.

Communication between leaders on the theatrical team can be impacted by several variables. This includes the institutional factors discussed in Chapter 2, such as mindfulness, power dynamics, identity and intersectionality, reporting structures, and more in relation to a culture of consent. Other major factors may include adjusting for diverse communication styles, identity and inclusion, awareness of space, and awareness of tone and body language, or 'metacommunication.'

Differing communication styles

Awareness and adjustment will likely be needed when methods of communication of the team are different than one's own. Anyone who has worked on several theatrical teams has likely noticed that sometimes there will be more tension on some teams, or sometimes teams will "click" into a healthy ensemble. Or, sometimes there will be healthy communication between two-thirds of the ensemble with a few outliers. Different personalities, backgrounds, and personal histories can lead to very different styles of communication; some people are direct and to the point, some people talk in circles, some pause and wait, while some try to govern conversations. While members of the creative team may be more measured in their actions and check in with others consistently, others may make assumptions about the way their communication is received and push forward without confirmations. Understanding and having empathy for these varying styles or negotiating methods that work for all parties involved may be necessary at some point in the process. These methods could be considered and communicated before the process begins or if misunderstandings arise.

Identity and inclusion in communication

Teams who seem to work cohesively more quickly may have members with similar conversation styles, and this may relate to equity, diversity, and inclusion. Deborah Tannen, Professor of Linguistics at Georgetown University and author of many books and articles about how the language of everyday conversation affects relationships[15] discusses this in her article "The Power of Talk: Who gets Heard and Why" for *Harvard Business Review*. She explains, "How you say what you mean is crucial, and differs from one person to the next, because using language is learned social behavior: How we talk and listen are deeply influenced by cultural experience. Although we might think that our ways of saying what we mean are natural, we can run into trouble if we interpret and evaluate others as if they necessarily felt the same way we'd feel if we spoke the way they did."[16] This may mean that what feels like easy communication in a historically white industry such as theatre contributes to the lack of opportunities for those from marginalized groups. Stage manager Winnie Y. Lok stated in *The New York Times*, "Producers and general managers are used to hiring the same people for comfort, and that's an issue when you're talking about bringing new people into the fold."[17]

This relationship between communication styles and the distribution of opportunities needs to change. Storytelling is made stronger and richer through the inclusion of diverse experiences and perspectives. By widening one's creative and cultural scope, teams can find new ways to connect effectively that are not centered in sameness. We suggest further research in this area for creative teams, including training in inclusion, implicit bias, active listening, and more to facilitate workplace communication in relation to equity and inclusion.

Metacommunication

Another part of communication to consider is not just verbal communication, but tone and body language. Anthropologist Gregory Bateson coined the term "metacommunication" to describe the underlying messages in what we say and do. Bateson states that "Metacommunication is all the nonverbal cues (tone of voice, body language, gestures, facial expression, etc.) that carry meaning that either enhance or disallow what we say in words. There's a whole conversation going on beneath the surface."[18] Bateson's work looked at "communication on communication," or one's ability to verbalize any perceived metacommunications in tone or body language. One could ask, "Could you help clarify what you mean when you say that?" This type of questioning can help to clarify or appraise both verbal and nonverbal communications. Bateson claimed that these comments were essential for successful human communication.[19]

As performers, actors work with body language and tone to communicate subtext within their performances, and the same is true for team members in real-life situations as well. Personal exploration and understanding of the subtext one brings to a conversation or a rehearsal will speak volumes to all of the team members involved. When it comes to conversations and communicating while navigating staged intimacy or other complex subject matters and supporting a culture of consent, being mindful and observant of nonverbal cues and feeling open to clarify messaging through inquiry is crucial.

Awareness of location

An awareness of location or space is another factor that can impact communication in the rehearsal of staged intimacy. "Location" or "space" in this context has several meanings, and any of these could impact respectful communication practices in the rehearsal hall.

Proximity: The location of people in the conversation in relation to each other. Example: IDs are trained to not stand too physically close to actors while staging choreography. Other team members may consider proximity when asking questions or giving notes to actors involved in intimate staging.

Social location: The location of the conversation. Example: The freedom one may feel when the conversation takes place in private versus in public.

Location in time: The timing of a conversation within the rehearsal day, the schedule as a whole or the perceived urgency. Example: Initiating an important and sensitive conversation with an individual right after the stage manager gave a "one-minute, please" to resume rehearsal may not be ideal.

Global space or location: Language and cultural barriers. Example: A turn of phrase may have very different meanings based on one's first language or cultural identity.

Location within one's career: A team member's level of professional experience, impacting their communication style. Example: A young inexperienced actor may be more fearful to ask for clarity during rehearsal than a more experienced actor.

Mental or emotional space: The emotional state or mental space of those involved. Example: If people start to become emotionally involved or charged during a conversation, sometimes taking a few minutes to re-center and pause the conversation can lead to a more successful exchange moving forward.

The key takeaway when considering how to navigate conversations involving creatives and complex content involves awareness. Being mindful of communication style differences may not always apply to every conversation, but being mindful and considering identity and cultural backgrounds, as well as being aware of proximity, body language, location, mental space, etc. when in the rehearsal hall, may help to mitigate any miscommunications while supporting the group dynamic.

Communication and the triumvirate of consent

Earlier in this chapter we discuss the "triumvirate of consent," or the important connective relationship between director, intimacy professional, and stage manager during the process of staging intimacy. Open and honest communication among these three positions may help to establish a tone or style of communication that will work its way to the entire company. This triad may have the power to create a rehearsal space that lays a foundation of trust, inclusion, confidence, and care in all manners of communication.

Conversational and working methods will differ among creative teams. We recommend a few questions to get you moving in the right direction. Knowing every production and every creative team can be drastically different; the key toward open communication is to ask questions and let the needs of the production lead the way.

Question 1: *What is the working relationship we (director, intimacy professional, and SM) wish to establish for the company once we get into the rehearsal hall?*

Exploring how all can complement the process will allow each member to facilitate this working relationship. If we use the metaphor of a sailboat captain as a director, each director will want to lead their ship differently. This will result in the intimacy director and the stage manager adapting their approach on or below deck. Through open and honest communication regarding the way the director prefers to work, these three can strategize the creative rehearsal game plan and put it in place. Alternatively, if new to working with an intimacy director, the director may need to adapt their process in collaboration with the specialized skills brought into the process by the ID. This leads to our second question, which may be answered predominately by the intimacy professional.

Question 2: *How can we best communicate with each other and with the company to support the rehearsal process around intimacy? And what type of language will be used when staging this work?*

Each intimacy director (or other intimacy professional) will have their own vocabulary and methods of working. Sharing this process with the director and stage manager ahead of time will allow them to follow the ID's lead in their area of expertise. The ID may also want to put into place verbal shortcuts or cues in communication when rehearsing, to be used when either a performer or individual in the room needs to pause for reflection, step away for a moment or to take a break. These cue words are called "pause words" by professionals in IDC, eliminating the need for actors to explain themselves if they need a brief break. Providing this language at the start of rehearsal shows everyone involved that their well-being is truly being considered.

When it comes to communicating notes that come out of this work to those not in the rehearsal room, whether through rehearsal reports or emails, it may serve the production to consider a smaller group and identify a single individual from the necessary departments who will receive these notes. This is helpful especially should the content be sensitive in nature. By identifying this smaller team of individuals at the beginning of the rehearsal process, you are being considerate of the entire team and hopefully will prevent any one person from feeling left out or offended. Identifying this smaller group not only helps when communicating sensitive information to various departments but is considerate of and respectful to the actors who may be referenced within these notes.

Question 3: *What are our expectations when it comes to the staging of intimate moments?*

This question will allow for open dialogue not only between the stage manager, director, and ID but should be asked again when the entire company is together. This could include discussions around who will take the lead in certain moments and how they are being rehearsed or discussed. If expectations are established at the start of the rehearsal process, everyone involved will feel informed and confident in their ability to meet these expectations on a day-to-day basis. These expectations can also include establishing personal hygiene rules (such as refraining from the use of strong perfumes or colognes on the day's when intimate scenes will be rehearsed), allergy concerns such as not eating peanuts, ways to pause the work when necessary, basic rituals to start and end the work, or more.

The team can also establish ways to communicate when an actor feels themselves to be growing ill, getting a cold sore, experiencing chronic physical injury flare ups, or having other concerns related to viral or physical health. These elements can greatly impact intimate staging, so knowing what to expect should this occur will make it easy for the team to navigate these scenarios more quickly. Every production will have its own needs, and no two acting companies are the same, so identifying expectations early on will help to build a cohesive team.

Question 4: *Can we establish a standard check-in process to review notation after staging moments of intimacy?*

This final question that we suggest relates to ensuring accurate notation or note taking of choreography and storytelling in intimate moments as they are created. Check-ins for notation ensure that all members of the team have no questions and are confident in their understanding of the established choreography or choreographic parameters. Accurate and concise blocking notation will establish a consistent resource throughout the process as the play is shaped and eventually opens. Clear documentation will also be key when understudies are rehearsed and put in and when or if future replacement actors are cast.

Stage management usually will track and notate this movement during all rehearsals, fine tuning these notations on an ongoing basis. However, established check-ins with all involved will ensure that the stage management's notation is accurate, the director's story is being communicated, the ID's practices are being utilized, and the actors are confident and comfortable in their movements.

 Creative team spotlight: Dramaturgs

If you want to find a link between dramaturgy and intimacy, there is no greater advocating document than the Five Pillars of Intimacy Direction (discussed in Chapter 1 of this book). The first pillar that is often taught and used practically in the room is context. The way context is used and defined by this document is nothing short of dramaturgy itself.

In the current US paradigm, dramaturgs are the advocates for the Big Why of the process. They are the reminders in the room that things mean things. They are deep listeners, consummate collaborators, and skilled question askers. Many questions that a dramaturg may employ while working with a playwright or director are exactly what an intimacy director might ask while engaging with the context pillar, including What story are we telling? How are we telling it? How has it been told before? What might an audience's relationship to this story be?

Since both the dramaturg and the ID are engaged in asking these context questions, it's easy to see how a dramaturg and an ID can be allies in creating nuanced and specific stories of intimacy.

Let's imagine that an intimacy director is brought in to stage a scene of intimacy in which two characters engage in a consensual sex act. Before beginning any choreography, the dramaturg facilitates a conversation with the director and actors to figure out the details of this consensual act, how each character approaches it, etc. But with the focus narrowed to the physical storytelling in one moment, a crucial detail is missed: Although it's not in the text, the director decided to have the two characters drink heavily in the previous scene. The dramaturg, explicitly focused on the meaning and storytelling of each choice made and its effect on the next, politely interjects to mention how the heavy consumption of alcohol in the previous scene might affect how consensual this sex act appears to the audience.

That dramaturgical focus can provide an invaluable bird's eye view for the intimacy director, while the intimacy director can bring the dramaturg's specialized research to life. Together these two professionals can help each other complete the cycle of nuanced and specific storytelling of how intimacy works in the greater context of the piece as it's being created.

Cristina (Cha) Ramos
(she/her/hers)
Performer/Movement Designer/Dramaturg

Chapter reflection

Reflecting upon the importance of effective communication, we can wrap up with a few main takeaways. When starting out on a production, explore, establish, and share rules of communication that relate to production needs so conversations can evolve successfully. Explore the level of directness or indirectness needed, and discover what will work for your production. Acknowledge the different ways in which individuals communicate, and be open to inquiry for clarification. And lastly, take advice from *Hidden Brain* podcast host Shankar Vedantam when he recommends that we approach conversations with "a little more empathy but also a little more compassion for one another."[20] This approach, when applied to creative endeavors, unites and builds a sense of community that enables us to tell meaningful stories that will transport audiences. A mindful approach, built with empathy, respect, and open communication is the first step toward meaningful engagement.

Chapter discussion / exercise / activity

Casting exercise

We encourage you to create your own sample casting notice.

Choose a script, and after reading it create a detailed casting breakdown. Include character details such as

- required physical storytelling elements
- psychologically challenging content or charged language within the script
- potential physical stories that may be explored in the rehearsal process

As you build this, ask yourself

- How much information should be included in a casting breakdown?
- How much is too much? How much is too little?

Clear communication is a crucial part of the process, especially when starting out. Casting notices are a great first step on a clear path to setting expectations from day one.

Notes

1 Laura Rikard is quoted using this term in the article "Adopt Best Practices into Theatrical Intimacy Work" by Bridgette Redman, Onstage Blog. Nov. 8, 2021, https://www.onstageblog.com/editorials/2021/8/5/adopt-best-practices-into-theatrical-intimacy-work
2 https://newplayexchange.org/dashboard.
3 Bentley-Quinn, Kari. *Wendy and the Neckbeards*, June 2020, https://www.karibentleyquinn.com/wendy-and-the-neckbeards.
4 For more information on recommended practices for devised theatre, see Appendix D.

5 "Intimacy Coordinator Resources." *SAG-AFTRA*, Mar. 2020, https://www.sagaftra.org/contracts-industry-resources/workplace-harassment-prevention/intimacy-coordinator-resources.
6 "Casting Director's Guide: Casting Roles for intimate scenes." *SAG-AFTRA*, Mar. 2020, https://www.sagaftra.org/files/sa_documents/Intimacy_Casting%20Directors_2_2021.pdf.
7 Fisher, Laura, et al. *Contact US – #Notinourhouse*. https://www.notinourhouse.org/contact-us/.
8 "Chicago Theatre Standards." Dec. 11, 2017, https://collin.instructure.com/courses/869926/modules/items/18116826.
9 Concept shared by intimacy director Claire Wilcher during collaborations for development of curricular materials for "Stage Managing Intimacy," IDC workshop, spring 2020, www.idcprofessionals.com.
10 In March 2020, Alexis Black and Sarah Lozoff (intimacy director) brainstormed the concept of and details surrounding acknowledgement forms as preparation for the course "Stage Managing Intimacy" for IDC. A similar concept is also discussed by Chelsea Pace in *Staging Sex: Best Practices, Tools, and Techniques for Theatrical Intimacy*. Routledge, 2020.
11 Liem, Caroline. "Everything You Need to Know to Nail a Chemistry Read." *Backstage*, Nov. 2020, https://www.backstage.com/magazine/article/everything-need-know-nail-chemistry-read-7436/. Accessed June 2021.
12 Haas, Ingrid. "What 'Chemistry Tests' with Hollywood's Leading Men Are Like." VICE, Aug. 2021, https://www.vice.com/sv/article/gqmk39/what-chemistry-tests-with-hollywoods-leading-men-are-like.
13 *Law.com Legal Dictionary*, May 2021, https://dictionary.law.com/Default.aspx?typed=AND&type=1.
14 "SAG-AFTRA Contracts & Industry Resources." *Sagaftra.org*, https://www.sagaftra.org/contracts-industry-resources/workplace-harassment/quick-guide-scenes-involving-nudity-and-simulated.
15 Tannen, Deborah. "Bio," *Deborah Tannen*, http://www.deborahtannen.com/bio.
16 Tannen, Deborah. "The Power of Talk: Who Gets Heard and Why." *Harvard Business Review*, June 2020, https://hbr.org/1995/09/the-power-of-talk-who-gets-heard-and-why.
17 Paulson, Michael. "Theater Jobs Skew White and Male, Study Finds." *The New York Times*, June 26, 2020, https://www.nytimes.com/2017/06/26/theater/theater-jobs-skew-white-and-male-study-finds.html.
18 Hartwell-Walker, Marie. "Meta-Communication: What I Said Isn't What I Meant." *Psych Central*, Feb. 2020, https://psychcentral.com/lib/meta-communication-what-i-said-isnt-what-i-meant#3.
19 Baltzersen, Rolf K. "The Importance of Metacommunication in Supervision Processes in Higher Education." *International Journal of Higher Education*, vol. 2, no. 2, 2013, https://doi.org/10.5430/ijhe.v2n2p128.
20 Vendantam, Shankar. "Why Conversations Go Wrong." *Hidden Brain*, April 21, 2021, Https://Hiddenbrain.org/.

4
In rehearsal

Consensual crafting

This chapter focuses on the first weeks of rehearsal before technical elements are added. The following will provide useful terminology, recommended practices, and protocols during the first days of stepping into the process. Rehearsals are an exciting time where everyone who takes part in storytelling works together to bring dynamic, consensual staged intimacy to life. This chapter will include the following:

- Supporting change in the process
- First rehearsal and orientation
- Ways the creative team can support responsible partnering
- Methods that intimacy professionals use to create and maintain intimacy
- Techniques for notating moments of staged intimacy

By bringing these techniques into rehearsal, the entire production team will work with contemporary theatrical practices no matter the era or setting in the script. After rehearsals are over, the audience will experience stories built from a healthier culture and ensemble, experiencing catharsis, empathy, or entertainment without harm to those who created it.

Key terms in Chapter 4[*]

Anchor points

Positions of pressurized touch on the body, set by the involved actors and the intimacy director, that use support boundaries and stabilized points of contact during intimate or violent movement.

[*] *See Terms & Language Acknowledgement and Glossary of Key Terms in Appendix E for citations, trainings and reference materials that informed definitions.*

DOI: 10.4324/9781003206064-5

Boundary checks

A system or ritual of verbal communication (and sometimes agreed-upon physical movements) that allow for performers to establish personal boundaries and confirm consent before engaging in theatrical partnering.

Exit strategy

A multifaceted approach that allows egress for the performer before, during, or after staging intimacy.

Guideposts

Set moments that serve as check-ins or bases for actors in a series of choreographed movements that includes both improvised and set moments.

Intimacy container

This term may be used to designate a specific section of the body or a series of movements in intimate storytelling. In practice, an intimacy director might say "The container for this movement is from the kneecap to the mid-thigh on the left leg." Alternatively, in referencing a series of movements, the ID might state, "The container for this story is from the moment you lock eyes with each other through when you disengage from the embrace and step away."

Intimacy mapping

A technique that clarifies intimate physical storytelling for actors and others on the creative team. Mapping the choreography or choreographic parameters for a moment of staged intimacy is done by applying definable physical elements such as tempo, distance, intensity, and shape to make movements more specific and repeatable.

Intimacy notation

Written documentation of the physical movements and other storytelling elements in the moments or scenes of staged intimacy.

Masking

An action by or position of the actor(s) that conceals a physical action or position from the view of the audience. For example, masking may be used to conceal that the lips of actors do not actually touch during a staged kiss.

Open questioning

The practice of utilizing "May I" language when asking questions regarding personal boundaries. ("May I put my left hand on your right shoulder?")

Pause words

Part of an exit strategy, this is an agreed-upon word or words that can be used by those engaging in staged intimacy to call for a brief pause.

Red zones

A shorthand phrase to include predetermined boundaries during the staging of a scene. This may be set by the intimacy professional, director, and/or actors before a fuller discussion of additional boundaries (also called "No Go" or "No Contact" zones).

Tapping in/out

An action that is utilized as a kind of "mental bookend" to moments of staged intimacy, creating a threshold into and out of the work, and/or separating the actor from the character (also known as "Checking In/Closing Out," or "Tagging In/Out").

Supporting change in the process

Starting rehearsals on a new piece of theatre can feel like exploring an entirely new world, especially if it is the first time working with an intimacy professional such as an intimacy director (ID). Established directors or other leaders on the creative team may have a core set of people with whom they usually work and may feel off-kilter when working with new specialists. For those uncertain of what an intimacy director does, they may not realize that

IDs are passionate collaborators, or they could be unsure of the energy or application of authority the ID might employ.

Claire Warden, a professional intimacy director who served as co-intimacy director for Broadway's *Slave Play*, found that communication is key to avoiding misconceptions about the ways in which IDs work during these first rehearsals. In an interview,[1] she reflected on an early conversation with Robert O'Hara, director for *Slave Play*, when he memorably said to her, "I don't want you making the actors comfortable. That's not the kind of theatre I do." Warden agreed wholeheartedly. For her, it's not about being comfortable; it's about having confidence. She said, "If you're confident, you can tell these really risky, powerful stories. We want to create something that will allow everybody to push the limits of their want-desire-risk so we can really make a difference with the stories we are telling." Having this conversation prior to the first rehearsal clarified their collaborative approach to the work before stepping into the room.

Whatever concerns, uncertainties, or questions a director or other leaders may have, communication between IDs and the theatrical team (and research materials such as this text and others) will clarify the intimacy professional's role and methods of working. Intimacy directors are specialists who can bring ease, confidence, and dynamic storytelling techniques to rehearsals of staged intimacy while supporting both the performers' agency and director's vision.

First rehearsal and orientation

First rehearsal is upon us. It's now time for the director, ID, and stage manager, who have already been working together, to establish a foundation for confident, brave spaces in which to rehearse and ways to welcome in the company. This first rehearsal is the time when they will share their intentions and expectations with the entire ensemble. For many, the first rehearsal may feel like an opening night of sorts, as it is finally time to reveal the plans that have been in progress for days, weeks, or even months, to this excited group of artists.

Introductions, forms, and consent workshop

Getting started at the first rehearsal usually begins with introductions. The producer or artistic director may welcome the company and formally introduce the creative team, including the intimacy director. During this first rehearsal, perhaps during design presentations, the ID could introduce themselves and the work, briefly defining their position, basic protocols, preferred practices, and expectations. These explanations can set expectations for the staging of intimacy and the culture of respect in the rehearsal hall. Defining this culture clearly on day one helps to build a foundation of trust for more than only performers. From producers, upper administration, and design teams to the director, stage management, and assistants, every member of the creative team (whether involved in the staging of intimate moments or not) must understand and support this rehearsal culture the triad is working to create.

After introductions and design presentations have concluded, the rehearsal may shift to management's order of business. This varies from theatre to theatre, and may be based upon type of contract, but usually includes

- Announcements
- Forms and paperwork
- A vote for cast deputy (union or non-union)
- Possibly a visit with an AEA business representative
- Sharing of harassment policies

As noted in Chapter 2, harassment policies may vary but at a minimum should include a definition of harassment and sexual harassment, harassment policies, a reporting structure, and methods for reporting. (If working under an AEA contract, according to the union's President's Committee to Prevent Harassment,[2] the company must also share and define its harassment policy at this time.) Whether working under a union contract or not, the cast and entire creative team should be informed on how to uphold such policies, and it is recommended that the acting company elect a cast deputy (when possible) to assist with communicating cast needs around these procedures and reporting. Regarding distribution of these policies, procedures, and reporting structures, these should be made available through the use of a printed handout, posted, and shared on the company callboard, as well as provided electronically so members of the company can save them to personal devices. Workshops for or verbalizations of harassment policies may be useful in some situations.

The intimacy director (or other intimacy professional) may also lead a consent practices workshop for actors during the first rehearsal or sometime before staging and blocking begins. The ID may open this workshop to the entire company for observation. It is a recommended practice that the entire creative team observe this workshop when possible, so that the vocabulary and working practices shared during this session can become common knowledge for all. During the workshop, the cast may step through introductory consent exercises, learn shared vocabulary, execute trust or ensemble building exercises, discuss boundaries and safety, learn about tools for checking in with partners, as well as setting community agreements, and more. At this time, the ID may further explain that they will be the liaison for all to ensure that everyone has all the information they need to consistently ensure that all actors can maintain agency over their bodies.

A consent workshop is not only useful when orienting the team toward established practices and common vocabulary but is an opportune time to address initial uneasiness that may occur when working with practices from intimacy direction. Additionally, whether participants are new to this specialty or not, direct communication around physical touch may cause nervous energy. This may result in strange things being said or giddy behaviors occurring as participants attempt to "off-gas" subconscious or conscious nerves.[3] Techniques shared in this workshop will help to refocus the room, facilitate consensual work habits, and reinforce respect for this new method of working.

Ways the creative team can support responsible partnering

Rehearsals of any theatrical scenes have a spoken or unspoken understanding of working respectfully and safely. Intimacy rehearsals have additional considerations, such as performers' level of confidence when engaging with physical storytelling, power dynamics, amount of time allotted for rehearsals, and more. Open discourse between the intimacy director and the creative team prior to rehearsal is preferred, to have a clear understanding of how rehearsals will be run (as discussed in Chapter 3). However, whenever the intimacy director joins the process, they will help set processes and protocols for these rehearsals.

The rehearsal process will vary based not only on factors mentioned above but also on complexity of movements, specific choreographer's and/or director's processes, and other considerations. There are some foundational elements[4] that every member of the creative team can support:

- *The Production Pillars of Intimacy* discussed in Chapter 1 (context, communication, consent, choreography, and closure) or alternative foundational practices from intimacy professionals.
- *Safety* (psychological, physiological) of the performers.

- *Boundaries* (psychological, physiological) of the performers, and if they change over time.
- The *Storytelling* desired from each moment of staged intimacy, which should be repeatable while still allowing for growth in some circumstances.

For those who work behind the scenes while supporting staged intimacy, focusing on the pillars, safety, boundaries, and storytelling are the areas in which they can best support performers in the rehearsal hall. These elements combine both process and product, allowing care for performers while creating a dynamic, repeatable story for future audiences.

Methods intimacy directors use to create and maintain intimacy

This section provides a rudimentary understanding of an intimacy director's choreographic processes. In this section we will briefly cover

- Major elements in the rehearsal of staged intimacy
- Communication practices for supporting boundaries
- Communication tips boundary breaches
- Mapping moments of staged intimacy
- Approaches to choreography

The goal for this section is to give creative team members an idea of the process they may experience with an ID in rehearsal and how to maintain these moments through coaching and notation after the ID has exited the rehearsal room. This is not meant to train the reader as an intimacy director, as that is a multifaceted and extensive training process. Just as one would not be able to safely choreograph Romeo and Tybalt's fight to the death in *Romeo and Juliet* after reading a book on stage combat, **one should not attempt to stage intimacy without extensive in-person educational experiences, practical training, and mentorship from a highly trained and experienced or certified intimacy professional.**

Major elements in the rehearsal of staged intimacy

Intimacy direction has many moving parts and is situational. Different kinds of intimate stories, personalities in the room, directorial styles, institutional circumstances, and more may impact what elements are utilized by an intimacy director at any given time. (We go over approaches to intimacy choreography in a later section of this chapter.) However, for intimacy directors trained with Intimacy Directors and Coordinators, some or all of the elements below may be used during the staging of physical touch or nudity.

Placeholders

In choreography, stand-ins for movements are commonly called placeholders. During intimacy rehearsal, placeholders allow for ease during multiple run-throughs. For example, when actors are rehearsing a scene where they have lip-to-lip contact, they might touch palms as a placeholder, or use cheek-to-cheek contact instead. During movement or fight calls, or if an actor wants to refrain from performing certain staged actions for any reason, placeholders allow for comfort while still reminding actors of set choreography. Placeholders are especially useful if actors are concerned about illness or injury from too many repetitions in rehearsal but are confident they can perform the real movement when it comes time to do so. It may be helpful to identify a *placeholder removal date* on the rehearsal calendar if needed, this informs actors as to when run-throughs will contain all physically intimate movements as they are intended to be run during performances.

Desexualized language

When working on a production, whether it contains intimacy or not, the use of more mindful language is recommended when discussing physical storytelling and anatomy. This language could be called desexualized, neutral, mindful, or de-loaded.[5] Even though the material being discussed may be that of intimate storytelling, which inherently will include terminology that relates to intimate content, prevent the use of offensive euphemisms or derogatory colloquialisms when discussing the content or anatomy involved. This approach should be taken when in the rehearsal room, when taking notes or writing reports, and when in discussion with the creative, production, or administrative team.

Private vs privacy

While privacy is always a concern when staging intimacy or nudity, this work should not remain private. It is a recommended practice in intimacy direction to have additional personnel in the room beyond the actors involved and the person staging or coaching the intimacy. The inclusion of an assistant director, assistant stage manager, movement captain, or other member of the team, who are at a similar level within the organization's reporting structure, is recommended to mitigate any concerns with consent, power dynamics, reporting, or liability. This applies when working with principal actors, during understudy/replacement rehearsals, and in movement calls.

Exit strategies

There is a three-branch approach that allows egress for the performer before, during, or after staging intimacy.

- Actors may use a predetermined "pause word" to stop an action during a scene. (See the term below.)
- Actors are permitted additional breaks or permitted to leave the space regardless of the break schedule during the staging of intimacy. (See the section "Additional Breaks" below.)
- Actors may use language such as "red, yellow or green zones" or other systems to clarify boundaries during the staging of intimacy regardless of the text if clarification is needed during improvisational work. (Boundaries are discussed in more detail later in this chapter.)

Pause word

An agreed-upon word or phrase which can be used by those engaging in staged intimacy to call for a brief pause. This pause may indicate not feeling safe or confident in continuing with the movement, an opportunity for a question, or simply a breath to allow focus and ease back into the process. The pause word can be a straightforward word or phrase, such as "Pause," "Stop," or "I need a minute." Some intimacy professionals may suggest using a more symbolic word, such as "Button,"[6] "Kentucky," or "Pineapple."

Additional breaks

Although taking breaks during the rehearsal of any production is standard practice, often using AEA union break rules as a standard or guide, it should be noted that when staging intimate content that involves vulnerability, permitting extra breaks as necessary is recommended. The ability to request an additional break should be established during either the first rehearsal meeting or the ID's orientation. When in rehearsal, the actors may be exploring heightened emotional content, which can be taxing and exhaustive work. Stage management and the director should be prepared for the request for an additional break, and if anyone in the room needs to step away and take a breath, support the ability to do so.

Boundary checks

In order to assure clear communication and facilitate consent during physical storytelling, intimacy professionals encourage a communication practice called a boundary check.[7] These verbal or verbal and physical rituals are practiced regularly by actors engaging in staged intimacy as a warm up or check-in. Additional practices around boundaries will be discussed in the Communication and Boundaries section.

Tapping in and out

Tapping in and out, also referred to as tagging in and out by some intimacy professionals,[8] becomes a healthy "bookend" that allows for an intentional transition into as well as out of the work. It's the technique an actor or member of the production team may utilize for checking in and closing out at the start and end of either rehearsal or performance. This technique will differ based on the needs of the actors or creative team members involved but will usually include several distinct elements:

- *Eye contact* as a visual connection and acknowledgement of presence with the scene partner(s). This may be adjusted to an auditory acknowledgement of presence when necessary.
- *Breathing* in and out together once or several times to release tension and transition between actor and character.
- *The use of a simple physical movement* that creates a distinct ending to the ritual (such as a clap, "high five," or other agreed-upon movement).

Anchor points

Anchor points[9] are stabilizing points of contact during more challenging intimate or violent movement. This term is utilized in stage combat as a method to cue fellow actors or provide stability during shoves, chokes, throws, etc. This concept is also used in dance during moments like dips or lifts. For staged intimacy, there are also many examples, but an example could be that when engaging in a story where hands are nearing genitalia, setting an anchor point for the wrist of actor A on a specific point on the thigh of actor B may allow for more confidence. For both performers an anchor point will serve as a check in and assure that hands will remain safely out of boundary zones.

Masking

A method to tell the story of physical contact while not actually connecting, masking is often used in stage combat for punches and slaps: through angles and agreed-upon timing actors are able to "mask" the space between the fist and the target in a staged punch and tell the story without physically connecting. Masking can also occur with stage kisses, as well as other intimate storytelling such as the story of penetration or oral stimulation to a character's genital regions.

Communication practices for supporting boundaries

Boundaries can be found in every aspect of theatre. From actors being asked to stand in a certain area for lighting or wear physically restrictive costumes to the use of the script itself, which limits actors to only speaking words written by the playwright, a variety of boundaries are always part of the process. Other choreographed physical work, such as fight work or dance choreography, will often have set boundaries to support physical limitations when working around a chronic injury. Yet the term "boundaries" has historically been seen as problematic when it came to actors performing vulnerable intimate storytelling, as though the bodies of actors should always be open to any type of touch in the name and support of art.

Thankfully, theatre practitioners are discovering that for storytelling, defined limits such as the words of a script, the positioning of a spotlight, or a physical boundary are simply another element of the creative work. Boundaries are structure, and structure creates freedom. In intimacy direction, communicating boundaries has proven to be a freeing process for choreography time and time again. Actors working in this informed, communicative way, can confidently make choices that they know are consensual. They may even be able to make physical choices they assumed would be off limits but are acceptable to their partner within the context of the story. They gain vocabulary and physical rituals to connect with their workplace colleagues during these sensitive moments.

As boundaries are different for each performer and each situation, clear communication practices around supporting actors in this area are needed. There are many methods to take an inventory of physical areas or types of touch that can be included in physical storytelling. We detail some here.

Common practices for boundary checks

Boundary checks have commonalities among many intimacy specialist/directors, and usually include some form of the following elements:

- *Time for self-analysis and reflection for each performer.* Each actor should do a self-scan and determine their own physical boundaries for that day in rehearsal. This could include where a touch may occur, where touch may not occur (e.g., back of knee), and the type of touch that is acceptable (e.g., a light brush would tickle the neck, but a press of the hand is acceptable).
- *Community-wide agreements for touch.* At times, community-wide boundaries may be set by the intimacy specialist/director for everyone involved in the intimate storytelling. These could be called "no-go zones". For example, an intimacy director may set "no-go zones" for all actors as the chest, front of the pelvis, and glutes before rehearsal begins. These no-go zones may be expanded based on design elements. For example, if all of the actors are wigged, the intimacy director may add the top and sides of the head as a universal no-go zone.

No zones can sometimes adjust to "yes zones" later in the process. For example, one of these zones could be included in script (such as a grab to a glut being written into the dialogue or stage directions), and the actors have agreed to this during the audition process. The intimacy director will then work with context and communication to move forward and build these moments with the actors. However, no-go zones are often useful even in these kinds of scenarios during early rehearsals while actors are gaining confidence and trust. They also are an opportunity to practice awareness of and respect for boundaries for performers new to consent practices.

- *Verbalization and confirmation.* Actors who are engaging with the physical storytelling will have time to communicate their boundaries and have them verbally confirmed (e.g., Actor B asks if there are any boundaries today; Actor A states their boundaries, including the no-go zones the ID set; and actor B repeats back what they heard).

- *Opportunities for adjustment.* Actors are invited to continue to adjust boundaries as needed during the rehearsal process. The actors may grow more confident with movements and remove boundaries or discover previously overlooked boundaries. Adjustments can be made at any time.

In addition to these standards in boundary checks, some intimacy professionals may utilize concepts such as

- *Green, yellow, and red zones.* This expands conversation from purely yes zones and no zones to areas that are maybes. Yellow zones are areas of the body or types of touch that can be opened up for consideration as storytelling requires.
- *An agreement to not explain reasons for boundaries during boundary checks.* Actors may feel the need to explain or justify their boundaries due to nerves, embarrassment, or other reasons. This is discouraged in intimacy direction. A boundary is a boundary, and does not need to be proven as worthy through evidence or explanation on the part of the performer. Performers and intimacy directors may communicate about reasons privately if this is necessary for health, safety, or a consensual desire to expand physical storytelling as an actor works with the discomfort scale (discussed in Chapter 1).
- *Exercises in physical touch.* While the standards for boundary checks described above are more reflective and utilize verbal communication, some boundary checks may include elements of physical touch, such as rubbing one's own hands over yes zones or actor A taking actor B's hands and placing them on an agreed-upon area to allow for very clear and active consent.
- *Verbalizing yes zones instead of no zones.* This is the practice of giving permissions to specified options for physical storytelling instead of declaring boundaries. IDC-certified ID Adam Noble calls this "offering blessings."

Notes from the field ... Adam Noble on "giving blessings"

In my work with performers, I have found the implementation of what I call "blessings" to be a very useful tool. A blessing is simply a possibility, apropos of the physical moment being explored, that offers one's partner a way in—a place to begin. These permissions can offer a useful starting place for exploration, but still necessitate that the other performer consent to the action.

In my experience, discussing personal boundaries can generate anxiety in performers, and not just for those sharing but also for the partner receiving the information. Boundaries alone can sometimes make performers feel as though they are navigating a mine-field in rehearsal. Blessings offer options, a map of sorts, so that performers can tread more boldly into their moment of intimacy.

Pedagogically, offering blessings gently moves the artists from a discussion of "no" to a discussion of "yes." The process of considering and verbalizing their blessings to a partner is another opportunity for them to know themselves deeply and to become more facile at expressing their boundaries, ideas, and preferences to other people.

While this addition to process has borne the most fruit with young and less experienced performers, especially those fearful of treading on their partner's boundaries, I have employed the technique with students and performers working at every level, even at some of the country's most prestigious League of Resident Theatres (LORT).

Adam Noble
(he/him/his)
Actor/Director/Educator
Fight Director & Intimacy Director

Additional considerations for the creative team

- *Verbal vs physical boundary checks.* While verbal boundary checks between performers may be introduced by members of the creative team (such as stage management) as healthy, consent-based workplace communication, boundary check-ins that utilize physical touch should be introduced by an intimacy professional.
- *The duration of time needed for boundary checks.* While these checks may take a few minutes to complete when first introduced, they often may shorten to a ten-second check-in later in the process. After choreography is set, a question like "Are there any boundaries I should know about today" may adjust to "Are there any changes I should know about today?" As the movements have (hopefully) been built with respect for boundaries in mind, checking in on changes may be more appropriate

than re-checking on boundaries. During later rehearsals or the run of the show, adjustments to boundaries are more likely to occur due to a sore muscle, illness, or other temporary circumstance.

Communication tips for boundary breaches

When supporting boundaries in physical storytelling, there may come a moment when a performer or creative team member makes a misstep. A boundary may be crossed due to a lapse in communication, a discovery of a new boundary, or by accidental physical mistakes. If this is not an issue of harassment (as discussed in Chapter 1) but is perceived as a genuine misstep or miscommunication, there are methods to reconnect and mend the relationship and methods of working together. An intimacy professional, trained in several ways to rebuild trust, will serve as a liaison between parties or necessary actions. Below are a few methods that could be utilized by the creative team with or without the assistance of an intimacy director.

Taking accountability

Actors engaging in intimate staging should continuously check in and observe their partner to avoid mistakes and take accountability and apologize if they believe they have erred. In "How to Give an Apology," Mia Mingus talks about flipping the script when it comes to accountability: "Accountability should be proactive. We should be forthcoming about our mistakes, rather than hoping no one finds out about what we've done." She says that, preferably, "We would not put the labor of reaching out and checking in about our accountability on someone else, especially those we've harmed. We would proactively do the work to be accountable for ourselves."[10]

Being proactive in this way may be new or humbling for an unintentional aggressor, especially if they were unaware of creating a negative impact. They will need to work to accept the experience with grace and view this incident as an opportunity to grow as a responsible partner in the consensual workplace. It is key to not take up time explaining a behavior, but accepting harm was caused and doing what it takes to learn and grow. "We use the discrepancy between intent and impact all the time to tell us where our skills need refinement. If someone tells you that something you said or did was hurtful, and that was not what you meant to happen, don't use that as an excuse. Instead, take it as a cue that your skills need improvement."[11] We explore more ways to improve communication skills in the sections below.

The four-point script

Broadway intimacy director Claire Warden describes the use of a four point "script" as a method to assist communication between actors when boundaries are being pushed or unintentionally breached. The following script is comprised of four statements in specific order, that can be customized to the situation:

> "When you do _____, I feel _____.
> I imagine _____. I request _____."

This exercise is about helping the person experiencing the breach to speak what they experience, identify and name their feelings, share the interpretations or judgments around the situation, and then make a request. The script template above might be used in the moment as demonstrated in the sample script below:

"**When you** joke around about this embrace moment, **I feel** distracted and insecure. **I imagine** you are trying to ease the awkwardness of the situation, but **I request** we remain story-focused as we are working on this."

Utilizing this scripted tool can help to clarify for all involved what actions are causing what impact, then allow for an interpretation of that action, and finally indicate a clear request for a change.

> ### Notes from the field ... in the moment communication
>
> *We spoke with Claire Warden about the benefit of considered communication, especially verbal connection when in rehearsal. It became clear that creating a space where one feels confident using direct and clear communication with a scene partner can greatly benefit from some guidance. Providing a structure that guides open communication is not as difficult as one may think and can be extremely beneficial.*
>
> "This four-point structure aims to focus communication and give the speaker a template, which they may utilize to express their feelings and verbalize what they need in the moment. The script also allows the

speaker to move away from explaining or defending themselves or their feelings and to refrain from judgment of the other person.

Providing a method to verbalize feelings, to own and name them, hopefully will reduce judgment or blame around them. This scripted exercise purposely segments the stages of reaction to become, in turn, an action plan.

The template works as follows:

"When you…..
I felt…….
I imagine(d)…..
I request ….."

For example, a sample situation may be

"When you improvised slapping my butt on stage last night, I felt violated and shocked. I imagined that you were objectifying me to assert your dominance. I request that you do not improvise any touching of me and that we both talk about and agree to any future changes with our physical interactions on stage."

The "I feel" segment names the emotion/feeling that came up. Part of the practice of this direct communication structure is to help the speaker stay with the feelings that occur in the moment and to name them, rather than skipping straight to naming the consequences of the behavior resulting from them or judgment of their scene partner.

Naming feelings vs consequences is an essential distinction in this exercise. There has recently been a subtle but pervasive and powerful shift in the language we use in American society that obfuscates or entirely moves away from the naming of our actual feelings. For example, "I felt like you are not listening to me," which is not actually a feeling, but an interpretation of the other person's behavior and perhaps a judgment upon them. What is actually happening is "It seems like you are not listening to me, that makes me feel… (hurt, dismissed, isolated, angry, etc.)"

At first it may seem pedantic, but in fact, the real and damaging consequence of this language shift is that by not naming our feelings, we are not allowing ourselves to feel them or to share them, and therefore our humanity, with others. The avoidance of expression of feelings may in future contribute to our inability to even recognize them. Eventually, we may shut ourselves down to the expression and recognition of feelings to a level where we no longer consciously feel them, which then works against our ability to gauge our own consent levels moment to moment. This is also contrary to what we ask of actors as part of their work, which is their ability to engage in complex and varied portrayals of a myriad of emotions. From this more precise use of language the emotions occurring may become clearer to the person feeling them and therefore assist them in understanding what they need in the moment to enhance and/or create safety in the situation and the actors can work together on more helpful communication tactics to improve their working relationship.

Another reason to investigate this shift in language is because it may result in jumping straight to naming judgments disguised as feelings. Hearing these judgments spoken out loud may put the scene partner into a defensive mode, which makes it more difficult to openly discuss boundaries and the dynamics of the relationship and/or behavior. It can also reinforce inaccurate or untrue assumptions on the part of the observer, putting them in a place of defense rather than communication and resolution. For example, "I feel like you are not taking this seriously," "I feel you are dismissing me," "I feel you don't care about this." When this occurs, utilizing the "I imagine" segment of the four-point script is a very useful step. It allows the speaker to avoid sitting in a statement of judgment and provides a direction forward for the conversation.

In deeper consideration of the "I imagine" part of the script, currently I am honestly of two minds. On the one hand, it is a handy tool for us to share the impact or the interpretation of someone's behavior, which can be very helpful as we all learn and grow together in this shifting moment of our industry. However, it often does have a powerful impact on the receiver. Hearing "I imagine you are trying to ease the awkwardness of the situation" may not be challenging, but hearing "I imagined that you were objectifying me to assert your dominance" may put them in a place of wanting to defend their intention, deny the impact, or simply create big feelings in the moment. Then, if they are not skilled at managing these big feelings or they move into denial, the focus of the conversation may shift to coping with their feelings instead of listening to the request, which is the opposite objective of this tool.

However, it can be hugely beneficial, when these situations are facilitated by someone who understands this structure or when the parties are practiced at managing their feelings. So, it may be a judgment call on the speaker's part as to whether they include "I Imagine." The flip side is, without "I imagine," the receiver can be left feeling in the dark in trying to understand the speaker's feelings in the context of their behavior if they are unaware of the difference between their intention and the impact of their behavior. So to take it out might also unsteady the structure of the communication.

I realize that we need to provide more education and guidance for those who find themselves in a situation where they have caused concern or harm. While it is important to support those experiencing harm, we do not want to leave scene partners out in the cold on how to heal relationships if they have unintentionally caused that harm. Both partners have to be fully considered and equipped to make a change!"

Claire Warden
(she/her/hers)
Intimacy Director/Coordinator
Fight Director & Actress

The "Oops and Ouch" method

In the *Chicago Theatre Standards*, an adjusted form of resolution in the moment is referred to as the "Oops and Ouch" method.[12] An artist on the receiving end of an unwanted action could indicate the need to pause work with a simple "Ouch!" On hearing this, initiators of the comment or behavior would realize that harm had potentially just occurred and would respond with "Oops!" This response would indicate their awareness and regret for the words or actions. The person who called "Ouch!" would then decide if it would work to move on or if more conversation needed to occur. Overall, this type of resolution includes three steps:

- Showing accountability through self-reflection
- Apologizing
- Working to repair and change behaviors

This resolution will allow all parties to move forward. Additionally, the "Ouch" caller can be anyone in the room who perceives possible harm, not necessarily the direct receiver of the problematic words or actions.

The person receiving the injury need not spearhead resolution in the moment. As people become more aware of healthy communication and see inherent problematic behaviors in a new light, anyone in the community might communicate an Oops even before the Ouch.

Mapping moments of staged intimacy

Using clear, definable, straightforward physical elements is key to codifying and repeating movements in staged intimacy. Using a technical vocabulary for building and documenting intimacy, instead of casual or colloquial language, also allows for a professional workplace experience when staging and performing physical stories. The use of technical terms is not unusual for staged movement; creative team members have likely experienced certain vernacular from staged violence such as the sword numbering system or standard terminology in dance. Now there are clear systems for staged intimacy.

When approaching the notation process for choreographed and staged intimacy, numerous elements may assist in creating and documenting this movement. For professionals at Intimacy Directors and Coordinators (IDC), creating moments of intimacy is known as *intimacy mapping*.[13] Mapping elements include the following:

- Audio cues and breath
- Distance
- Initiations
- Duration and tempo
- Gaze
- Intensity
- Location and shape

Some or all of these may be used in a production containing intimacy. Outside of IDC, other intimacy professionals and organizations have named the documentation of these moments in different ways. At Theatrical Intimacy Education (TIE), for example, their choreographic terms are referred to as "ingredients" and their choreography "recipes,"[14] and in Adam Noble's method of extreme stage physicality, he refers to the choreographic framework as "blueprints."[15]

Audio cues

Audio cues are defined as emotional expression through sound that has been incorporated into the storytelling as a set verbal element of the choreography. These expressions may be loud and explosive, soft and timid, or any blend based on level of emotion and character intention. One example: Actor A initiates a kiss to Actor B's left cheek and when lip to cheek contact is made, Actor B *"giggles quietly"*.

Broadway fight director David Leong[16] speaks often to the importance of building a "soundscape" into a staged fight, mentioning that an audience should be able to determine the story unfolding even without visual help, as if their eyes are closed.[17] This importance and specificity of sound applies to intimacy specialists/directors as well, many of whom build detailed audio stories along with the physicality. Just as the senses of taste and smell may enhance each other, so might sight and sound when melded with intimacy direction.

Emotional audio cues are important elements to monitor when in performance for safety and repeatability. Laurie Goldfeder, Production Stage Manager[18] for the 2019 Broadway revival of *Frankie and Johnny in the Clair de Lune*, believes that especially in fight and romantic scenes, the sounds actors make are what "sell it," and when the sounds change that is an indicator that something is different and may need to be looked at in the next movement call.

Breath

This is the audible inhalation or exhalation of air as storytelling for characters or a cue for actors. When the inhalation or exhalation of breath of a character has been intentionally set by the ID or director, noting that breath, along with the other choreography, will assist with maintaining that director's intentions. Breath is one clear way to measure time and maintain repeatability for the actors in moments of intimacy. It also may be key in defining the story of consensual or non-consensual touch for an audience.

Examples: "Actor A reaches out slowly and embraces Actor B. Actor B audibly exhales over a count of two as Actor A's arms close around them" (Figure 4.1). Or, "As Actor A's left hand grips Actor B's right wrist, Actor B takes in a quick inhale through their nose" (Figure 4.2).

Figure 4.1 Two figures in an embrace with arrows depicting inward and outward breath choices. Artwork by Karen Schierhorn.

Figure 4.2 Two figures holding hands, with one figure leaning away; arrows depicting sound and breath choices. Artwork by Karen Schierhorn.

Distance

Distance can reference the space between actors, as well as the actions of their hands, faces, and bodies. As in staged fighting and staged intimacy, refer to both "opening" and "closing" distance to indicate when actors get closer (closing distance) or further apart (opening distance).

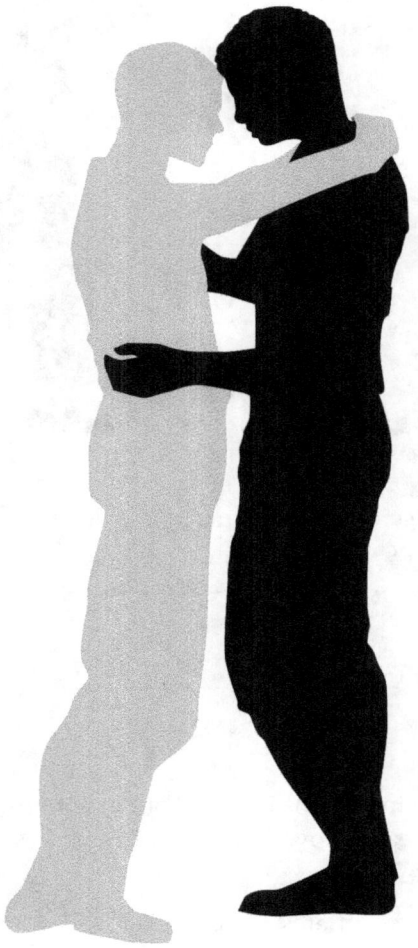

Figure 4.3 Two figures engaging in an embrace with closed distance. Artwork by Karen Schierhorn.

Example: "The embrace between actors A and B begins with three inches of distance between their hips and chests, foreheads touching" (Figure 4.3). Or, "Actor A closes distance to attempt an embrace, but Actor B steps back with an arm up and reopens distance" (Figure 4.4).

Figure 4.4 One figure keeping distance from another approaching figure. Artwork by Karen Schierhorn.

Initiation

This can indicate initiations into and out of actions. Who is initiating the beginning of each move or sequence of moves? Who is initiating the end of the move?

Example: "Actor A initiates a kiss to Actor B's forehead, then disengages and opens distance, turning their back to actor B. Actor B then closes distance, reaching out to touch Actor A's cheek, initiating a turn of Actor A's face to meet eyes with Actor B."

In rehearsal

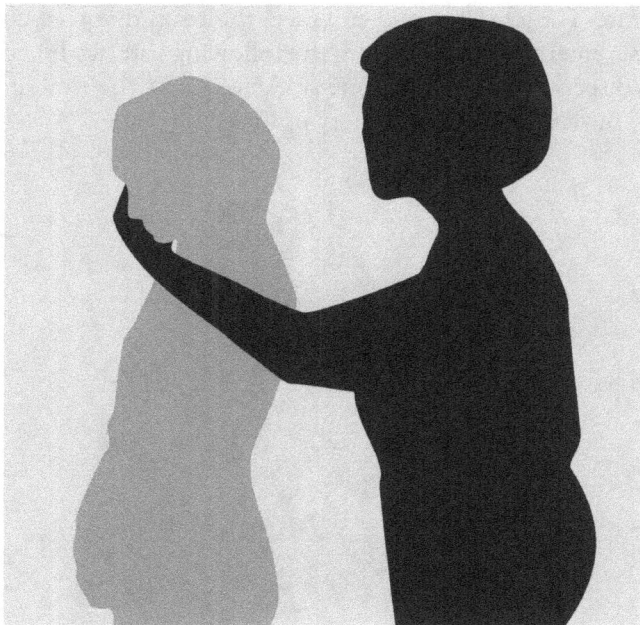

Figure 4.5 One figure initiating a moment of intimacy by walking up behind another person and reaching to turn their face toward them. Artwork by Karen Schierhorn.

Duration

Duration indicates the amount of time the actors engage in a movement or the length of stasis between movements. The measurement method may consist of seconds, beats, breaths, a character's line, a lighting effect, or physical action taking place on stage. If choosing a more subjective form of duration, such as breaths or beats, the actors involved should take the lead on determining what that method of duration means in their partnership. Once a method is set, it should be documented in notation to ensure consistency and repeatability.

To illustrate: For a brief staged embrace, the team involved could pick one measurement of duration from the following list: two breaths, three beats, two seconds, the entire line of Actor C, or the time it takes to complete moving a piece of scenery upstage.

Figure 4.6 Two figures embracing for an extended duration while one looks impatiently at their watch. Artwork by Karen Schierhorn.

Tempo

Tempo is the speed at which the actors close or open distance, or engage with an action. Without the use of music or a stopwatch, tempo is subjective. Thus, tempo for a moment should be defined by the actors involved in a way that works for them. This can be defined through a numbering system referring to inner or outer tempo. Inner tempo refers to the "inner engine" felt by actors that ranges from calm and slow to anxious or excited, but could change in speed without much movement on the outside. The speed of the breath can often indicate the inner tempo of an actor. Outer tempo is the speed of gestures, movement through space, or other full-bodied movements that occur at different speeds, such as a run versus a walk across the space.

Example: "Actor B opens distance at a tempo of three and turns down stage. Actor A closes distance at a tempo of six. Actor A initiates a hug to Actor B's back when they arrive down stage left." Or, "Actors A and B run onto the stage, pause and see each other, both of their inner tempos at an eight. Actor A runs to the embrace at an outer tempo of eight. As they embrace, and take several deep breaths together, their inner tempos lower to three" (Figure 4.7).

Figure 4.7 A person running into an embrace with a kiss at a high speed. Artwork by Karen Schierhorn.

Gaze

This refers to eye contact or the movement of the eyes of the actors. Actors' gazes may be focused on each other, focused away from the other, one focused on with the other looking away, or a myriad of combinations with a variety of intensity levels of glances, stares, peeks, etc. Similar to breath, notating eye contact or gaze is helpful when it has been intentionally set by the ID or director.

Example: "Actor A seeks eye contact from Actor B as they close distance. Actor B continues to look away from Actor A, who wraps their arms around Actor B, and then both actors close their eyes" (Figure 4.8.) Or, as actor A kneels, they seek eye contact from Actor B, who turns and looks down into Actor A's eyes" (Figure 4.9).

Figure 4.8 One figure looks at the other, who has turned their gaze away. Artwork by Karen Schierhorn.

Figure 4.9 Two figures gaze into each other's eyes, one in a kneeled position. Artwork by Karen Schierhorn.

Intensity

The level of pressure or tension in a moment of intimacy, usually indicated as a number between 1 and 10. The amount of energy in a moment of intimacy has a lot of potential for storytelling.

Example: "Actor A and B hug. Actor A's embrace is at an intensity of two. Actor B starts at an intensity of four, then both increase their intensity to eight as actor B brings their hands to actor A's face" (Figure 4.10).

Intensity numbers are subjective and should be defined by the actors involved. Additionally, the acting of intensity may be used to tell a story while keeping the actors safe. For example, a character may grab another character's arm "violently" at what looks like a level of eight to the audience through full body engagement, but in reality the actor is grabbing at a level of only four. This difference between actor's action and character's story would be utilized to prevent bruising during the repetition of performance. Both the story of intensity and the actual intensity should be notated by stage management when necessary.

Figure 4.10 Two figures engage in a higher intensity embrace, gripping each other tightly. Artwork by Karen Schierhorn.

Location

When applicable, notate the location of the actors' hands, face, hips, feet, etc.

Example: "Actor A places their hands on their lower belly and turns to face stage left. Actor B closes distance and embraces Actor A from behind. Actor B places their hands above the hands of Actor B on the belly" (Figure 4.11).

Or "During the kiss, Actor A's hands are on the shoulders of B. Actor B's hands are on Actor A's hips."

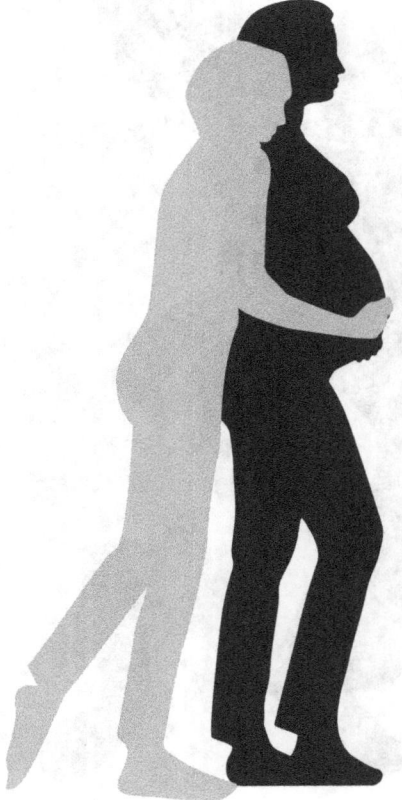

Figure 4.11 One figure embraces a visibly pregnant figure, with hands located on the pregnant belly. Artwork by Karen Schierhorn.

Shape

This is the form or shape in space formed by the bodies of the actors engaged in a movement or a moment of stasis.

Example: "Actor A and Actor B are seated, legs crossing over each other, with Actor B leaning on Actor A's stage left shoulder" (Figure 4.12). Or "Actor A and Actor B hug, shaped in an "A" (heads and upper chests together with feet and hips farther apart)."

Figure 4.12 Two figures create a unique, seated, intertwined shape during their moment of intimacy. Artwork by Karen Schierhorn.

Approaches to choreography

Just as there are differences in how dance, movement, and fight choreographers approach physical scenes or notation, there are multiple ways intimacy professionals may choose to work. These differences are due to multiple circumstances and can be related to the context pillar in the Pillars of Intimacy. Concerning choreographic approaches, context will include the background of the intimacy specialist/director; both in training and artistic style. Context also includes the scope of the intimacy in the project. After elaborating on the elements of education, experience, and scope further, we will look at a few distinct stylistic approaches that may arise due to them.

Differences in intimacy training

The way a story is choreographed will be influenced by a professional's intimacy education background. Training in choreographic methods will differ depending upon the organization and mentors under which they learned their craft. (For reference, a partial list of staged intimacy training organizations is included in Appendix A.) If the training background of a hired intimacy professional is known, it may be helpful to research vocabulary or methods that organization utilizes and, when possible, to ask for time to confer with the professional prior to the start of rehearsals to establish common understanding and language.

Differences in artistic backgrounds

Many intimacy directors come from movement backgrounds, as movement specialists are typically already trained in working with actors' bodies and physical contact and in creating through corporeal storytelling. However, this means that a preferred movement methodology may influence an intimacy specialist/director, and the style of movements might reflect that preference. Of course, not all choreography will match a specific technique. Still, for example, an ID trained in the imaginative techniques found in the Michael Chekhov method may have a different choreographic style than one drawn to the rigorous energy and concentration of the Suzuki technique. The vast and varied spectrum of movement methodologies makes for myriad styles for staging intimacy, and trained choreographers will use various tools for varying stories. Thus, it can be helpful for those working with intimacy choreographers to expect individualized approaches in connection with standard protocols and understand it is normal to witness IDs working with actors in different ways.

If not a theatrical movement specialist before training in staged intimacy, an ID also may have a background in directing, acting, stage combat, dramaturgy (see contribution by Cristina (Cha) Ramos in Chapter 3), dance, administration, or other experiences that impact their methods. To expand on this briefly, we have included contributions from intimacy professionals on ways in which their work with intimacy relates to another area of theatrical expertise.

 Artistic collaboration: Dance choreographers and intimacy

As a former professional dancer, I've so enjoyed the process of bringing intimacy direction to concert dance. The collaboration with concert dance choreographers is truly unlike any collaboration I've experienced. Not only are we often speaking the same language as choreographers and movement specialists, but because dance is, in its nature, physical storytelling, we get to laser focus on intimacy choreography even more. Thus, these moments can be further heightened.

Another thing I've discovered is that so often when it comes to choreographing intimacy, it's the choreographic aspect that gets balked at immediately. However, in concert dance, everything is choreographed, even down to finger movement. So, choreographing micro gestures, moments of stillness, or an intimate embrace is not at all a foreign concept.

While having two choreographers in the room may sound challenging to navigate, I've found that the shared vernacular, valuing of detailed movements, and commitment to set choreography can encourage an extraordinary level of trust in this working relationship.

Sarah Lozoff
(she/her/hers)
Intimacy Director/Movement Director/Gyrotonic Trainer
Partner with *Production on Deck*

> ⚔ **Artistic collaboration: Fight choreographer and intimacy**
>
> There were several years that I worked as a fight director prior to my intimacy training. In addition to general staged violence such as sword fights, this included being hired to do sexual assaults, intense physical contact, or violence against women. Although I always tried to make the actors safe to the best of my ability, I found the missing key when introduced to intimacy direction. The expansion of my vocabulary that I learned through training empowered me as a fight director and as a person.
>
> On the same note, intimacy training has also improved my work as a fight director. How I approach conversations around boundaries and triggering and how I approach trauma on stage is tremendously more intentional than before. It is to the point where I honestly can't see doing one without the other. I am hired to be a storyteller while keeping the actors safe, both physically and emotionally. Having trained in both disciplines (and continuing to train and evolve in both) has only benefited me to becoming a better storyteller and leader.
>
> As a fight director, when collaborating with an intimacy director I love starting the process with them in the lead. They will set the room up with consent-based practices from the start while allowing me to also have knowledge of the needs of the actors. A trained, consent-forward ID makes my job as an FD smoother because the trust and physical awareness built by the ID spans the bridge between the intimacy and the violence.
>
>
>
> **Rocio Mendez**
> (they/she)
> Fight Director/Intimacy Director
> Actor & Educator
>
>

Time, scope, and collaboration

Situational differences in choreographic style may also occur. Is there a lot of complex intimacy, or a few brief moments? Does the choreographer feel there has been an appropriate amount of time allotted for a moment to be worked thoroughly, or have they realized they need to work in a different way to adhere to the scheduling as set? How many actors are involved in a moment? Has the choreographer been brought in at the start of the process, or as an emergency "fix" for challenges that have occurred? There are many elements that can adjust the methods of working by the intimacy professional. If an intimacy choreographer knows they have only three hours with the actors to restage a problematic scene of intimacy, for example, they might approach that very differently than when working on a project in which they are fully engaged from the beginning of the creative process as an ID. *Scope* may also include other design or storytelling elements. An ID working on a contemporary scene that contains staged nudity will have different methods than when staging intimacy with actors performing in upper-class, corseted Renaissance era clothing. Working with actors dimly lit in silhouette on a proscenium stage will be approached differently than a moment of brightly lit intimacy in a theatre in the round. Set design can also impact intimacy; a raked stage will affect the choreography, as will a set with multiple levels, large furniture pieces, or, as seen in Broadway's *Slave Play*, a set with the back wall made entirely of mirrored panels. Variety in environmental design may be the impetus for different choreographic approaches to staging scenes of intimacy.

Differing styles for building moments

Training, artistic background, and scope all contribute to stylistic differences for choreographers. These stylistic differences may include the use of one or more of the following foundational elements to their techniques:

- Guideposts
- Improvisation
- Setting multiple options
- Written agreements or "contracts"

Guideposts[19] are set moments that serve as check-ins or bases for actors in a series of choreographed movements that include both improvised and set moments. These guideposts may take the form of body shapes, stage pictures, moments of eye contact or breath, or simple movements that the actors come to in a specific order. These could also be referred to as grounding moments, or choreographic checkpoints. Using guideposts is a way choreographers can meld set movements with safely improvised movements: keeping intimate storytelling both repeatable and slightly flexible from show to show. Actors working in this way will be given tools to improvise between guideposts safely and responsibly.

> ### An example of guideposts in action
>
> Two actors cross to stand two feet apart (*guidepost 1*), and slowly improvise to an embrace (*guidepost 2*); and then one actor improvises how and when they sink to their knees and look up, while the other moves to put a hand on the top of their head (*guidepost 3*).
>
> - Guidepost 1 – stance: two feet of distance
> - Guidepost 2 – embrace
> - Guidepost 3 – position on ground, hand on head
>
> Clarifying and notating each guidepost helps to provide consistency in movement while still allowing for improvisation.

Live theatre is a living and breathing art form, and slight changes are bound to happen from night to night. If the actors are working with consent, these moments of improvisation can enliven the set story and create organic nuances that might arise from the slight changes in emotion or in their character's relationship formed in that specific performance.

When taking notation, the stage manager may choose to notate only the shape of each guidepost, noting that the movement from guidepost to guidepost is improvised and will adjust each night. When maintaining the movement or putting in understudies or replacements, the guideposts are what will be key in communicating character intentions and actor movements.

Improvisation, mentioned as a transition between guideposts, may be used for an entire moment of uncomplicated intimacy when actors are communicative, having built trust and are confident in working together consensually. Improvisation may be used in slow motion to build moments from the start or may be encouraged for an entire embrace or moment of touch that is fully within boundaries for actors. Actor A might say, "You can rub my shoulders, back, and neck in any way for this moment of connection between mother and child. We know the story and I think we can let this come out of the moment each night." If Actor B enthusiastically consents to this mode of working, the moment can remain improvised. However, if one party prefers setting movements, the moment should not be improvised. Additionally, if an issue of the bordering or breaking boundaries arises, choreographic parameters will need to be adjusted to set movements and the team will need to work to repair communication and trust before moving forward.

Setting multiple options may be a tool an intimacy professional uses to create flexibility in movements while maintaining boundaries and storytelling. Sarah Lozoff, who has served as resident intimacy director for Oregon Shakespeare Festival and RudduR Dance, sometimes uses this technique to give actors multiple choreographic options when staging intimacy. She employs this method to support the organic styles of some directors, actors, or entire productions, allowing for active listening and slight changes to the relationship in the moment leading up to the intimacy. After setting multiple options, within the run of the scene the actors may explore this flexibility. An example might be actors determining in the moment if the intimacy will be just a brief embrace, a longer more intense embrace, or an embrace with a kiss on the forehead, having rehearsed each option previously. Predetermined, non-verbal communication would make the upcoming choice clear to both actors, and the scene would then flow naturally to one of the set choices. By giving actors multiple options, all built within boundaries, the organic nature of the dialogue could flow into the intimate moment as well.

Written agreements, or "contracts," are done by writing out the intimacy choreography in full and having the performers, stage manager, ID and director sign a written choreographic agreement as a commitment or contract. This more formalized process regarding notation is one way to clarify movements for pre-professional actors or for productions with intimacy in academia. Written agreements may positively impact scene work for actors who have trouble learning choreography and a written reminder helps them commit the work to memory. These kinds of contracts for intimacy are also useful for creative team members who prefer both written and verbal communication due to liability or company-based issues in the past.

Techniques for notating moments of staged intimacy

Similar to when one is blocking text or staging violence, it may be necessary to create written documentation for staged intimacy. Known as notation, this documentation should be detailed and specific to document and maintain movements. Clear notation is vital; filming staged intimacy, either in rehearsal or performance, is not an appropriate practice, and could lead to privacy or harassment issues if filmed and mishandled.

While not all moments of intimacy may require detailed written out choreography, IDC recommends that moments of complex intimacy such as extended kisses, simulated sex acts, stories of sexual assault, and moments that contain staged nudity should be notated. Working with the intimacy professional, actors, and the SM team should establish standard notation for the intimate actions. This notation will be shared with those involved in the scene, referred to if there are discrepancies and concerns, and may be signed as a contractual agreement to the movements by the actors if necessary or desired. Depending upon the level of discrepancies that may occur during these movements after choreography has been set or when in performance, the stage manager or director may address the situation, or the intimacy director may need to be contacted.

Before starting out, especially for actors and stage managers, there are a few guidelines we recommend one follow when notating staged intimacy:

- *Notate by character*—Always use the character name or a symbol that represents that character when notating their set movements, do not use the actor's name playing that character. Not only does this make it easier during understudy rehearsals or if a replacement actor comes in to take over a role, but it helps to maintain a clear separation between actor and character.
- *Use clinical language*—Approach the method of writing the character movement in a clinical, mindful and desexualized manner. This means when notating set choreographed movements, be specific to what the *actor* is actually doing with their body in order to tell the *character's story*. For example, if the story of the character's movement is grabbing another character's genitals, that is not what the actor will actually be doing. It may actually be "Character A firmly pushes palm of right hand to upper inner left thigh of Character B." By notating the specific movement in a clinical and character-based manner, it is easy for an actor to clearly understand what movement they will do and easier for stage management to maintain their correct physical actions.
- *Notate director's intention*—Look at the movement from the perspective of what the director and ID want the audience to experience. What is the story that is being told? Notate how the director speaks of the movement to capture their intentions behind the story. If the director is repeating certain phrases or words to express what the emotional context of the movement is, those may be important descriptors to notate. For example, when a character is "grabbing" the other character's arm, do the directors and actors describe it as seductive, violent, teasing, timid? If repeated several times in coaching, including this kind of language in notation may be a useful addition to technical elements from mapping (such as intensity, tempo, etc.). *Please note*—as a stage manager, this does not mean that you take creative liberty to impart your own interpretation to this notation. Be mindful and be concise; include only what is crucial to maintaining movements and storytelling.

Tips for taking notation

We recommend when notating intimacy movement to incorporate the terminology and phrasing used by the intimacy professional during the process. When writing this notation, one should keep in mind that details to notation can be adjusted and added each time the scene is rehearsed. So, begin by capturing broad movements, then add detail as rehearsals progress.

Although each stage manager or ID will have their own style (see Figure 4.13 for a notation example from an ID) and preferences, below is an example of a notation method that may be useful:

Write a **number** on the script page to notate the location of movement within character dialogue, and write a corresponding number for your notation. (Each script page uses a new sequential numbering system to track movements for that specific page.)

Write **the character symbol** to start the specific notation that will indicate the individual character involved in the action. (These character symbols can be the first, or first and second letters of the character's name and should all be listed on a "notation key" for easy reference)

Within the script, the notation would then be scaffolded with increased detail as rehearsals progress, and may develop as indicated below:

Notate first: Broad movements or guideposts for each character

Add a slash, then notate: Detailed movement(s) involved (position, shape, tempo, etc.)

Add a slash, then notate: More levels of specifics regarding movement(s) (such as counts, breath or audio cues, gaze, etc....)

Notate last: The director or intimacy director's details regarding intentions

This would then read something like

Number, Symbol: Guideposts / detailed movements / even more details or specifics / intention notes.

See Figure 4.14 for a more fully realized example.

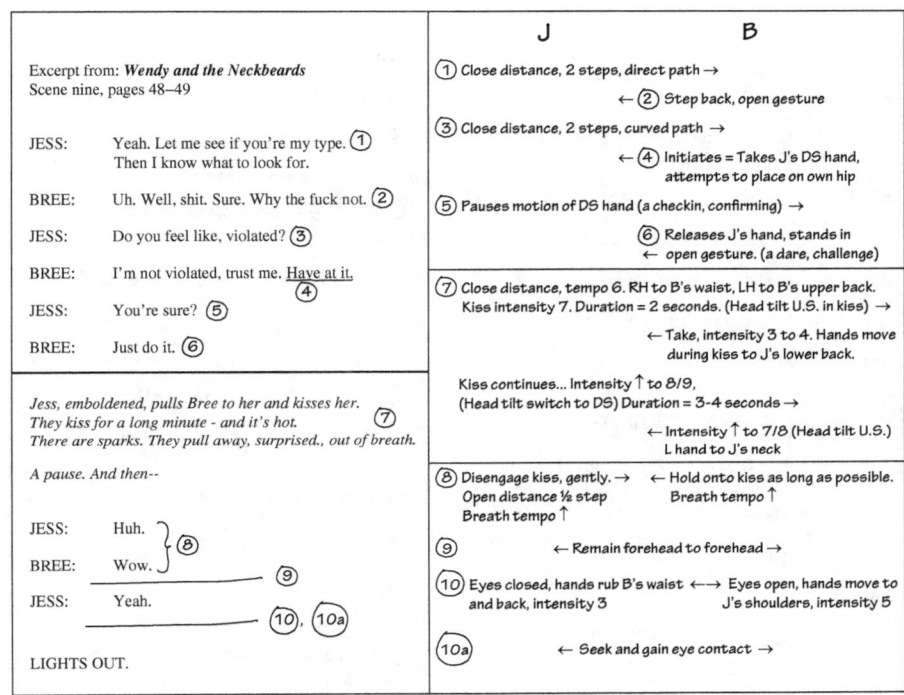

Figure 4.13 An example of written notation by an intimacy director. Created by the authors.

Style of notation

When documenting movement and writing intimacy notation, it's important to understand that each individual may use their own writing style, method of shorthand, and notation symbols. Additionally, the layout of their notation may vary if notating scripted dialogue, musical lyrics, dance, or opera. Whatever the style and layout, methods of notation are usually customized based on who is taking the notation, the speed of rehearsals, and the director's and ID's methods of working. While documenting in the moment, stage management's notation may look different from the intimacy director's, for example, but hopefully a universal language between the ID, director, actors, and stage management is understood. While symbols or layouts may change, using the same terminology and phraseology for notation will ensure consistency in understanding, clarity in communication, and ease when maintaining choreography.

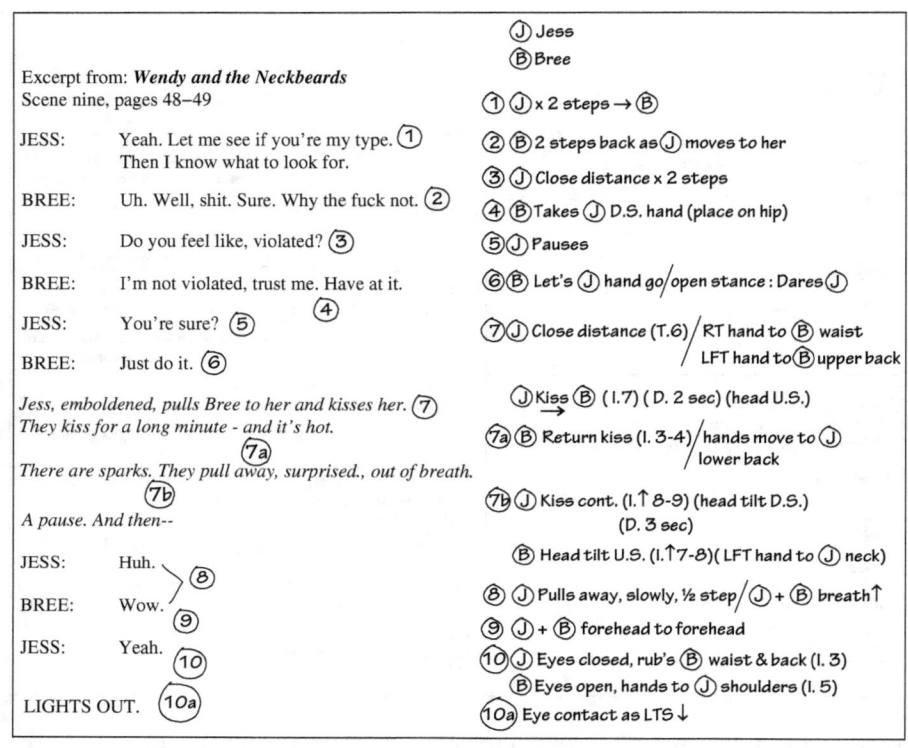

Figure 4.14 An example of written notation by a stage manager. Created by the authors.

Once the production has opened, notation should be finalized as thorough, coherent, and specific. Beyond movement and safety, it also needs to accurately convey the director's story. This can be done by specificity in the intimacy map, and by including key words or phrases repeated often by the director or intimacy director. Whatever works best for those maintaining it should be used; for some the word "passionate" may make a movement repeatable, while for others, using physical tools such as intensity and tempo will be much more useful.

As mentioned at the top of the chapter, the job of the creative team is to maintain boundaries, safety and storytelling, and notation is key in this endeavor. These three elements must be maintained throughout the run to protect the actors, the experience of the audience, and so understudies or replacements can be properly rehearsed and put into the production.

Privacy concerns in notation and rehearsal reports

As movement and blocking are being explored during closed intimacy rehearsals, details may arise that need to be shared with the production team. When this is the case, it is preferred to be thoughtful about the possibly sensitive nature of rehearsed material. Information gathered during the staging of intimacy may contain personal details directly or indirectly related to privacy concerns of performers working in those scenes. These details may not need to be shared with every member of the production team in daily rehearsal reports. Stage management may need to create a smaller group, identified in advance, who will receive information that comes out of the closed rehearsals of intimacy. This smaller group may consist of department heads such as costumes and wardrobe, lighting, props, and sound. The team members who should receive more sensitive material will vary from production to production and should be identified before rehearsals begin. Clarifying the needs behind this decision can also help prevent anyone from feeling dismissed or offended; being mindful of sensitive information and how it is communicated and distributed shows support and respect for those being asked to be vulnerable.

Accommodations for performers

In Chapter 3, we briefly explored accessories and safety equipment for performers. It may be relatively easy to create a preliminary list of items required before rehearsals start, especially when working with an intimacy director. However, accommodations for the performers may need to be clarified, updated, or reconsidered within the rehearsal process as things change. Maintaining a space where performers are confident and secure in knowing that their physical well-being is a top priority will empower them to take more significant risks and experiment with complete confidence. Stage management should be in continuous dialogue with the performers and the intimacy professional regarding personal accessories and safety equipment to maintain privacy and physical safety. Specific physical accessories may also help eliminate any opportunity for repetitive strain injuries during rehearsals and through the entire run of the production.

When working with an ID, protective accessories have likely been discussed with costumes, set design, or other creative team members before the final choreography has been set. Stage management should confirm with design and the ID what protective accessories actors will wear during the performance. It may be vital for the costuming department to test these accessories when fittings occur, when costume rigging is being determined, or when quick changes are choreographed. When finalized, equipment to be used during the production should be communicated to the entire creative team.

Early rehearsals are also the time to begin conversations regarding backstage accommodations. As the story surrounding intimate staging is rehearsed, stage management should be looking for accommodations that will need to exist in backstage areas and communicate these requests once they are apparent. Careful consideration of backstage privacy early in the process will allow for creative solutions to play out more easily. Backstage accommodations will be discussed further in Chapter 5, but one should begin to explore backstage considerations for performers and wardrobe, visibility and privacy issues for backstage staff and crew, as well as personal accommodations that may be needed for navigation between scenes. Establishing a backstage space that is crafted with a mind toward privacy and well-being, not only for actors but also for crew and company, supports the culture of care that is core to this work.

Remember the riders

One last element that should remain in the minds of those in rehearsal is any specific accommodations that have been negotiated on behalf of the actors during their contracting stage. Notated in Chapter 3, when finalizing contracts, actors may have made arrangements that were documented in a rider that outline specific accommodations relating to their performance of intimate content. When this is the case, stage management, company management, or other members of the administrative team will need to ensure that these arrangements are being upheld.

Chapter reflection

Rehearsals are an exciting time to apply and work alongside growing, contemporary practices from intimacy direction. Tension within or dismissal of the creative possibilities when staging intimacy has dominated rehearsals of physical storytelling for too long. After absorbing the tools found in this chapter, such as introducing team members to a space that allows for brave, confident choices and utilizing new, clear terminology for creating physical stories, actors and directors can feel rejuvenated when approaching this work. Awareness of notation techniques and differences in choreographic styles can also help production teams feel better prepared.

It is now clearer than ever how modern methods of storytelling foster a trusting environment in which actors, the creative team, and everyone involved in bringing the production to life can support taking more risks and commit to more dynamic choices. Next, teams have the opportunity to transition out of the rehearsal hall and into technical rehearsals to finish filling out the sights, sounds, and mechanics of these powerful stories.

Chapter discussion / exercise / activity

Notation exercise

As a fun exercise, when streaming a TV show or movie and you notice a scene that tells an intimate story, use that scene to help you begin to identify elements of intimacy mapping and begin to practice taking intimacy notation. (Watching a show that utilized a trained intimacy coordinator, such as *The Deuce, Euphoria, Wu-Tang: An American Saga* or *Bridgerton*, would be ideal for this exercise.)

To get started,

- Watch the scene all the way through to follow the arch of the story and to track general movements.
- Watch a second time with a focus on broad intimate movements of the characters, and notate these movements using your own shorthand notation.
- Watch the scene again, look for more specific elements found within the Intimacy Mapping section of this chapter.

As you watch the scene, try to watch from start to finish as though watching a run-through in rehearsal, instead of stopping and starting the video. You may want to play the content several times in a row, as though watching multiple run-throughs in rehearsal.

Questions to ask include

- Can you determine which character initiates movement, or can you get a sense of the duration of their movements?
- Which character closes or opens distance during the scene?
- Does one of the characters use audio cues or breath to tell the story?
- Where are their eyes focused? What shapes do their bodies make?

With the goal of identifying specific elements used within intimacy mapping while watching scenes of filmed intimacy, one can begin to train the eye to notice nuances of storytelling in live performance as well. Practicing notation in this manner helps one to understand how the layering of action and intention allow complex stories to be told clearly and concisely.

Notes

1 Zoom interview with Claire Warden and authors Newhauser and Black, Apr. 26, 2021.
2 "Actors Equity Announces New 'President's Committee To Prevent Harassment.'" *Actorsequity.org*, 2018, https://Www.actorsequity.org/News/PR/PresidentsCommittee/. Accessed Feb. 2021.
3 Concept described by certified ID Sarah Lozoff during the curriculum development for IDC's Stage Managing Intimacy course, first taught Summer 2020.
4 Developed by Black and Newhauser as part of the curriculum development for IDC's Stage Managing Intimacy course, first taught Summer 2020. www.idcprofessionals.com
5 Rikard, Laura, quoted in Redman, Bridgette. "Adopt Best Practices into Theatrical Intimacy Work." *Onstage Blog*, Nov. 8, 21, https://www.onstageblog.com/editorials/2021/8/5/adopt-best-practices-into-theatrical-intimacy-work.
6 Pace, Chelsea.. *Staging Sex: Best Practices, Tools, and Techniques for Theatrical Intimacy*. Routledge. 2020, https://www.amazon.com/Staging-Sex-Practices-Techniques-Theatrical/dp/1138596493.
7 Concept shared with Alexis Black during mentorship under Alicia Rodis in intimacy direction, 2017.
8 Concept discussed in relationship to intimacy direction during February 2019 "Intimacy Directors International O'Neill 9-day Intensive" in-person training attended by Alexis Black. Training held at Eugene O'Neill Theatre Center, Waterford, CT.

9 Concept discussed in relationship to intimacy direction during February 2019 "Intimacy Directors International O'Neill 9-day Intensive" in-person training attended by Alexis Black. Training held at Eugene O'Neill Theatre Center, Waterford, CT.
10 Mingus, Mia. "The Four Parts of Accountability: How to Give a Genuine Apology, Part 1," *Leaving Evidence*, Dec. 18, 2019, https://leavingevidence.wordpress.com/2019/12/18/how-to-give-a-good-apology-part-1-the-four-parts-of-accountability/. Accessed May, 2021.
11 Kardia Group LLC. "Intent vs. Impact: Narrowing the Gap." August 6, 2020, https://kardiagroup.com/intent-vs-impact-narrowing-the-gap/. Accessed May, 2021.
12 *Chicago Theatre Standards* December 11, 2017, p. 32, https://www.notinourhouse.org/wp-content/uploads/Chicago-Theatre-Standards-12-11-17.pdf. Accessed May, 2021
13 Mapping element descriptions were expanded and adapted from concepts shared at the "Intimacy Directors International O'Neill 9-day Intensive" in-person training, held in Waterford, CT, February 2019.
14 Pace, Chelsea, with contributions by Laura Rikard. *Staging Sex, Best Practices, Tools, and Techniques for Theatrical Intimacy*. Routledge. Taylor & Francis Group. 2020.
15 Noble, Adam. "Sex & Violence: Practical Approaches for Dealing with Extreme Stage Physicality." *The Fight Master*, Spring 2011, https://earlhamtheatrearts.files.wordpress.com/2018/06/extreme-stage-physicality-adam-noble.pdf.
16 www.davidsleong.com
17 Quoted from discussions during mentorship for Alexis Black at Virginia Commonwealth University, 2014–2016.
18 Interview conducted January 26, 2021, Alexis Black, Brian Bogin, Laurie Goldfeder, Tina Newhauser.
19 Concept introduced in relation to fight direction by David Leong during mentorship for Alexis Black at Virginia Commonwealth University, 2014–2016.

5
Technical and dress rehearsals

Collaborating with care

Technical and dress rehearsals are an opportunity for all elements in the production to finally come together. Moving into the performance space and adding design elements often energizes the entire team as they feel opening night drawing near. There are many moving parts during this exciting time, and knowing how to plan ahead can help mitigate any issues with consent or safety that could occur due to rushed time frames or fatigue. With preparation and awareness on the part of those already behind the scenes, along with methods to orient any new team members joining the process, bringing staged intimacy to technical rehearsals and runs can be incorporated seamlessly and safely.

This chapter details some key terminology, recommended practices, and protocols that should be undertaken during this exciting and challenging time, through the following sections:

- Moving into the theater
- Communication and crew
- Accommodations for actors
- Intimacy captains
- Intimacy movement calls

> **Key terms in Chapter 5**[*]
>
> **Consent check-ins**
>
> Brief check-ins to see if any adjustments need to be discussed regarding set choreography due to a shift in boundaries, an injury, an illness
>
> [*] *See Terms & Language Acknowledgement and Glossary of Key Terms in Appendix E for citations, trainings and reference materials that informed definitions.*

requiring a return to a placeholder, or other circumstances (new venue sightlines when on tour, for example). These check-ins may occur during warm-ups, movement calls, or at the actors' daily call, and may consist of a phrase such as "Is there anything new I should know about today?" Consent check-ins often replace boundary checks (defined in Chapter 4) after choreography has been set. If significant changes need to occur to choreography, the intimacy professional and director should be contacted to set and rehearse these adjustments.

Intimacy captain

The person responsible for maintaining movements involved in intimate storytelling while supporting safety and consent practices during the intimacy call and performance. They are also responsible for maintaining communication between actors and necessary team members (SM, IDs, Directors or more) in regard to actor well-being and storytelling throughout the run of a production.

Intimacy movement call

An "intimacy call" is similar to a fight call when stage combat is present in a production, and also may be called a "movement and safety call." This is a brief rehearsal before a performance that is set aside for the actors to check in with one another, reaffirm boundary agreements, and assess if there are any obstacles that need to be addressed. Preferably, movement calls are scheduled only when the intimate physical movement is demanding or complex and involves movement such as leaps, catches, falls, or other strenuous physical actions. These calls may also be scheduled if requested by actors performing in these scenes.

Moving into the theater

When the time comes to move into the theater as technical rehearsals approach, early and open communication regarding how the show will progress is imperative. Information about staged intimacy may need to be provided to the production's various technical departments, such as run crew, company management, production management, designers, front-of-house (FOH), ushers, and custodial staff. Basically, anyone who may have access to the theater space during the technical rehearsal process will need to be informed about when areas will be accessible, when they will not, how moments of intimacy will be handled while adding technical elements, and more. This company information should provide expectations as well as explain personnel requests to prevent any surprises.

Company information regarding staged intimacy during technical rehearsals may include the following:

- When intimate staging takes place within the production and a rough schedule of when those moments will be spaced on set and rehearsed, and if these rehearsals will be closed.
- The company's closed rehearsal protocols, such as who will be permitted to stay in the theater or backstage during closed rehearsals and when the stage and theater space may be off-limits to the company.
- Clarifications on signage that will be posted on theater doors, when closed rehearsals are in process, to prevent individuals from coming into the theater at inopportune moments.
- A directive that cell phones and recording devices will not be permitted in the theater during staging and run-through rehearsals that involve scenes with intimate staging (to avoid any video or images being taken without permission of performers). This refers to both open and closed rehearsals.
- Content notices (written and/or verbal) for the staged intimacy, especially if nudity, simulated sex acts, or sexual violence is being depicted.
- The context behind intimate material within the show, especially if emotionally charged or violent. (Research or resource material may be provided to help clarify context as requested or when recommended.)

We highly recommend that company communications begin at least one week before starting the technical rehearsal process. This way, questions and potential issues may be addressed and information shared throughout departments before tech week begins. Based on the staffing structure of an institution, this communication may be sent from stage, company, or production management and should include everyone involved with the production.

Notes from the field ... moving into the Broadhurst Theatre

Laurie Goldfeder, Production Stage Manager for the 2019 revival of Frankie and Johnny *in the Clair de Lune (the first Broadway production to have an ID on their creative team) recalls the company's pre-tech communications as they were preparing to move into the Broadhurst Theatre.*

The team was guided by the general management office to communicate clearly with the entire production staff: crew, FOH, cleaning staff, anyone who would be in the theater during technical rehearsals. This was in the form of an emailed memo that clearly and thoroughly communicated everything about the show regarding intimate moments and what would transpire. Recalling this memo, Ms. Goldfeder shared, "The good part of that memo was that it was clear to everyone what was going to happen, and there were no surprises. So, if you were locked out of the theater that day, which was really only one time for maybe half an hour, I didn't have to then turn to everyone in the theater and say "everyone get out." They knew it was going to happen. Everyone was asked to leave except maybe five people, which is very unusual. No assistants were allowed; no crew was allowed; no FOH staff; no one. And that's a real closed rehearsal. When they say closed rehearsal, sometimes there are still 30 people in there. And then after that day everyone was allowed in, and the cast was very comfortable. It was the first time the actors rehearsed the scene with technical elements and with no clothes. Extreme care was taken for their ability to feel comfortable and confident in this moment."

Clear and concise communication helps to create a workplace environment where everyone feels informed and respected, creating an inclusive, supportive culture.

Laurie Goldfeder
(she/her/hers)
AEA Stage Manager

Communication and crew

As the production prepares to move into the theater, plans to bring together designers, cast, crew, theatre administrators and staff are taking place. This is also the time to inform those who are new to the production and will be working closely with the team regarding the intimate content that takes place within the production. This can be achieved with a simple gathering at the start of technical rehearsals.

Crew orientation

At the beginning of tech week, as rehearsals get started, the intimacy professional (such as an intimacy director) may conduct an orientation meeting with the production crew, similar to the orientation provided to the acting company at the beginning of rehearsals. This crew orientation aims to provide everyone who will be taking part in technical rehearsals or running the show, information regarding the production's intimate moments (such as content and context) and provide time to connect in-person about essential protocols. Overall communications may cover any number of the following points:

- Information on sexual harassment and reporting
- Notices about explicit or challenging content
- Mental health resources if there is explicit or challenging content
- Explanation of desexualized language and other professional communication practices
- Other workplace etiquette reminders as needed in connection with the context of the staged intimacy
- Clarification of protocols regarding actor costume changing areas, or any exits utilized after staged nudity
- Protocols around photographic and other recording devices

While some of the above and other more basic protocols may be shared via email or through crew department heads ahead of time, some time for in-person connection at the start of technical rehearsals is recommended. Being in the same room simultaneously with the intimacy director (ID) allows for consistency in the protocols being communicated and provides an opportunity for questions or clarifications in the moment.

Backstage access

When considering the transition from the rehearsal hall to the theater, both onstage and backstage environments should be considered. Oftentimes, backstage areas may be accessed by many more groups than just stage management, actors, and run crew. These offstage areas, including hallways, bathrooms and dressing rooms, may be open to a wide variety of individuals who work for the production company or theater facility, cleaning crews, security officers, and more. Due to this unknown list of personnel who may have the opportunity to wander backstage and the impact that may create regarding privacy, these spaces need to be thoughtfully considered for productions that contain charged content.

In preparation for the technical rehearsal process and considering traffic patterns that will exist backstage, a few things should be considered for those navigating this space. First and foremost is access for actors, especially when intimacy is involved. There are a few key questions to ask when determining the needs for the backstage space:

- What space will performers need to access, and what setup will be required to accommodate their needs?
- Where will costume quick-change areas or private spaces need to be set up?
- Who will need access to these spaces, and who will not?
- How can spaces be organized to allow for actor privacy, crew accessibility, safety and ease?
- Will these spaces need to be closed off to others at certain moments during the performance to accommodate performers' privacy? If so, will additional masking or curtains need to be installed to allow for ease and speed of access? How can we best communicate when access is limited?

Each production will have its own unique requirements; what is crucial is looking at these backstage spaces with a mindful eye for those who will navigate them as part of the run of the production, while also accommodating the needs of the entire creative team.

Camera use and visibility

It can be standard practice for productions to use cameras and monitors backstage to aid with visibility for those performing in and running the show. Cameras may focus on everything from the front view, musical director, and backstage areas to scenic pieces, automation, and trap rooms. These "extra sets of eyes" become necessary for stage management and crew to maintain safety, call cues, and watch automated scenery and actor movements. These cameras may also make visible things that shouldn't be, such as when working on a production that contains nudity. When cameras/monitors are being used on productions involving staged nudity during technical rehearsals, stage management and crew should be mindful of what is being displayed on these monitors when staged nudity is being performed. When nudity is happening onstage, consider whether the cameras need to stay on or if they can be temporarily turned off to prevent the streaming of actors performing nude to every monitor located throughout the theater. This consideration is especially crucial during technical rehearsals when every designer, assistant, and manager may also have a video monitor on their tech table located throughout the house. Turning off monitors as part of the technical process as cues are being worked, whenever possible, shows consideration and care for those on stage and off. After working through the play, setting and running cues, and as technical elements are becoming solidified, stage management can work with the crew to determine if and when any cameras will still need to be turned off or remain on for final run-throughs as opening night approaches.

If using infrared cameras that provide visibility during blackouts and extremely dim lighting, consider turning off this camera as well unless it is vital for safely executing cues. While infrared cameras are beneficial during dark scenes, the privacy of performers should be taken into account and accommodated whenever possible.

> **Notes from the field ... consistency in communication**
>
> *During the 2020 Broadway Stage Management Symposium, founder Matt Stern hosted a panel discussion on intimacy direction during which stage manager Jhanaë Bonnick shared their team's method of communication when staging intimate moments during Broadway's* Slave Play.
>
> Bonnick recalled that while in the rehearsal hall for *Slave Play*, "the signage for outside the doors used a red/yellow/green streetlight sort of approach. The signs informed the company that if the room was totally open, this was a 'green light;' You could come and go as you needed to based on what was being rehearsed. The next level was more cautionary; this informed the company that sensitive material was being rehearsed so you needed to wait until a break was called to enter. The last level was a full stop or a 'red light,' informing those in the hall that it was a completely closed rehearsal. For this, those in the room were the only ones permitted, and if you needed to enter, even during a break, you had to text stage management first and check to see if you were permitted. This method was very clear and kept the entire team feeling informed and comfortable in what was expected during the entire rehearsal process. This also helped to keep visitors informed so they didn't accidentally barge into rehearsal during a particularly sensitive or vulnerable moment.
>
> This method of communication was used twice; first in the rehearsal room when initial staging was taking place, and again in the John Golden Theatre when these moments were being staged and adjusted during technical rehearsals on set. Repeating this method of communication

made the transition into the theater much easier because the acting, management, and design company was already familiar with this method. Once moving into the theater, adding an entirely new group of individuals from FOH to the crew, they just needed to be informed of the signage used and what it meant. Now the entire team is in the know and rehearsals can flow more easily."

This experience illuminates how important it is to maintain established methods of communication when transitioning into the performance venue. Whether verbalized or conveyed through the use of signs or other methods of communication, consistency is key for clarity and ease within established community agreements.

Matthew Aaron Stern
(he/him/his)
Broadway Stage Management Symposium
Founder & Executive Director
Jhanaë Bonnick
(she/her/hers)
AEA Stage Manager

Accommodations for actors

When working with staged intimacy, some accommodations may need to be made for the physical or psychological comfort of the actors and those in the wings during technical rehearsals. These accommodations may include the reintegration of placeholders, specified accessories, and a mindful look at quick-change procedures.

Placeholders when adding technical elements

In Chapter 3 we discussed protocols for early rehearsals of intimacy, which included the use of placeholders. These substituted movements may need to be utilized again during the long technical rehearsal period for the comfort of the performers. If the final kiss of Act One is being run by performers numerous times for the designers and director to finalize setting cues, these actors could utilize a kiss placeholder of cheek-to-cheek while working with the same hand placements, body movements, and timing that would happen while making the lip-to-lip contact without needing to perform the kiss repeatedly. For simulated sex acts, actors can mark through movements or use substitutions as well until the final couple of runs. For staged sexual violence, actors can use both physical and emotional substitutions to avoid unnecessary fatigue or trauma to their voices, bodies, or emotional health.

Overall, using placeholders[1] during technical rehearsals is one way to support performers who may be experiencing fatigue from repetitive physical movement. During these rehearsals, the focus is mostly on design elements and cuing, so the actual act of lip-to-lip contact is not as important to maintain. Allowing the actors to "mark" this action with placeholders will make it easier for them to maintain physical positions and repeat movement during the long hours of tech week. Utilizing stand-in movements may also help to mitigate the spread of illnesses, such as colds.

Accessories

We explored the need for accessories during early rehearsals in Chapter 3, and as we move into the theater and are preparing for technical rehearsals, it is worth a revisit. Some accessories may have been needed only during rehearsals, when movement is being created, due to the amount of repetition occurring with those movements or other concerns. Now that staging is mostly set, actors may find that they no longer want or need them. But temporary use of some accessories may still be wise as we prepare for the long hours of tech and dress rehearsals. In addition, some items, such as dance belts, athletic cups, briefs, adhesive modesty patches, or skin-colored garments of various types, may need to be added as costumes are introduced. For moments in tech where actors are engaging in the intimate staging for longer periods of time, or waiting for technical adjustments, the use of skin-colored body stockings may be an appropriate option to maintain modesty while allowing for lighting and other departments to create their stage picture. It may also be helpful to have robes at the ready for performers either on stage or nearby off-stage when rehearsal is paused for longer periods of time.

At times, these accessories may not feel necessary to an actor, but may support professional etiquette in the space. For example, an actor may not object to walking around nude during long technical rehearsals, but this is not an appropriate situation for the director, crew or designers also working these moments. Consent culture is for all members of the creative team.

Costumes: quick changes and crew

One area of design that usually comes to mind when working on productions that contain intimate or physical storytelling is costuming. Given the inherent personal nature of this area of design and the proximity to actors' personal space, it makes sense to apply the same care and consensual practices found in intimacy work to this area of design, especially when approaching technical rehearsals. Reflecting on the production pillars outlined in Chapter 1, one can easily apply this approach when integrating costumes into the production. The way in which interactions are established and relationships are built when bringing together cast and wardrobe crew can be achieved through open and mindful communication when considering the following:

- Costumes, changes, and dressing room locations
- Wardrobe personnel and proximity to actors' bodies
- Quick changes that need to take place backstage or on set
- Choreographing quick changes in regard to speed and actor privacy
- Establishing a working relationship between actor and wardrobe crew when personal touch is required

This approach to the work was expertly explored in an article titled "Offstage Intimacy: Best Practices for Navigating the Intimacy of Costuming" and is highlighted in the costume spotlight below.

 Creative team spotlight: Costumes

"Offstage Intimacy: Best Practices for Navigating the Intimacy of Costuming"

Authors Daugherty, Hertzberg, and Wagner state in their article for Johns Hopkins University Press that when working backstage with actors and costume crew, "Whenever practical, costume changes should happen in the dressing room. However, we acknowledge that this is not always best in the logistics of a particular production. The next best option is to find an area backstage that will facilitate the storage of costumes and the space to layout presets for quick changes. If possible, this should be separated from the rest of the backstage area by a curtain or temporary room divider to offer some privacy for costume changes. It is usually necessary to consult with the technical director and/or stage manager about this. As with any part of running a show, quick changes must be rehearsed or choreographed with the actor, wardrobe attendant, and the wardrobe supervisor or designer. First, provide an opportunity for introductions and the exchange of consent. Similar to choreographed onstage intimacy, costume changes should be crafted as a series of physical actions that are specific and repeatable. Identify which costume pieces are coming off and which are going on and establish a choreography for the change. Identify who is responsible for handling each piece of clothing, accessories, and even the process of fastening and securing the garment. These changes should be worked through slowly at first to allow for the planning of the mechanics of the change and incorporating any necessary adjustments. Once the changes can be done accurately, speed can be increased. Continued check-ins between actor and wardrobe attendant will aid in furthering open communication and comfort. Run the change enough times so that everyone involved knows their movement and timing. As the quick change is integrated into the overall backstage sequence, any other members of the backstage crew should be included in the conversations regarding context and consent as they become part of (even peripherally) the intimate backstage environment." Incorporating the entire production team into the process of choreographing movement both onstage and off is crucial and necessary when maintaining a supportive and consensual workspace, especially when staging intimate stories.

Authors
Elaine DiFalco Daugherty
(she/her/hers)
Central Michigan University
Deborah Hertzberg
(she/her/hers)
Brooklyn College
Darrell Wagner
(he/him/his)
Casper College

Scenic and properties

Scenic and properties teams have a consistent focus on actor safety, and this same level of attention should be applied to scenes of intimacy. Specific issues that may require attention from scenic design may include set dressing that incorporates bed padding required for a scene of simulated sex or strategic adjustments to a set piece in order to provide coverage or masking for actors engaging in a story of intimacy. Certain movements may also require extra safety considerations, such as a safety mat for two actors rolling off a bed, or extra set bracing for an intimate yet violent moment when an actor is pushed against a wall. It is important that constant communication between scenic and prop designers, technical director, director, intimacy director, and stage management be maintained. Connecting prior to tech regarding intimate staging and how it relates to scenic elements is crucial. Making sure there is open dialogue between those in the rehearsal room and those in the shops, especially in the early stages of choreography, will help to ensure that the transition to the stage can be seamless.

Lighting

Lighting designers may also need to be made aware of certain requirements that result from the staging of moments of intimacy. Communicating these actions and needs, such as requesting a quick black-out to preserve actor modesty or support storytelling, will assist designers as they conduct pre-production planning and cuing.

There may also be contractual obligations that involve areas of design that are linked to moments of nudity or transitional movements between intimate scenes; these will need to be considered. Requests may be made from the actor and agreed to during the contracting stage, as part of the mutual agreements around the performance of intimate staging. These negotiations may include limitations to lighting; an actor who will appear nude may negotiate very dim lighting that is more sculptural or provides only a silhouette of the body to the audience, for example. Finally, lighting designers may need to be informed about modesty garments, such as a nude body stocking or a robe, that may be worn by an actor during tech rehearsals. These temporary coverings may impact lighting levels and looks during the creation stage.

Sound

Sound design may also have considerations regarding staged intimacy, including navigating lavalier battery pack placement, especially if actors appear scantily clad or if there is staged nudity. Sound designers may also want to have additional conversations around soundscapes or environmental music that relates to or enhances intimate staging. Maintaining communication with the staged intimacy professional, director, and stage management throughout the process will help to inform and prepare the sound department and avoid any surprises.

> **Creative team spotlight:**
> **Sound department and mic packs**
>
> When working backstage on productions that will be using lavalier body microphones for the actors, the same care and attention that wardrobe and costume crew will take when executing quick changes should be applied to the sound crew when mic'ing up actors. Determining microphone placement on actors' bodies can be a puzzle. Finding the right location on their body where the mic pack can securely and comfortably live, while not being visible or impeding the actor's ability to freely move, is often a challenge. This challenge, while not unusual, will frequently result in strategic placement in very vulnerable locations. When this is the case, and in all instances when a sound person needs to assist with the placement of a mic pack on an actor's body, respectful and consensual practices are required. One may look to similar recommendations regarding costume quick changes by finding a private location for mic placements to occur.
>
> When an actor is unable to place their own mic pack on their person, always have at least two individuals, in addition to the actor, there to assist with placement. The technician placing the mic should maintain a professional demeanor and always inform the actor where they will need to touch in order to place the mic pack. Ask for permission prior to touching the actor and maintain a proper distance when not adjusting or placing the mic. Communicate with the actor by informing them of what you will need to do in order to place the mic, and using desexualized, neutral language, inform them (before placing hands on their person) where you will need to touch. This practice may seem awkward at first, but by creating a step-by-step routine that is repeated for every performance, this action will easily become a quick professional action that is respectful of all parties involved.

Intimacy captains

When it comes to maintaining set intimacy choreography or staging, exploring the position of an "intimacy captain" may be an option for the team. Similar to the position of a fight captain or dance captain, an intimacy captain is an individual whose focus is to maintain the safety of the physical movements that make up choreographed intimate staging.

The responsibilities of the intimacy captain in rehearsals may include observing and confirming that intimate physical movements are being maintained as choreographed or discussed during rehearsal runs and serving as a liaison of communication between actors and stage management as well as director and assistant director or intimacy professional when necessary. During the run, intimacy captains may run an intimacy or movement call, serving as an imperative outside eye for the actors in order to make sure that angles and sightlines for masked moments are being maintained. They may bring up changes or shifts to set staging that occurred during a run of the show as a reminder for the actors in order to maintain choreography for the duration of the production. They may also assist the stage manager (and possibly the director, assistant director or intimacy professional if they are brought back in) when understudies or replacements are being rehearsed in preparation for performance, which will be discussed more in chapter six.

Candidates for intimacy captain

If an intimacy captain will be utilized, it is recommended that the team discuss with the intimacy professional, such as an intimacy director, as to who would be the most qualified or appropriate individual to serve in this capacity and maintain the movement. There are many different mindsets when it comes to the training of an intimacy captain. For example, Ann C. James, founder of Intimacy Coordinators of Color, offers an Intimacy Captain Certificate workshop that aims to create "safer rehearsals and braver performances, for union and non-union actors and allies."[2] Other specialists may prefer to work one on one to train someone project by project, perhaps to support that ensemble or choreography's individualized needs and vocabulary, or to ensure the intimacy captain's working methods are appropriate. Whatever the approach, there will be differing opinions regarding who should serve as the intimacy captain, or whether one is necessary, and these variations are based on the needs of the production and working philosophy of the intimacy professional. What is important to keep in mind when exploring the position of intimacy captain is that supporting actor boundaries and safety while maintaining the story is key.

For some staged intimacy professionals or intimacy directors, the most appropriate individual to serve as the intimacy captain may be determined to be a member of the acting company. The ID may choose a member of the acting company because of known prior experience or qualifications around intimacy, similar to how the fight director chooses a fight captain or a dance choreographer chooses a dance captain. However, choosing an actor should not be a lightly made decision; complicated staged intimacy inherently contains more liability and requires a nuanced understanding of consent practices and power dynamics. If using a performer for this position, they should have staged intimacy training, not be engaged in the staged intimacy they are observing, and not have the position of cast deputy or any position of power on the creative team (such as an assistant director also acting in the show) to balance the dynamics of power. They also should be willing to not attempt to choreograph or adjust any of the moments without approval of the staged intimacy professional and the production's director.

Other intimacy professionals believe that if an intimacy captain is needed, it should be a member of the stage management team. Claire Warden (IDC-certified intimacy director/coordinator and Broadway's first intimacy director) believes this choice directly relates to power structures and may help to alleviate or prevent any complications.[3] Stage management is in the room when the movement and staging is being set, and they have an eye on the actors as they navigate choreographed movements throughout multiple rehearsals. From the repetition of viewing, they will know the specific moments of staging that raised challenges when setting movement and the moments that were set more confidently. Stage managers and assistant stage managers are usually the most familiar with movement and content within the show due to this consistent and attentive connection to the production.

Whoever is chosen to serve as intimacy captain, it is preferred that they be fully trained in consent-based practices whenever possible. However, their main objectives should be those as described in Chapter 4: maintaining movement with an emphasis on safety, boundaries, and storytelling. Intimacy captains should also be clinical in their observations, trying not to design or redesign moments. They should have access to clear notation and understand the elements involved. They should know who to report to if there are any changes, such as the need for adjustments or placeholders for a specific day, and know who to connect with regarding any incidents or issues if something should arise. They should be able to witness the intimacy during the show as well as beforehand to maintain or give notes accurately.

Finally, intimacy captains preferably will have worked alongside the intimacy professional hired for that particular production. Their working relationship may not have necessarily been that of an assistant but may have allowed the chosen intimacy captain to be deeply aware of the established language, set movements, and processes unique to this directing team, ensemble, and production.

Intimacy captains in the industry

In regard to the actors' union for live performance, as of publication, there was no mention of the position of "intimacy captain" in their various rulebooks.[4] It will be interesting to see where the industry moves as this new practice takes hold and the role of the intimacy captain develops and evolves. With other captains such as fight and dance, these position-holders are sometimes actors who receive a role in the ensemble due to their expertise and relationship with the choreographer. This creates the opportunity for their expertise to aid in building a more trustworthy relationship with the entire team, but is not always possible. If an intimacy captain is chosen after casting has occurred from the acting ensemble, careful consideration must occur in league with the intimacy professional. An overall goal would be not to empower an intimacy captain to do the work of an ID, but to empower them to step in and maintain the ID's work (as long as they have the proper training to do so).

Intimacy movement calls

Movement calls are common for fights, dance, and other moments in shows that require a quick reminder for safety or storytelling. The same may be necessary for staged intimacy. The first questions that should be discussed with the intimacy professional, stage manager, and actors are Should there be an intimacy call? If so, what moments should be included?

When determining answers to these questions, it is recommended that the intimacy professional, cast members, stage management, and director meet to consider the needs of production team members, choreographed movements, and the confidence of the actors involved in those moments. To expand, a movement call may be necessary due to the following factors:

- *Cuing/Production*—If the action is complicated and connected to technical cues that need to be executed identically night after night, the stage management team may request a call to mark or run those moments.
- *Physicality*—If the choreography includes any physical movements that are demanding or complex and involve actions such as leaps, catches, falls, or other strenuous action, a movement call may be needed to maintain safety.
- *Inconsistency*—If, during the run, set movement is noticeably changing, the intimacy professional, director, stage manager, actors, or intimacy captain may request a movement call to reestablish the set choreography.
- *Performer confidence*—Confidence is essential; there may be a time when an actor asks to have a call so they can walk through a moment for their own level of comfort. Whether or not this movement seems consistent or physically simple from the outside, the movement call should be scheduled.

Whatever the reason, safety and storytelling are paramount and accommodating the needs of the actors as well as the needs of the production is key.

If moments are recommended for movement call, the following should also be considered:

- Do the actors and creatives believe these should be done full out or marked through with placeholders? (This may adjust from moment to moment or from night to night)
- Do any technical elements need to be included in this run-through, such as a set piece, costume piece, or a lighting shift, and who else would need to be involved in the call due to this?

Intimacy captains and stage management should also include the following practices:

- Encouragement that the intimacy movement call is in a space that is not completely private. This space needs to be safe but not create a situation where actors work alone with the intimacy captain.
- Flexibility in adaptations to movement call for long-running shows. There may be a need for intimacy calls at every show early in the run,

but this can adjust to once weekly or bi-weekly as the run progresses (with brush-ups as necessary).
- Creation of a clear communication or reporting process. Actors may wish to request that an intimacy moment be added to the call at a later date, or actors who are experiencing any issues with the movement or their fellow performer(s) may need to communicate these issues.
- Creation of a clear communication process for actors who may feel, once you are into the run of the production, that an intimacy call is no longer needed. However, note that for a movement call to be removed all actors involved, stage management, and the intimacy professional (when applicable) should be in agreement.
- Methods for check-ins with the intimacy professional as needed throughout the run. If the moment of intimacy seems off, there should always be the possibility to contact the ID. This contact could be a request to have them come in to take a look at the movement or to speak with the actors to see what they feel is off.
- Establishing a plan for replacements or understudies (discussed in Chapter 6).

Through communication and the utilization of the recommended practices that fit their situation, the intimacy captains, intimacy professionals, and stage managers can work together to determine how best to accommodate the needs of the production.

Notes from the field ... intimacy calls

Marie Percy, Chief Content Officer and certified Intimacy Director with IDC, spoke with us about the routine of conducting nightly intimacy calls and the established structure she has found to work well.

I always have an intimacy movement call consisting of these simple steps:

1. How did the choreography go last time?
2. Are we good to go with what we usually do, or do we need to make any adjustments tonight?
3. Do we need to mark through anything tonight?
4. If they say yes to adjustments or marking, then we take time to work with the choreography in that way.

> A structured intimacy call is important. Having formal time scheduled for the conversation normalizes the practice of giving and receiving ongoing consent, even if nothing is actually marked or adjusted.
>
>
>
> Marie C. Percy
> (she/her/hers)
> Intimacy Director/Choreographer/Movement Specialist
> Laban Certified Movement Analyst & Registered Yoga Teacher
>
>

When working with intimacy movement calls, it should be noted that "fully acting" each moment is not always a requirement. In fact, if there is highly charged emotional content, it may not be a helpful practice for actors to experience it more often than necessary. The point of these calls is to assist the performers and stage management team in maintaining confident performances of these moments. If working with full emotional stakes is necessary for the safety, consistency or timing of the moment, the emotional content can be negotiated, but the hope is that the actors are able to work through these moments with the correct mechanics without creating any unnecessary physical, vocal, or emotional strain prior to performance. Just as fights, dance, or acrobatics can be "marked" through during pre-show calls, this may be the case for staged intimacy choreography as well.

Chapter reflection

Technical rehearsals are a time when the culture of consent integrated into the rehearsal process can be fully introduced to the creative and production teams. The addition of new designers and more assistants, along with theater staff and run crew, means there are more individuals who will not only become involved in the production's process but will also be introduced to the production's staged intimacy. This is a time when intimate storytelling shifts from the creation phase to the preservation phase. It is during this phase that the company will build confidence and consistency in the execution of these moments. With patience and preplanning, clear communication and thoughtful attention to detail, the practices launched and established in rehearsal can be incorporated and normalized for every member of the production team. With these tools, everyone behind the scenes can support staged intimacy not only during the technical process but through to opening night, during the run, and beyond.

Chapter discussion / exercise / activity

Discussion on perspectives

While this chapter has explored technical rehearsals from a professional theatre perspective, an interesting topic for discussion is, What happens when we look at this from an academic perspective? When your creative and production team is composed entirely of students, how might that affect the way in which you bring these different departments together and how might you approach establishing and maintaining the practices described in this chapter? Explore these protocols from the perspective of a student:

- Designer
- Crew member
- Cast member
- Technician
- Front of house staff/usher
- Other

Extend this exploration to other disciplines within live performance. How might these practices be integrated into the various needs of technical rehearsals when working in

- Opera
- Cruise Ships
- Theme Parks
- Circus
- Dance
- Other

Notes

1 Concept discussed in relationship to intimacy direction during February 2019 "Intimacy Directors International O'Neill 9-day Intensive" in-person training attended by Alexis Black. Training held at Eugene O'Neill Theatre Center, Waterford, CT. Concept is also discussed in multiple publications, including 2020's *Staging Sex* by Chelsea Pace.

2 James, Ann C. "Courses by ICOC EDU." *Ann C. James*, Feb. 2022, https://anncjamesintimacy.com/icoc-edu/.
3 Zoom Interview with Claire Warden and authors Newhauser and Black, April 2021.
4 Several attempts were made by the authors to communicate with staff from Actors Equity Association about this topic. While AEA did reply to emails, they did not respond to requests for information.

6
Running the show

Continuity and closure

Once the show opens, and the production slowly starts to settle into its groove, the team may begin to feel a sense of ease. Now, the creative machine is fully assembled, and those who will keep it running establish a routine where everyone knows their job and can perform their role; operating procedures become set. Yet every machine requires maintenance, attention, and safety checks. It may need a replacement part, a tweak or two, or recalibration every so often. This chapter details methods for this stage of preservation or upkeep, including terminology, recommended practices, and protocols for supporting intimate staging until the final curtain call.

Through the topics listed below, this chapter will explore ways to responsibly introduce understudies or replacements into intimacy choreography, how to maintain choreography during a long run, and methods to support mental health and closure practices for cast and crew. The full list of sections is listed below:

- Adding the audience
- Standard checking in and out
- Maintaining performance for the long run
- Tips for note-giving during the maintenance of staged intimacy
- Understudies and replacements
- Accommodations while touring
- Transference energy and responsible communication
- Emotional resilience and self-care
- Building a closure practice

During ongoing maintenance, it is necessary to ensure that the entire team understands how to best work with and maintain staged intimacy so that the story established in final rehearsals is still the one told in performance.

> **Key terms in Chapter 6**[*]
>
> **Audience content notice**—written or verbal notices that are intended to inform the audience of content that will be explored within a staged theatrical production. Content may range from special effects (gunshots, smoke, haze, or strobe effects), charged physical interactions (intimacy, sexual or domestic violence, abuse) to strong language and/or sensitive themes.
>
> **Replacement performer**—an actor who takes over a role when the current actor performing that role leaves the production.
>
> **Show advance**—the verbal and written communication(s) between the staff of the presenting organization and the touring production when details, requirements, and schedule are clarified and confirmed before the tour's arrival at the venue. Based on the size and scope of the touring production, their communications may begin anywhere from one month, one week, to one day before the tour's scheduled arrival and performance.
>
> **Technical rider**—an addendum to a touring production's contract that sets forth their specific technical, production, hospitality, and other requirements or accommodations that need to be provided or arranged for by the presenting organization.
>
> **Understudy performer**—an actor hired to learn the part(s) of another actor in a production, so that they can replace them on short notice if necessary (i.e., if the actor is sick or unable to perform).
>
> [*] *See Terms & Language Acknowledgement and Glossary of Key Terms in Appendix E for citations, trainings and reference materials that informed definitions.*

Adding the audience

Introducing an audience to a new reality, one that has been created just for them is a moment like no other. As temporary residents in this new world, the audience members become a vital part of the experience and must be welcomed with care and consideration, especially when exploring charged content and staged intimacy. Some of the processes used during early rehearsals to inform actors or production team members are revisited here to create an environment in which the audience can confidently choose to experience this new world of the play.

Audience content notices

Chapter 3 discussed content notices regarding informing both actors and the creative team of show content. Similarly, audience content notices are used to notify incoming observers of the subject matter to be explored and executed within a specific production. Informing consumers of content is standard practice in most industries, seen everywhere from ingredients in packaged materials to notices popping up at the beginning of movies, TV shows, and live entertainment. Notices used for productions are not there to restrict creativity in any way; nor are they intended to assume that consumers cannot handle the experience. Instead, this information allows the audience to decide for themselves whether or not to engage with that material. Every observer comes to the creative arts with unique lived experiences; what may cause discomfort for one may not do so for another. By neutrally informing the audience of what content will be explored, it not only allows them to consider in advance whether that experience is one they wish to have, but it also builds a stronger relationship with them through considerate and mindful communication.

When presenting theatrical work containing intimacy, intimate content, violence, strong language, or visual and atmospheric effects, one should always explore the material with an eye toward what may be considered sensitive or provoking for the consumer. What experiences may members of an audience have had, and how may the content of the production resonate? In order to include the audience within a culture of care, providing this information is a must.

Below is a partial list of what may be appropriate to include in content notices:

- Simulated sex acts
- Simulated sexual assault or abuse
- Nudity
- Charged racial/gender/ableism content or language
- Graphic violence
- Stories of self-harm/suicide
- Prop firearms or sound of gunshots
- Haze/smoke/smoking
- Strobe or rhythmic light effects

Methods for sharing content notice information vary between types of institutions and kinds of productions, but may include the following:

- Emailed information for those who purchased tickets in advance
- Information made accessible and clearly posted on the company's website for the event, especially on pages where tickets are purchased
- Requiring an acknowledgment sign-off before tickets can be purchased
- Posted signage that is clearly visible on the doors of the performance space
- Signs leading to more information provided at box office via pamphlet or verbalization by box office staff
- Information readily visible in the event's program
- Announcements made by management or staff prior to the performance

While it is impossible to account for all potential elements that may affect an individual audience member, it is possible to establish trust in the fact that the theatre company is evaluating the production's content from all angles to be as inclusive and informative as possible.

Notes from the field ... a jaw-dropping moment

While serving as assistant director on a production at a university during her graduate studies, Alexis Black had an interesting experience with an audience member about intimate content within the production.

I was observing a high school matinee performance, to be available for support if the visiting middle school students became rowdy or if the chaperoning teachers had any questions or needs. After a scene that depicted a long, passionate kiss between the main characters, one of the teachers angrily motioned at me that she needed to speak with me in the lobby. We quietly moved out of the theatre as the performance continued. Once in the lobby, the teacher demanded to know why the school administration was not informed about the intimate content. (At this time, this was not an established practice, as intimacy protocols were not yet introduced into theatrical culture or my own methods of working.) I apologized that this was overlooked, and said I would make sure to let the administrative team know so they may change this practice in future. She then demanded, "Will there be any

MORE inappropriate content that we need to know about for the rest of the show?" I thought for a moment, then purposefully replied, "Well, there will not be any more kissing in the show, but there are several graphic depictions of brutal murders, including the simulated killing of an eight-year-old boy." Her face brightened immediately as she said, "Oh, that's fine! As long as there isn't any more KISSING." I stood in shock as she cheerfully turned and reentered the theatre, relieved, reassured, and relaxed.

One can never underestimate the variety of reactions audience members may experience in response to staged intimacy and violence; which is proof enough that content notices are a valuable proactive method of communication.

Standard checking in and out

Getting into the routine running of a show is what many consider to be the "sweet spot." Audience reactions become more regularized; actors begin to feel more confident and comfortable in their roles; and crew are finding the most efficient ways to manage backstage. The crew and the acting company start to find ease in their collaborations and may start to establish more close-knit relationships. But even when productions are running smoothly, there can be times when individuals need to connect to talk through what may have felt to be an awkward exchange during a specific moment in the performance, either backstage or on stage.

To facilitate this connection, a standardized check-in and check-out process is recommended for those engaged in performing or witnessing intimacy. This set activity could include actors involved in choreography, actors on stage when the choreography occurs, as well as dressers or other run crew members who assist with production elements, quick changes, or other means of off-stage support. These communication procedures are meant to serve as conduits between team members working to maintain safety, boundaries, and storytelling. These procedures encourage us to ask, Is the intimacy choreography feeling cohesive, clear, and continuing as established in rehearsal? Are actors and crew members working together as needed? Are there any psychological concerns that need to be addressed about the staged intimacy, especially if the staged content is graphic or violent?

Having a simple check-in, as established by either the intimacy director or stage manager, can help to create space for team members to engage with each other as necessary. These check-in and check-out rituals may

- Involve individuals or small groups
- Utilize available space for connection without interfering with pre-show or post-show duties
- Allow for actors and crew to check in with each other if needed
- Include stage managers and assistants if needed

These may be as simple as a nod and "thumbs-up" for some situations, or they may require a more in-depth verbal check-in. If issues arise during check-ins, these can be resolved through either discussion or being addressed during a movement call before the next performance. The hope would be to have the SM and the ID set up these communication procedures as a standard practice but then leave these to occur at the discretion and request of those involved. Not every team member may require a check-in, and communication with the SM regarding check-ins may not be necessary for those who use the process. However, if issues arise more consistently or escalate, the SM may need to ensure proper communication and resolution during check-ins.

Maintaining the performance for a long run

Planning for and maintaining a live theatrical production when scheduled for a limited, extended, or open-ended run can be both thrilling and challenging. Whatever the length, all shows have similar elements to oversee and manage, such as actor and crew safety, technical upkeep and maintenance, paperwork, and payroll. There may be crew and substitute crew training, understudy or replacement rehearsal; and of course, maintaining and building overall company morale. But when we add to this mix intimate staging that may be physical, sexual, violent, or any combination, it can add layers of complexity.

Long-running productions evolve and grow just as shorter-running productions, but with the added time comes the inevitable need for rehearsing new understudies and replacement actors on a revolving basis. Maintaining a production should be approached with the same care and attention as maintaining movement on any other type of production. Actors are human, and they make mistakes, line mishaps, mental errors, and physical missteps. These unexpected shifts are part of what makes live theatre an art form like no other. Every show can feel as fresh and exciting as it did on opening night, but this takes attention, time, care, and effort, especially when working with intimate complex staging.

Being mindful of the following can assist stage management and the acting company in telling the director's story night after night, for as long as there is an audience to experience it.

- Staged intimacy is blocking and should be documented as such, just like any other part of the show. This approach helps to remove much of the subjectivity from notetaking or note-giving, which can become a source of disagreement when left vague.[1]
- Detailed, definitive intimacy notation supports specificity, and, regarding maintenance notes, it makes the process easier for all involved.
- The Production Pillars of Intimacy can be utilized and reinforced as an ongoing reminder of shared agreements.
- Staged intimacy mapping and placeholders provide a framework from which adjustments can easily be made to accommodate illness or change of circumstance regarding actor boundaries.
- If needed, actors or stage management can speak with the director and ID regarding artistic growth and the possible need to connect again, especially when on long-running shows. Alternatively, if there is an assistant director still on contract, connection can start with them.
- When working with replacement actors, the possibility of having the ID return as part of the put-in rehearsal can be explored. They will be able to help adjust the movement for these new bodies and their different shapes and sizes and maintain safety of movement for all involved. (See more information on understudies and replacement later in this chapter.)

Having eyes on the action

When it comes to stage management's responsibility for maintaining the show, one must consider how the stage manager actually "sees" the show. Are they in a booth at the far back of the house? Are they backstage on the jump above the stage and to the side? Or are they able to "see" the performance only by using a camera and monitor setup tucked in a backstage corner? Location, sightlines, and quality of stage visibility can play into the stage manager's ability to watch the performance and physical movement with an eye toward safety and storytelling. If their line of sight to the stage is impeded or possibly only visible through a camera/monitor setup, especially if it is an infrared set up, what they "see" when they are running the show may not be at all what the audience experiences. Their ability to see the stage and actors, especially on productions that contain intimate staging, must be considered when determining the best way to keep eyes on the action, actors, intimate movement, and nuances so storytelling can be maintained for the long run.

Should the stage manager's visibility be an issue, one solution could be to utilize an assistant stage manager (ASM). If the ASM has no other duties during those specific moments in the show, they could find a location either on stage, backstage, off to one side, or any spot in the theatre that gives them a clear line of sight to the stage. From this vantage point, they could assume the responsibility of watching the staged movement for safety and storytelling. This individual becomes the dedicated eyes on the performance for those specific moments and communicates with the stage manager or intimacy captain (when applicable) as needed. Should the ASM be assigned this responsibility, it may become a part of their role as intimacy captain should they be designated as such. Maintaining eyes on the movement is essential to preserving actor safety and intention.

Tips for note-giving during maintenance of staged intimacy

- Give notes to the actors only if authorized to do so (stage management, intimacy captain, or similar agreed-upon positions)
- Learn and use the same vocabulary established during rehearsals by the actors, director, ID (when applicable), and stage management team
- Use quantifiable choreographic terms such as "The tempo in this moment should be a three; it seemed to be closer to a six during the last run" and "Your right hand remained on his thigh during that last run; it was choreographed to move to his left hip" rather than ambiguous or intention-based phrases such as "That looks messier now" or "You should be more passionate in this section."
- Utilize verbal adjustments only: do not physically model, perform movements, or step in as one of the characters.
- Lead with empathy and a neutral-to-warm tone during note-giving for vulnerable moments, as perceived briskness or frustration may be detrimental to the process.
- Give the notes early enough to provide time to mentally process them before the show. This may mean in an email the night before a performance or a conversation before half-hour call.

- Allow the actors to physically work any adjustments that are needed to maintain the story, and/or protect the physical or emotional safety of the actors. This physical review may occur during an intimacy call if regularized, or a brief rehearsal may need to be scheduled before the next performance.
- Do not adjust or change the choreography of the hired intimacy professional without consultation with them and the director.

Final takeaway—the established methods of working, set by the intimacy professional at the start of the rehearsal process, help to create open communication, allowing for an easier process when maintaining movement. And remember, the production's intimacy professional is usually only an email or phone call away if questions or concerns arise after they step away from rehearsals/performances.

Understudies and replacements

In many live performances, there will come a time where an actor involved in staged intimacy will be unable to perform, or finish a contract, and they will need to be replaced by a new performer. When incorporating new performers in roles that involve staged intimacy, an understanding of and respect for their personal boundaries is imperative. Therefore it is a beneficial practice to involve these alternate performers in as many of the actor-based elements mentioned in this book as possible and as soon as possible. This includes

- Informing possible replacements of intimate content at auditions
- Noting any contract rider requirements for the new performers
- Providing new actors with the company's reporting structures and policies
- Providing time to introduce and explain consent basics, the pillars of intimacy, established protocols, and vocabulary
- Initiating boundary checks and check-in rituals with principal performers as needed
- Adjusting the intimacy map of the moment of choreography or utilizing placeholders in response to personal boundaries
- Having replacement accessories (such as modesty barriers) for hygienic purposes as needed
- Scheduling closed rehearsals if necessary (for staged nudity) prior to running these scenes with an audience

When welcoming replacements and understudies whose characters are involved in staged intimacy, it's important to also engage in the same mindful rehearsal protocols and methods of communication that took place and involved the original cast of actors. Staged intimacy is inherently individualized and needs to be handled with individual care and attention.

It is understood that this process may not always be possible or feasible. Every situation is different, and every organization has its own constraints on budgets, schedules, and staffing complexities, which may not be flexible. What is possible and preferable will change for each individual context, and the goal for this text is to use the tools, protocols, and suggestions in this book in individualized ways. We hope that after reading this book organizations will reflect upon their current standard practices and consider how they may introduce new ideas and concepts covered here when working with replacement actors, including informed consent during auditions, clear reporting structures, the use of mapping practices and boundary checks. Introducing these basic consent practices will enhance the process not just for the betterment of replacement actors but for all performers and the show itself.

Understudies

If working with an intimacy director (or similarly titled professional) who has been given the opportunity to communicate with members of the production ahead of time, it is possible that some additional practices may be put into place when working with understudies. For example, the ID may request

- *The inclusion of understudies in the consent workshop during the first week of rehearsal.* This will be a time-effective and inclusive practice, creating an opportunity for unity and trust among the entire cast.
- *The inclusion of understudies in intimacy rehearsals.* When understudies are involved in the production, it is recommended to consider their input when intimate staging is being set. Building choreography to support actor boundaries means all boundaries should be considered, including those of understudies. Ensuring consent from all performers that will be involved in the staging will ease transitions and save time, money, and energy. Exploring new boundaries after opening could involve hours of rehearsal time or require the ID and/or director to return. In addition, the variances in height, body types, and sizes of understudies may prohibit certain movements that could be avoided if understudies are engaged from day one.

- *That consent and mapping exercises be executed with "understudy and principal" pairings in addition to pairings between the main performers.* It is far more likely that an understudy would be going on with the other principal rather than with their understudy counterpart.

If understudies cannot join early introductions and choreographic rehearsals, next steps could include the following:

- Call back the ID and director or assistant director to work with understudies.
- Have the ID discuss "wiggle room" or possible alternative movements during original staging that would be acceptable to the director, and then adjust movements accordingly with understudies.
- Employ masking techniques or placeholders as needed to tell the story with consent from the understudy; this can occur even if masking or placeholders are not used with principal actors. This version may be preferred for principal actors when performing with understudies to maintain consent.
- Have understudies work on the basic physical movements of the intimate story before adding in "acting." This does not mean marking the movements; they are done full out but without added intention until understudies are confident with the physical movement and muscular text.

Planned replacements

For replacement performers, the intimacy director would return to work with these new individuals whenever possible, as variance in boundaries and physical elements may occur. If the ID is unable to join in person, a beneficial practice could be to inquire about the possibility of virtual rehearsals through a video chat platform. An intimacy captain (if assigned) may be another option when rehearsing replacements, especially if the choreography is less challenging or complex. However, the training and trust of the intimacy captain's ability to stage this material must be determined in consultation with ID, director and SM, actors and possibly members of the administration if additional payment is required.

Emergency replacements

Should understudies or replacements be put into the show because of an emergency situation, the following may need to be considered: What is the essence of this story? How can these actors tell this story as simply as possible with consent? Do we need to remove phrases of choreography for one performance to better support this emergency replacement and their acting partners?

As in fight choreography, when an emergency situation occurs that involves a sword fight, for example, what was a one-minute fight routine could be cut down to two moves to ensure actor safety. While not ideal for the director's vision, the show must go on and it must be safe. In a staged fight situation, individual safety always takes priority over staged movement, and the same should be the case with staged intimacy.

Archival video taping when a production contains nudity

After the production opens, the opportunity for digitally capturing this staged work for archival purposes may be explored. If working under an AEA contract, productions may be recorded or broadcast only under the terms of the contract or code under which the production is governed or if the producer has secured written permission from Equity.[2] If working on a nonunion production, it is recommended that during the initial contracting phase, the producer or upper management introduce the option to the acting company as well as the creative team. (See Chapter 3.) Archival recordings are made for numerous reasons, such as the company's historical documentation, future marketing efforts, and plans to share with performing art libraries or others. Whatever the purpose, videotaping a staged production that contains nudity needs to be discussed and negotiated. When working on a union contract, these negotiations will be assisted by the union business representative. If working nonunion production, actors may work through their agent or manager or reach out to the production's intimacy professional for guidance (when possible) if they feel unable to manage negotiations themselves.

Once final decisions have been made and agreed to, being mindful of union rules and negotiated riders, actors can be confident that theatre management will ensure agreements are adhered to. Whether involving staged nudity, sexual violence or other charged intimate staging, it is recommended that questions are asked regarding how digital recordings will be stored and who will have access to the content, as actor privacy is paramount.

Accommodations while touring

When taking a show on the road, preparations may begin months or even years before trucks hit pavement. Whether one is mounting a children's production that will fit into a van along with its cast and crew, remounting a season favorite, or taking the latest Broadway musical out of the city, each will be booked at venues and contracted in advance. This process can be relatively smooth when negotiating for a show that has already been on the road for years, or the process may have a few unknowns if one is booking the show before the production has begun rehearsals. Whatever the timeline, each touring production will need to communicate their show's needs, technical requirements, and content as part of the contracting process.

For the most part, these details live in the technical rider that accompanies the contract, which is possibly the most relevant section when preparing for the show to arrive at the loading dock. The rider attachment is composed of sections that cover technical requirements, schedules for load-in and out, local stagehand needs, specifics regarding dressing rooms, catering/hospitality needs, merchandise plans, trucking, parking, and security. In addition to technical details, it may be essential to communicate the show's content during the early phase of contracting.

Content notices and show advances

When booking a tour, production contracts usually provide general content information, such as notices of mature content, nudity, or violence. Yet general themes and basic content information communicated may lack specificity. Should the production still be in the early stages of rehearsal when sold to venues and contracted, providing specific content information may not be possible until after the show is fully staged and begins touring. When that is the case, this detailed information can be provided to the presenting venue during their show advance. The show advance will be the time when final technical requirements, as well as complete content information, can be shared with the presenting venue staff. This conversation, between the presenting organization and the tour, is the time when every detail is discussed and every need is clarified.

Based on type, size, and scope of the touring production, the show advance may start one month, one week or even one day before the scheduled performance, and the content details discussed may need to be shared with several different departments. For marketing and FOH staff, if content notices were unavailable during original negotiations, details regarding intimate or challenging content will be needed for composing audience notices. For the production staff, the same content notices shared with audience relations may also need to be shared with the production crew. It will be at the discretion of the presenting organization as to how this information will be made available to their staff and audience. (There is information on "audience content notices" earlier in this chapter.)

Spacing and sightlines

Once the tour arrives and trucks are unloaded, the next crucial process regarding intimate or challenging content involves the acting company and relates to the new space. When the tour's stage management team arrives at the venue, they will need to prepare and acclimate their cast to this new theater layout and their audience sightlines. Regarding intimate staging, stage management should pay particular attention to site lines related to actor movement and intimate choreography. Adjustments may need to be made not only to actor movement but also with the positioning of scenic elements and accommodating audience sightlines. And finally, the tour's production stage manager and technical supervisor may communicate about show content with the local crew during their orientation upon arrival at the venue or during a production meeting with the run crew before the first rehearsal or first performance.

> **Notes from the field ... when on the road**
>
> *In a conversation with Richard Rauscher, production stage manager of numerous touring productions, he discussed life on the road, communicating with presenting houses, and handling theatre sightlines on shows with intimate or challenging content.*
>
> When you're touring a show, you are presenting this show in its original format. If it's a Broadway show you're trying to replicate that Broadway production as closely as possible. These tours run years, so the rider is set, and nothing is changing in that regard. When doing the show advance, it's mostly to confirm that they are aware of the content. There may be questions from the venue to clarify content, so they may ask "What do you mean by violence or intimidation?" As one doing the advance on behalf of the tour, I would basically mention what the show contains, a sexual scene or sexual violence; as well as confirming other needs, such as we need 12 dressing rooms and so forth. One big thing that's different in each theater is the physical space and relationship to the audience. So, we must look at sightlines and see if there will be something that's going to be more visible now because the audience is wider or steeper or the balcony protrudes over the audience a bit more.

You don't want the actors doing something different than they normally do; you don't want surprises onstage in that way. And you don't want the audience to experience it differently than you have staged it for them to experience. So that is the bigger challenge when on tour. I ran into something on a tour where we were at an outdoor covered stage, outdoor seating, and therefore, ambient light from the sun not being fully set meant more light was on a specific scene than we wanted, this was designed to be a very low light situation. So, we physically altered the set. We brought in a scrim that didn't normally play in that scene to lower the light situation because it would have been too visible with the setting sunlight. So there are a lot of different changes that may be made necessary by the venue, by the physical layout of the space, or if performing outdoors."

As a follow up, we asked Richard "When it comes to the show's run crew and intimate content, how can you communicate crew expectations on touring shows that contain charged intimate content, when you have huge crews and little or no rehearsal time?"

Generally speaking, at the beginning of load-in for the show there is a meeting with everyone to make general announcements to the crew. And then after load-in, in preparations for either rehearsals or the actual first performance, there's a meeting with the run crew to explain the show and content, etc. Whenever there's any nudity on stage or quick changes happening that's visible, perhaps from backstage, there are always measures taken to block it off and to keep the crew out of that area. A touring crew member heads up a team of a number of local crew, whatever is needed in that department, and that touring crew member is responsible for letting their local crew know what's happening, when it's happening, and keeping them clear from the situation or keeping an eye on what they're doing. The responsibility is given to the touring crew head to communicate with their local crew about content. During the run, as those scenes approach, the touring crew will inform the local crew as to what is coming up. Once the shift into that scene is complete, the local crew can step away if needed based on the content of the scene or they may need to stay to execute cues based on the needs when running the scene.

Richard C. Rauscher
(he/him/his)
AEA / AGMA / AGVA
Production Stage Manager
Broadway & National Tours

Transference energy and responsible communication

The passion that performers express when on stage can be captivating for an audience to witness. Their passion can also become all-encompassing and may take hold of the actor, impacting their psychological well-being and maintaining a tight grip as their character's story unfolds. This grip, while magical on stage, can sometimes affect behavior or be detrimental off stage. For example, if this grip is so tight the actor can't release the emotional life of their character, they may still be riding an emotional rollercoaster when stepping backstage, unable to fully disengage from the storytelling. This extreme ride then may alter their ability to have composed personal exchanges backstage, creating an emotional toll not only on the actors but on the crew as well.

Unfortunately, many theatre artists have experienced or heard stories about actors behaving backstage in the same manner that their characters were behaving on stage. This may include behaviors that are emotionally charged, angry, or abusive. This conduct is never acceptable, and so there may be times when challenging content prompts a need to script the narrative backstage as carefully as the story on stage. It should be assured that everyone who engages with the story has a way to work through the emotion in a healthy manner, or have resources for further support if they feel they are losing personal control. This effort needs to be mindful of the mental health and treatment of actors telling the story and the crew witnessing and supporting it. Creating an atmosphere where everyone is able to process and experience charged emotions in a professional manner is key.

The question is then, How best may this atmosphere be achieved? After all, backstage areas are a complex space. Scenery is moving; actors are rushing by as the crew navigates the dark. This mysterious dark world was created primarily to serve another in the limelight, so placing value on backstage spaces and the interactions that transpire within is not usually a concept that is fully considered. One who works backstage may believe they are only there to serve and support the action and actors, no matter what they may experience behind the scenes. However, every member of the company matters; the entire team should be supported as equal contributors and everyone appreciated as professionals and as individuals. When working on productions that contain challenging and charged content, supporting a backstage atmosphere that allows for a professional and respectful workspace is essential to a production's holistic success during the run.

Building an atmosphere that provides for healthy backstage communication could include some of the following options:

- Plan in advance with the ID and SM team, and strategize a support system for actors and crew should anyone feel emotionally charged during or after a performance. (Closure practices discussed later in this chapter may be a place to start.)
- Communicate with the entire team that it's okay to reach out, letting them know who to go to if resources are needed.
- Establish check-in protocols with stage management at different stages of the run to ensure that healthy and professional behavior is consistent.
- Support self-guided mental health practices by providing or posting self-care and/or counseling resources for actors and crew.
- Provide a more private space for an actor to decompress after an emotionally charged scene.
- Connect with HR for additional resources on how to maintain appropriate workplace culture.

Notes from the field ... "taking a breather"

Emotions can be difficult to control, especially when feeling the pressure and stress of a performance. Finding a routine or method for channeling emotional stress is vital, especially when on a long-running production. While stage managing a successful and long-running production many years ago, Tina Newhauser was able to work together with an actor to help them process their emotional stress in a healthy way.

The actor was mesmerizing on stage; their performance was transformative, and every night calling the show, I was in awe watching them embody the character and transport the audience. What was not fun was how this performer came off stage one night after the curtain call. Once the curtain hit the deck, they stomped over and began to yell expletives into my face. This was not done with malice towards me; I instinctively knew that. It was done with malice toward themselves. They were so passionate about our show and their work that any moment during their performance that didn't "click" would just pick at them and fester inside their mind. I think their only method of dealing with this was to explode the moment they stepped off stage. Unfortunately, that was precisely where I stood to call the show. The first time this outburst happened I was kind of taken aback, I looked at them and said firmly, "Go hang outside, and I'll meet you there in ten minutes." I then explained that I had to wrap up the show before I could help them. This had never happened before so I had no idea what was wrong, but by the time I joined them outside, they had calmed down enough to rationally explain what was going on.

I realized that their extreme emotional high prevented them from being able to have a logical conversation and resulted in this emotional release. I could understand but couldn't allow it to continue. It was after this first exchange that we set up a system: when this performer felt overwhelmed and upset based on their performance and came to me at the side of the stage ready to burst, I would calmly say, "I'll meet you in the alley in ten," and off they'd go. In ten minutes, when I joined them, they would have calmed down and could rationally explain what felt "off." We would then discuss this until they felt better. Eventually, this connection became my favorite part of our time together on this show."

Finding a method for channeling and releasing energy and creating a space for individuals to express their emotions calmly and rationally can be therapeutic. It can also establish a routine that builds healthy relationships and supports professional behavior.

Emotional resilience and self-care

A career in the performing arts contains many exciting attributes: working with dedicated or revolutionary artists; encouraging empathy through intentionally crafted storytelling; and getting the opportunity to reach audiences and experience their energy, emotional release, and even praise or appreciation. However, these careers also involve long hours, financial challenges, emotionally draining exchanges, and moments when any amount of gratitude seems to be miles away. Those who work in the theatrical arts know this ever-changing journey can mean that one moment they are thriving, while the next feels more like surviving. Navigating this world of polarity may, at times, take a toll on each artist and every creative team member and may require mindful attention to stockpiling reserves of mental and emotional energy. Building and maintaining reserves of energy takes flexibility, patience, self-care, and understanding: it takes "emotional resilience."

Psychologists define emotional resilience as having three building blocks: physical, mental or psychological, and social elements.[3] Deliberately dedicating time and energy to explore these elements and building emotional resilience takes conscious effort. One can work towards stability and strength through a few individual activities, such as creating a healthy way to step away from work at the end of the day. Or one can establish a method for releasing emotional attachments to the art, allowing a respite from these attachments until the next rehearsal, allowing themselves to close the door to the theatre space for a few hours or days so they may more fully step into their personal space. Whatever is chosen, any of these methods will help establish a closure practice as part of a healthy work/life balance. Ultimately, one should determine what personally works best to navigate a well-conditioned relationship between home and work life.

Building emotional resilience takes self-care routines built through physical, mental, and social elements, and may be achieved through the exploration of and focus on the following:

- Interpersonal connections—prioritizing relationships
- Healthy lifestyle choices—exercising, building energy levels and vitality
- Self-confidence—flexibility, maintaining a positive outlook
- A sense of humor—self-enhancement and laughter
- A sense of purpose—maintaining inner motivation

When exploring and embracing these elements that help us build emotional resilience, one can also develop the capacity to persevere. Perseverance strengthens when one intentionally shapes their self-care routine with an end purpose in mind. Perseverance is supported when one's positive outlook creates positive energy. One may especially persevere when personal connections motivate laughter; it's been widely documented that laughter may indeed be the best medicine. Research by Dr. Rod Martin, a professor of clinical psychology, "gave support to the idea that people who have more of a sense of humor are better able to cope with stress and therefore are less adversely affected by it."[4] Whatever the routine, building a mindful self-care practice that leads to perseverance should feed and fuel one's energy, nurture one's spirit, and allow for healthy interactions. This balance builds emotional resilience and allows everyone to place value on and prioritize self.

Building a closure practice

A healthy transition between one's work identity and personal identity may be supported by creating a closure practice. Closure practices, an important part of self-care techniques, are an established routine that creates a sort of threshold or line between our public life and our private life. This threshold is created through uncomplicated mental and physical rituals, consisting of simple or easy movements and thought patterns. Examples include breathing exercises, physical stretches, a brief group activity with colleagues, or even something as simple as a deep sigh after walking out of the theatre.

When starting out with building a closure practice, you could try one or all of the following:

- Breathe—deep slow breaths will trigger your nervous system to calm down.[5] When feeling stressed or when ending a long day, close your eyes and focus on slow controlled breathing, or utilize intentional breathing patterns that work for you.
- Mindful movement—the way you move can affect the way you think and feel.[6] Easy physical actions such as walking, stretching, and controlled repeated movements can relieve depression and ease tension. After standing or sitting in one position for a period of time, like when running or calling a show, take a few minutes after the curtain comes down to move, stretch, and walk.
- Connect—personal connections have a calming effect, lowering levels of anxiety and depression, building self-esteem and empathy.[7] One of the best ways one can step away from work may be with friends. Gather with your tribe and unwind; doctor's orders.
- Disconnect—disconnecting from work activities after that curtain comes down will lower levels of fatigue, burnout, stress and anxiety.[8] When you leave the theatre, leave the job behind as well, relax, and enjoy the calm. Disconnecting can be supported through a variety of activities, such as reading, taking a long bath, listening to music, or enjoying a calming cup of tea.

A creative life is a busy life, and there can be stressors that can overwhelm anyone. It's okay to dedicate time to mental health during your day, especially when working on productions that challenge and provoke. Artists may not realize how much of an emotional buildup can occur when running a show that depicts intimacy, violence, or abuse. Mindful reflection, self-care, and taking time to process your emotional experience is sound advice, and placing value on your mental health is smart thinking. Allowing unhealthy emotional tension to accumulate may result in unhealthy interactions with friends, family, and colleagues.

Intentionally working to build emotional resilience and closure practices is becoming standard for artists and other creatives working in live performance with charged storytelling. By understanding the worth in building rituals that support emotional resilience when starting out, one can support a long, healthful career in what can be a challenging art form.

> ### Notes from the field ... creating closure
>
> *The section above explores one way that a closure practice can look. We spoke with Dr. Jessica Steinrock (CEO of IDC) on how she structures closure.*
>
> These four elements are often present in successful closure practices, regardless of if they are individual or used as a part of co-working.
>
> - **Multi-sensory stimulation**—Engaging more than one sense invites mindfulness of the present moment. Subtle sensations that require attention can support emotional grounding. Examples may include physical contact of one's own or another's hand, one's hand on the chest, the swishing of water in the mouth, an audible sigh, the rubbing of hands together to create heat, among others.
> - **Presence and gratitude**—Central to the work of building a consent-focused workspace is gratitude and care both to your colleagues and to yourself. This allows for the entrance of trust, which is built over time and through practice. Centering the closure process in gratitude helps to reinforce the agreements housed within the working relationship.
> - **Breath**—Intentional breath actively changes the rhythm of the body and can increase introspective awareness. It involves physical and sometimes auditory stimulation and can offer additional grounding benefits that help separate the real and imaginary.
> - **A distinctive ending or button**—Like the button of a piece of music, this element signifies the end of the closure practice. It is a cue to let go of that which is unhelpful and reinforce that which is helpful. Sometimes, after performing this ending,

> practitioners may realize that they are still holding onto something that is not serving them. This may indicate that more than one closure method is needed or that the closure practice should be repeated. This button can serve as a checkpoint with which to assess the effectiveness of the closure practice. Common endings look like clapping hands, patting the ground, or stepping over an imaginary line.
>
> With the repetition of a closure practice, it is possible for the impact to lessen over time. As the rehearsal process goes on, sometimes I often find myself or my colleagues simply "going through the motions" of a closure practice. When this occurs, the structure above becomes incredibly useful. By naming why the practice works, and the specific components that make the practice whole, your closure practice has a higher likelihood of being successful and impactful.
>
> Jessica Steinrock, PhD
(she/her/hers)
CEO of Intimacy Directors and Coordinators, Inc.
Intimacy Director for Live Performance
Intimacy Coordinator for TV and Film

Chapter reflection

It takes ongoing vigilance and care from all creative team members to maintain a show, especially one that contains moments of complex, challenging, or vulnerable storytelling. Care means supporting the audience, cast, and crew, along with understudies, replacement performers, and anyone experiencing this story night after night. Remaining vigilant means determining proper communication practices for backstage interactions, finding a path to emotional resilience, and establishing closure routines that allow team members to make a relaxed and centered transition back to their personal lives.

Whether the show runs for days, months, or even years, it is important to come to the work with mindful attention, patience, and compassion. Striving every day to create a world that values both the people within it and the art crafted together will help to ensure that we can maintain a culture of consent and care through the final curtain call.

One final note from the field ... observing and embracing a shift in institutional culture

In the years of building staged intimacy–related curriculum and course materials and engaging professionally with this work as movement professionals and managers, and during the last year and a half while writing this text, we have witnessed the beginnings of a possible tectonic shift in theatrical workplace culture. We have standardized the use of staged intimacy practices from pre-production to performance in university productions at Michigan State and have worked with mental health professionals and cultural consultants on some of our productions as well. We also are witnessing and taking part in deep conversations regarding psychological and physical health, race, gender, and disability during rehearsals at regional and Broadway theaters.[9] We have witnessed members of theatrical teams, both those appearing in productions as well as behind the scenes, becoming more intentional about their workplace customs and communications as individuals. At the institutional level, organizations and ensembles, whether academic or professional, seem to be rapidly creating policies and moving toward a more mindful culture.

Production on Deck (PoD), a "talent and consulting firm for theatrical production roles that identifies talent from marginalized communities" and a company that works to "increase pathways for marginalized communities to access jobs in theatrical production"[10] articulates important change occurring with theatrical teams through a survey on changes in workplace conditions over the pandemic.[11] Within an article documenting a survey by writer Bear Bellinger, one respondent is quoted as saying, "The company I work for took great care of their employees over the pandemic. Since returning, the workplace has been consistently working to change the status quo and make working in theater a humane and sustainable career. I want to be involved in that work."[12]

We found this quote to be inspiring. We want the theatrical team's work with staged intimacy and consent to also be a contribution toward making theatre work a humane and sustainable career for all, whether working on stage or beyond the fourth wall. And most of all, we want everyone to join movements and changes happening in the industry and enjoy the ride as the ground keeps shifting beneath us, creating a brand-new landscape for better, healthier storytelling in live performance.

Bellinger also seems to be inspired by the aforementioned quote by stating, "This is a foundation for the future of the theater industry: acknowledging that there is work to be done, understanding that it is ongoing, and committing to participate in that work together. We can create a more humane industry. We can create a more sustainable industry. But it will take an honest examination of our past faults and a radical reimagination of our future.... There is hope. We can do this together. Let's get to work."

We enthusiastically consent.

Alexis Black and Tina M. Newhauser
Authors of *Supporting Staged Intimacy*

Chapter discussion / exercise / activity

Improv activity: Practice scenarios for during the run

Sometimes it's difficult to know how to handle a charged situation, especially if one finds themselves in the middle of an emotional exchange. As it is unfolding around them, one may freeze, unsure of what to do or say. To help learn how to navigate these emotional situations, create a few different scenarios. Using improvisation techniques, develop a script that can be practiced through acting them out.[13] These scenarios can involve a few different players and explore a few different situations.

For example, if an actor is creating an unhealthy work environment for a crew member backstage, determine who needs to be involved, and to what capacity; then, with improvisation techniques, work through the navigation of this situation. What are some plans for resolution in the moment that can be learned from this activity and shared with others?

Next, explore additional scenarios, role play, and create a plan that engages a variety of positions, such as

- Understudy performers
- Run crew
- Assistant stage managers
- Dressers
- Others

Closure activity: Establish a self-care routine

Create your own self-care ritual and try to utilize each area of closure mentioned above:

- Breath
- Mindful movement
- Connecting techniques
- Disconnecting techniques

Notes

1 Concept discussed in relationship to intimacy direction during February 2019 "Intimacy Directors International O'Neill 9-day Intensive" in-person training attended by Alexis Black. Training held at Eugene O'Neill Theatre Center, Waterford, CT. Concept is also discussed in multiple publications, including 2020's *Staging Sex* by Chelsea Pace.
2 "Recording and Broadcast." *Actors' Equity Association*, June 2021, http://www.actorsequity.org/resources/Producers/recording-and-broadcast.
3 Chawdhury, Madhuleena Roy. "What Is Emotional Resilience and How to Build It? (+Training Exercises)." *PositivePsychology.com*, Feb. 2021, https://positivepsychology.com/emotional-resilience/.
4 Martin, Rod, and Nicholas A Kuiper. "Three Decades Investigating Humor and Laughter: An Interview with Professor Rod Martin." *Europe's Journal of Psychology*, PsychOpen, May 2020, https://www.ncbi.nlm.nih.gov/pmc/articles/PMC4991054/.
5 "Breath Meditation: A Great Way to Relieve Stress." *Harvard Health*, Apr. 2019, https://www.health.harvard.edu/mind-and-mood/breath-meditation-a-great-way-to-relieve-stress.
6 Pillay, Srini. "How Simply Moving Benefits Your Mental Health." *Harvard Health*, Mar. 2019, https://www.health.harvard.edu/blog/how-simply-moving-benefits-your-mental-health-201603289350.
7 Seppala, Emma. "Connectedness & Health: The Science of Social Connection." *The Center for Compassion and Altruism Research and Education*, June 2020, http://ccare.stanford.edu/uncategorized/connectedness-health-the-science-of-social-connection-infographic/.
8 Park, Young Ah. "Mental Break: Work-Life Balance Needed for Recovery from Job Stress." *Kansas State University*, Feb. 2020, https://www.k-state.edu/media/newsreleases/feb13/worklifebal20513.html.
9 Alexis Black had conversations on these topics in early 2022 while working at the Denver Center of the Performing Arts and while rehearsing a spring 2022 Broadway show.

10 Stewart, David, and Sarah Lozoff. "Home." *Production on Deck*, http://www.productionondeck.com/.
11 Bellinger, Bear. "Production on Deck: Eliminating Excuses." *PLSN*, Feb. 2022, https://plsn.com/articles/stage-directions-articles/production-on-deck-eliminating-excuses-2/?fbclid=IwAR0KsmaP0kEUe48H5vv_ajmB6275oldjTsjFONuUvu3Kcn2reKAbY4V0pmE.
12 Bellinger, Bear. "Production on Deck: Eliminating Excuses." *PLSN*, Feb. 2022, https://plsn.com/articles/stage-directions-articles/production-on-deck-eliminating-excuses-2/?fbclid=IwAR0KsmaP0kEUe48H5vv_ajmB6275oldjTsjFONuUvu3Kcn2reKAbY4V0pmE.
13 One may find more guidance by looking at Augusto Boal's technique, "Theatre of the Oppressed." Boal, Augusto, et al. *Theatre of the Oppressed*. Theatre Communications Group, 1985.

Appendix A

Intimacy organizations

A partial list of intimacy direction, coordination and education organizations

For stage
- Centaury.co — www.centaury.co
- Heartland Intimacy Design & Training — www.heartlandintimacydesign.com
- Humble Warrior Movement Arts — www.humblewarriormovement.com/intimacy
- Intimacy Directors & Coordinators — www.idcprofessionals.com
- Intimacy Coordinators of Color — www.intimacycoordinatorsofcolor.com
- Intimacy Professionals Association — www.intimacyprofessionalsassociation.com
- Theatrical Intimacy Education — www.theatricalintimacyed.com

For screen and film
- Centaury.co — www.centaury.co
- Intimacy Coordinators Alliance — www.icaft.org
- Intimacy Coordinators Education Collective — www.intimacycoordinatorsed.com
- Intimacy Directors & Coordinators — www.idcprofessionals.com
- Intimacy Professionals Association — www.intimacyprofessionalsassociation.com

SAG-AFTRA industry protocols and resources for intimacy coordination
www.sagaftra.org/contracts-industry-resources/workplace-harassment-prevention/intimacy-coordinator-resources

International companies (stage and/or screen)

Intimacy Coordinators Australia	www.intimacycoordinatorsaustralia.com
Intimacy Coordinators Canada	www.intimacycoordinatorscanada.com
Intimacy Practitioners South Africa	www.intimacysouthafrica.org.za
Intimacy on Set	www.intimacyonset.com
Intimacy for Stage & Screen	www.intimacyforstageandscreen.com
SAFE Sets	www.ssintimacycoordinators.com
The Intimacy Collective, India	www.facebook.com/theintimacycollective

A partial list of practitioners whose EDI work has impacted the field of intimacy direction

These individuals are among many whose work helps to advance diversity, equity, inclusion, anti-racism, anti-oppression practices and cultural competencies in the field of intimacy direction.

Narda E. Alcorn (www.drama.yale.edu/bios/narda-e-alcorn)
Nicole M. Brewer (www.nicolembrewer.com)
D. Christian Bolender (www.linkedin.com/in/d-christian-bolender)
Kaja Ajado Dunn (www.kajadunn.com)
Megan Gilron (www.megangilron.com)
Maya Herbsman (www.idcprofessionals.com/bios/mayaherbsman)
Brian E. Herrera (https://gss.princeton.edu/brian-e-herrera)
Ann C. James (www.anncjamesintimacy.com/)
Teniece Divya Johnson (https://www.idcprofessionals.com/bios/teniecedivyajohnson)
Sarah Lozoff (www.productionondeck.com)
Sharrell Luckett (www.sdluckett.com)
Rocio Mendez (www.rociomendez.com)
Adam Noble (www.uh.edu/kgmca//theatre-and-dance/about/faculty/noble-adam)
Chelsea Pace (www.chelseapace.com)
Lisa Porter (www.theatre.ucsd.edu/people/faculty/stage-management/lisa-porter)
Siobhan Richardson (www.siobhanrichardson.com)
Laura Rikard (www.laurarikard.com)
Alicia Rodis (www.idcprofessionals.com/bios/aliciarodis)
David 'dstew' Steward (www.productionondeck.com)
Sasha Smith (www.elle.com/culture/movies-tv/a33850492/black-intimacy-coordinators-interview/)
Tonia Sina (www.idcprofessionals.com/bios/toniasina)
Cristina (Cha) Ramos (www.callmecha.com)
Claire Wilcher (www.clairewilcher.com)

Appendix B

Practice scenarios

Discussion Exercise: Practice Scenarios

Read through the different scenarios below. How would you approach these different situations, and what action could be taken or explored that may help mitigate or handle the situation? After each scenario there are additional focused questions to inspire deeper discussion.

Scenario I: Perspective of the director, intimacy director, and/or SM

The script that is to be staged next in your season has scripted scenes that require full nudity with two characters, as well as one other character appearing scantily clad. One of the actors who has been cast in a role that is scripted with nudity negotiated with the producer and outlined in their rider that they will not appear nude. The other two actors have been contracted and will appear nude or scantily clad as noted in the script. How can the creative team navigate these agreements to be respectful to all actors cast in this production? What are some steps you could take when navigating this situation?

Follow-up questions for this scenario: How can the ID, director, and stage management plan for this scenario during pre-production? How can the director and ID communicate with the cast to build confidence and a culture of consent during the rehearsal process? How can stage management communicate with the design and production teams regarding these arrangements?

Scenario II: Perspective of the stage manager or assistant director

A director has been hired to direct a show that contains a significant number of intimate moments in the script that would benefit greatly by the expertise of an intimacy professional. When asked, this director declines the offer to bring an ID onto the creative team, claiming that they have been directing theatre for over 40 years and they don't need another set of eyes in the rehearsal room. Knowing you will be in the rehearsal room for the entire rehearsal process, how would you navigate this situation and what are some steps you could take?

Follow-up questions for scenario II: How might you use "The Pillars" in this situation? How might one communicate with the cast regarding the complex moments in the script and their expectations and confidence in staging them? How do power dynamics come into play in this situation? Who might be allies in the room, and how can they help if needed?

Scenario III: Perspective of artistic director, designer, production manager

You are working at a union summer stock theatre company with a long history. For the first time, an ID has been brought on by theatre management to work on every production that will be produced this summer. A returning actor, who has a long history performing for this company every summer for over 10 years, is openly resistant to this and loudly disagrees with the ID during early rehearsals of the first show of the season. As a member of the creative team, what are some steps you could take to remedy this situation and support the intimacy specialist/director?

Follow-up questions for scenario III: What private conversation might you have with this actor to work through this situation? What public conversations might you have with the entire acting company to work through this situation? Who in upper management might be an ally when working through this situation?

Scenario IV: Perspective of assistant SM, SM, fight choreographer

There is an actor in the company who has a challenging time learning intimacy movement and choreography. It is also challenging for them when learning dance movements and sometimes even regular blocking. An ID was on the team to stage the intimate moments and they were in rehearsal for a week to set movement, and this actor was able to get to a consistent place during this time. However, during the continued rehearsal of the staged intimacy they are a frequent, seemingly genuinely accidental, boundary breaker. The actor they are working with within these scenes lets the deputy know that they personally are becoming increasingly uncomfortable and frustrated with this actor's continued mistakes. The director seems unaware or unconcerned. What are some steps you could take to remedy this situation?

Follow-up questions for scenario IV: What questions could you ask the director when trying to work through this situation? What questions could you ask the actor who is having trouble maintaining the movement? What type of reassurances could you offer the actor who brought this issue to the deputy? How could you adjust the rehearsal schedule to help resolve this situation?

Scenario V: Perspective of director, ID, SM and lighting designer

During tech rehearsals of an outdoor drama that contains nudity, as the stage manager you realize that when performing during matinee daytime hours, the lighting will be different, and during the scenes that involve nudity, the daylight will illuminate the stage much more than what is preferred for the scene. How would you handle this situation in regard to actor nudity and visibility?

Follow-up questions for scenario V: What questions could you ask the director when trying to work through this situation? What questions could you ask the ID? What accommodations could be explored in order to help mitigate this situation?

Scenario VI: Perspectives of crew heads and run crew

A member of the run crew comes to you about an incident with an actor backstage—the actor is quietly mumbling after exiting from a scene; they are pacing and have knocked items off of a prop table (during audience applause to mask the sound). They seem to be more unstable as the show progresses. The crew member has been trying to avoid them backstage but is now fearful of possible escalation to physical action. What are some steps you could take to remedy this situation?

Follow-up questions for scenario VI: As the person handling the situation, who on the reporting path is the best person to speak with in regard to this situation? What questions could you ask upper management when trying to work through this situation? What type of reassurances could you offer the crew member who brought this issue to your attention?

Appendix C

Partial guide to desexualized language

Desexualized Language and Staged Intimacy

Desexualized language, as defined in Chapter 3, is the practice of using language that is more clinical, innocuous, or neutral in regard to staged intimate content or scenes. Even though the material being discussed may be that of intimate storytelling, which inherently will include terminology that relates to intimate content, prevent the use of offensive euphemisms or derogatory colloquialisms when discussing the content or anatomy involved. Examples include using a word such as "glutes" instead of "butt" or calling a scene "the reunion scene" or another neutral term instead of "the sex scene." This approach should be taken when in the rehearsal room, when taking notes or writing reports, and when in discussion with the creative, production, or administrative team.

When navigating rehearsals that involve intimate staging, choreography, or movement, try to use non-gendered, anatomical, clinical, or simplified medical terminology for physical areas of the actors' body. Sample terms by area of the body include the following:

Head and neck area

head, neck, skull, hairline, forehead, nose, base of skull, cheeks, ears, mouth, eyes, chin, jawline

Thorax area

armpit, ribs, shoulder, breast, chest, pecs, shoulder blade, breastbone, backbone

Abdomen area

abdomen, lower abdomen, lower back, buttocks, glutes, bend of hip, pelvic area, front of pelvis, pubic area, groin area

Upper extremities

forearm, upper arm, underarm area, tricep, bicep, inner elbow, elbow, wrist, hand, palm, fingers

Lower extremities

front of leg, inner thigh, upper inner thigh, outer thigh, outside of hips, quads, hamstrings, front of knee, back of knee, shin, calf, ankle, foot, arch of foot, toes

For additional information on language, reference medical websites that offer simple medical terminology and an approachable roadmap of the body that could provide a starting point for building your own list of intentional terms and phrases.

Appendix D

Checklists for staging intimacy

Devised Theatre and Intimacy Checklist
Staging and Managing Intimacy for DEVISING and NEW WORKS
Keep in Mind: Recommended vs Available practice

Pre-production

- What are stories (if any) we know we will tell?
- What are possible content and movement notices we could give to actors auditioning?
- What is in the current script (if available)? Can we connect with the playwright about possibilities to help with consent?
- What are the must-haves for the creative team—dramaturgy, design, acting, cultural, etc. (e.g., "required backflip," or "the story of…")?
- Can we hire an intimacy professional, or arrange for a consent workshop?
- How will the choreographers/directors be working/communicating?

In auditions

- Clearly disclose the process or the undecided nature in the work to inform consent.
- Clearly disclose any "must-haves" if this might impact consent.
- If there is an intimacy specialist or will be a consent workshop, this can be disclosed to auditioners during callbacks to inform consent.

In rehearsals

- Post Pillars, ESP method, or other similar foundational resource.
- Post mental health resources.

- Post organizational harassment policies and chain of reporting.
- Post additional resources or materials as needed based on possible storytelling/content.
- Support and model healthy communication as the team navigates changes to the script, content and/or movements.
- Ensure exit strategy is clear for actors (pause words, safety of egress).
- Have a system in place to call extra breaks if needed.
- Director, staged intimacy professional, SM team connect to make sure you're on the same page.
- As always, help facilitate and support community agreements.
- Communicate content notices to administration and company management as needed (e.g., marketing purposes, FOH, box office, and ticket sales).
- Remember closure and self-care (post resources, and remember for yourself!).
- Provide accessories for the show, tech, etc.
- Prepare design, tech, crew, production, front-of-house with content notices and/or community agreements.

Stage Managing Intimacy—A Condensed Checklist

Before signing on to a project, a few things to consider

- Is this non-profit or commercial?
- Is this union or nonunion?
- Is there a company manager?
- Is there a production manager?
- Is the production devised, a restaging, or new work?
- Are there any high-profile artists working on this project?
- What is the organizational culture when working for this company?
- Is there any "history" within the company of which you should be made aware?
- What is the company's definition of harassment and sexual harassment?
- What is the company's harassment policy and reporting structure?
- What resources does the theatre have available for the company (intellectual, physical, emotional, etc.)?

Pre-production

(Keep in mind: lists are not in chronological order and each project will have its own requirements; so always remember preferred versus available practice)

- Confirm production staffing: Will there be a staged intimacy professional (ID, etc.) on this production? If not, can the pillars or a similar resource be introduced to the company?
- Confirm production staffing: Will there be a dramaturg or other cultural specialists on this production?
- Understanding the working relationship: If there will be an ID, do the show's director and the ID already have a working relationship or are they new to working with each other?
- Examine your working relationship: Do you have an existing working relationship with either the director or the ID, or are you new to each other?
- Create and establish an open dialogue between SM / Director / ID. Meet and set expectations.
- Intimacy moments list: Make a list of any moments identified from the script analysis that may need the support of a movement/intimacy specialist. Compare and compile a final list with that of your director and ID. Be sure everyone is on the same page when starting out.
- Support the process: Director / ID / SM—discuss and agree on how you will support the rehearsal process based on the specific needs of this project.

A few things to discuss

- Identify and agree upon all moments in the script that will be part of the intimacy work.
- Identify and agree upon all actors who will be involved in these staged moments. (Discuss understudies and their role in this process.)
- Establish rehearsal room protocols:

Closed rehearsal: Agree to communicate at least 24 hours in advance when you will have closed rehearsals.

Limited support: Not all company members need to be in the room when moments of intimacy are being rehearsed; identify and agree upon those who do.

Rehearsal reporting: Do you need to limit who receives rehearsal report information regarding these scenes? If so, establish who they are.

Actor requests: Identify what questions to ask of / communicate to before starting rehearsals, such as info from or expectations of the cast: any pre-existing conditions, possible allergies (limit use of perfumes and lotions), inform if getting sick, maintain personal hygiene, rehearsal needs, etc.

Notation/blocking: Discuss language, notation method, and established routine of confirming notation before moving on during rehearsals.

Understudy protocols: If there are understudies, establish how will they be incorporated/considered during the rehearsal process.

Running rehearsals

- Scheduling for actors: When possible, give 48 hours' notice before moments of intimacy will be staged or rehearsed. Under no circumstances should you give less than 24 hours' notice. (Take into account AEA rules)
- Company notices: Regarding the entire company, when possible, give 48 hours' notice; give no less than 24 hours' notice for "closed rehearsals."
- Accommodations: Discuss with the intimacy director and actors regarding needed rehearsal supplies such as knee pads, personal coverings, personal hygiene products, privacy screen, or coverings, etc.

Before technical rehearsals

- Scheduling: Confirm with the production team if there will need to be "closed rehearsals" scheduled for the initial spacing of intimate moments with actors once the company moves into the theatre (ideally before tech).
- Staff, designers & crew: Communicate content and context of intimate moments with those who will be in the theatre during tech. Inform of any restrictions: no cell phones, no access areas backstage, etc.
- Backstage: Determine and communicate backstage needs for actors' privacy that may need to be provided by tech department (e.g., privacy screens or quick change booths, etc.)
- Prop/costume: Determine and communicate personal coverings and other needs that may need to be provided for actors.

Before previews or opening

- Content notices: Communicate the content/context of intimate moments so audience relations/marketing can take appropriate measures. (This may already be in place—always ask.)
- FOH & audience management: When necessary, communicate and discuss protocols that may need to be in place based on possible audience reactions to extreme / violent intimate moments. Communicate these to FOH staff, acting company, and run crew etc.

After opening night

- Intimacy call: If requested, establish the schedule and attendees for movement/intimacy calls.
- Availability: Inquire whether the intimacy specialist can return or consult when putting in understudy or replacement actors
- Understudies, replacements, and put-ins: Communicate understudy rehearsal schedule and put-in rehearsals with partial/full acting company and if/when full tech elements will be added.
- Maintaining: Keep an eye on the action to maintain storytelling and safety.

Personal Hygiene Checklist during Staged Intimacy

For anyone in the room during rehearsals

- Be mindful of the smells that may exist on clothing, hair, or body such as hairspray, smoke, bug spray, perfume, aftershave, food smells, etc. It is recommended that folks avoid using strong-smelling body sprays during rehearsals
- Maintain a clean workspace, which includes rehearsal property items such as furniture, linens, and hand items. Use Febreeze, Lysol, and other cleaning/sanitizing items as needed to keep rehearsal items sanitized and smelling fresh.
- Maintain clean rehearsal clothing. Work with the costume department to establish a laundry schedule that will work with rehearsal clothing needs during rehearsal.

Personal hygiene kit for rehearsals

- When possible, put together a company personal hygiene kit that will live in the rehearsal hall.
- Items may consist of mints, Listerine (liquid or dissolving strips), menstrual hygiene products, spray deodorant, hand soaps and sanitizers, body or baby wipes, etc.

For those engaging in intimacy

Remember, you may be nose blind to your own personal smells or odor. Please take steps to maintain personal hygiene before engaging in any rehearsal that involves intimate staging. Be sure to do any or all of the following:

- Brush teeth, floss, use mouthwash or mints.
- Refrain from drinking coffee and/or eating during the break before staging intimate scenes. If that is not possible, be sure to brush teeth or use mouthwash prior to the start of rehearsal.
- Refrain from smoking before rehearsal. If that is not possible, wear an outer layer of clothing that can be removed to avoid bringing smoke smells into the room with you, and be sure to brush teeth or use mouthwash prior to the start of rehearsal
- Check with coworkers regarding possible allergens (nuts or other foods) and avoid those items on days when intimate staging will occur.
- Wash hands or use sanitizers thoroughly and often.
- If you feel under the weather or that a cold is coming on, alert stage management immediately; if COVID protocols are in place, follow as required.

Appendix E

Glossary of key terms

Terms & Language Acknowledgement

As noted in our introduction, this book contains vocabulary terms that are challenging to cite effectively given commonalities in language that are based on and evolved from general theatrical movement practitioners and the field of fight direction. Over the past decade (or more) existing language has been adopted or adjusted by intimacy professionals.

We find it important to note that as you read through these key terms in this text and in this glossary below, our usage and definitions stem from a variety of resources, such as workshops taken as part of the road to certification with IDC, most notably a workshop Alexis Black attended with lead instructors Tonia Sina, Claire Warden, Dan Granke, and Alicia Rodis, the Intimacy Directors International O'Neill's 9-day intensive intimacy workshop in February of 2019. In addition, Black and Newhauser gained knowledge from collaborations with many industry professionals, engagement with stage management students at Michigan State University in a classroom setting, experiences in the professions of movement direction and stage management, and while researching, building curriculum, and workshopping the course "Stage Managing Intimacy" created for IDC first taught in early summer 2020.

The following publications/trainings have also been resources when building out this glossary:

- The Pillars of Intimacy, crafted by Tonia Sina, Alicia Rodis, and Shioban Richardson
- Mentorship in staged intimacy practices for Alexis Black under Alicia Rodis (ID/IC), starting in 2016

- Mentorship and workshops in movement direction for Alexis Black under David Leong (Broadway fight director and Fight Master with the Society of American Fight Directors)
- Multiple workshops in intimacy direction from 2016–2020, including at conferences such as SETC and ATHE. Instructors were intimacy professionals such as Tonia Sina, Laura Rikard, Chelsea Pace, Dr. Kate Busselle, Alicia Rodis, and Teniece Divya Johnson.
- *Staging Sex: Best Practices, Tools, and Techniques for Theatrical Intimacy* by Chelsea Pace
- *Intimacy Direction: A New Role in Contemporary Theatre Making* by Jessica Steinrock, PhD.
- *Stage Management Theory as a Guide to Practice Cultivating a Creative Approach* by Lisa Porter and Narda E. Alcorn
- *We Commit to Anti-Racist Stage Management Education*, by Narda E. Alcorn and Lisa Porter, Howlround Theatre Commons, July 2020
- *Hold, Please*, by Miguel Flores, R. Christopher Maxwell, John Meredith, Alexander Murphy, Quinn O'Connor, Howlround Theatre Commons, October 2020

We acknowledge there will be ideas, terms, and themes that may have been utilized by like-minded professionals in addition to those cited above. It is important to note that there is a common vernacular within the theatrical field of movement and within the study of consent practices and that this common vernacular has become interwoven into the fabric of this industry.

Glossary of Terms

Acknowledgment Form—the written form that confirms performers' awareness of intimate storytelling involved in a role prior to their acceptance or declination of that role

Anchor points—positions of pressurized touch on the body, set by the involved actors and the intimacy director, that use support boundaries and stabilized points of contact during intimate or violent movement

Audience content notice—written or verbal notices that are intended to inform the audience of content that will be explored within a staged theatrical production

Audio cues—emotional expression through sound that has been incorporated into the set choreography and storytelling

Audition disclosures—written or verbal disclosures that include stage directions and/or directorial-based decisions on intimacy that may occur in the production (also known as content notices, intimacy moment lists or other terminology)

Boundaries—specific, defined areas on the body that are off-limits to touch for any reason, and any other personal limitations or adjustments regarding touch that will be respected by other performers (may include location and quality of touch)

Boundary checks—a system or ritual of verbal communication (and sometimes agreed-upon physical movements) that allows for performers to establish personal boundaries and confirm consent before engaging in theatrical partnering

Breath—inhalation or exhalation of air as storytelling for characters or a cue for actors

Choreography—the physical movements involved in staged intimacy, which may be impacted by elements such as tempo, duration, intensity, and more

Closure—the act, achievement, or sense of completing or resolving something[1]

Consent—voluntary agreement by an individual to a proposed action or series of actions. Consent in the practice of building physical theatre is a willingness to participate, partnered with the ability to say "no".

Consent check-in—a brief check-in to determine if any adjustments need to be discussed regarding set choreography due to illness, injury, or other circumstances

Context—the W's of a show: Who, What, Where, When, Why. Who is involved, what is the story, and where, when, and why is this particular story occurring? It is an understanding of the story that leads to staged intimacy, or the purpose of the scene or scenes to the overall arch of the story.

Contract rider—an amendment or addition to an existing contract

Cultural competency— required knowledge, research, training, and potentially lived experience that supports authenticity within culturally diverse storytelling in live performance

Cultural consultant—an individual who provides extensive knowledge (either through research and study or lived experience) of a specific culture or cultural experience; a cultural dramaturg.

Culture of consent—a workplace culture built upon respectful and conscientious communication, consensual preferred practices, mindful leadership and clear policies.

Desexualized language—language that is more clinical or neutral in tone regarding staged intimate content or scenes

Discomfort scale—a self-assessment tool that assists in understanding both boundaries and self-care

Distance—the space between actors, as well as the actions of their hands, faces, and bodies

Duration—the length of time the actors engage in a movement or a length of stasis between movements

Exit strategy—a multifaceted approach that allows egress for the performer before, during, or after staging intimacy

Expert power—the authority/influence a person has because of their educational background, knowledge base or expertise, or the perception of those things by others

Gaze—eye contact or the movement of the eyes of the actors

Guideposts—set moments that serve as check-ins or bases for actors in a series of choreographed movements that include both improvised and set moments

Harassment—any pressure or intimidation used to coerce someone into behaving a certain way, or behaviors that create a hostile work environment

Impact versus intent—intent: what the initiator of a behavior may have aspired to achieve from that behavior; impact: the experience a behavior creates for the recipient of the action or words

Informational power—the authority/influence a person has due to their holding of information that others may want or need, often exerted to protect a job or reputation

Initiation—initial movement into and out of actions

Intensity—level of pressure or tension in a moment of intimacy

Intimacy captain—the person responsible for maintaining movements involved in intimate storytelling while supporting safety and consent practices during the intimacy call and performance

Intimacy coordinator—movement specialists who choreograph scenes of intimacy and serve as an advocate for consent practices and procedures around rehearsing and performing moments of intimacy for the screen (film and television)

Intimacy consultant—a trained intimacy specialist who is brought on for a brief conversation or workshop that provides foundational tools for the performers within the run of a live production

Intimacy container—a term used to designate a specific section of the body or a series of movements in intimate storytelling

Intimacy content notices—verbal or written notices of intimacy movement contained within a script

Intimacy direction—a comprehensive approach to the creation of scenes or moments of intimacy on stage and screen

Intimacy director—a choreographer, an advocate for actors, and a liaison between actors and production for scenes that involve nudity/hyper exposed work, simulated sex acts, and intense physical contact in live performance

Intimacy mapping—a technique that clarifies intimate physical storytelling for actors and others on the creative team. Mapping the choreography or choreographic parameters for a moment of staged intimacy is done by applying definable physical elements such as tempo, distance, intensity, and shape to make movements more specific and repeatable.

Intimacy moment list—a list of moments in a production that clearly or potentially will contain staged intimacy

Intimacy movement call—a brief rehearsal before a performance that is set aside for the actors to check in with one another, reaffirm boundary agreements, and assess if there are any obstacles that need to be addressed in regard to intimate staging

Intimacy notation—written documentation of the physical movements and other storytelling elements in the moments or scenes of staged intimacy

Location—placement of hands, arms, or other parts of the actor's body

Mandatory reporter—an individual who, because of their position, is obligated to report incidents of harassment and/or violence to their relevant authorities (typically found in academia, social work, law enforcement, or religious institutions)

Masking—an action by or position of the actor(s) that conceals a physical action or position from the view of the audience

Modesty garments—robes, body stockings, or other garments that provide coverage for actors during breaks or pauses in rehearsals that involve staged nudity or scenes with scant clothing

Nudity—any full nudity of the chest, pelvis, or buttocks, or view of these body parts through sheer material

Open questioning—the practice of utilizing "May I" language when asking questions regarding personal boundaries

Pause words—an agreed-upon word or words that can be used by those engaging in staged intimacy to call for a brief pause (part of an exit strategy)

Permission—authorization for an action to occur; may be given by those in authority or in charge of leading a scene of staged intimacy, such as a director or choreographer

Personal barriers—hygienic coverings, support and/or padding for genitals and other sensitive areas that may be impacted during the staging and performing of more complex staged intimacy or nudity

Pillars—pillars for intimacy work that cover context, communication, consent, choreography, and closure (created by the founders of IDI)

Placeholder—substitute or "marked" actions in place of intimate actions such as kissing, simulated sexual movements, etc.

Placeholder removal date—a day agreed upon to end the substituting of movements and begin performing the fully realized movements choreographed in the staged intimacy

Power dynamics—real or perceived differences in power, hierarchy, authority, or knowledge in interpersonal and/or societal relationships that influence the ability for performers, crew, stage managers, etc., to consent fully

Punitive power—the use of threats and force or the implication of punishment for noncompliance

Red zones—a shorthand phrase, set by either a staged intimacy professional, director, or actor, that represents the physical area of the body that is prohibited to touch by others (also called "no go" or "no contact" zone)

Referent power—the authority/influence a person has due to an impression of their social or professional connections

Replacement performer—an actor who takes over a role when the current actor performing that role leaves the production

Reward power—the ability to offer rewards for compliance, expressed through motivation for others by offering raises, promotions, and rewards

Scantily clad—not fully clothed, such as appearing in a bathing suit or undergarments. May also be used to indicate the story of nudity, such as being wrapped in a towel or sheet

Shape—form or shape in space formed by the bodies of the actors engaged in a movement or moment of stasis

Show advance—verbal and written communication(s) between the staff of the presenting organization and the touring production clarifying and confirming details, requirements, and schedule before the tour's arrival at the venue

Staged intimacy—scenes with intimate physical contact, such as sex scenes and kissing (may be expanded to include familial and platonic intimacy, sexual tension, and "chemistry" where no touching occurs)

Tapping in/out—an action that is utilized as a kind of "mental bookend" to moments of staged intimacy, creating a threshold into and out of the work, separating actor from character (also known as checking in/closing out, or tagging in/out)

Technical rider—an addendum to a touring production's contract that sets forth their specific technical, production, hospitality, and other requirements or accommodations that need to be provided or arranged for by the presenting organization

Tempo—the speed at which the actors close or open distance or engage with an action

Thoughtful leadership—action and behaviors that are value-driven, do not induce harm to others, and work to create a conscientious and inclusive state of engagement; supports a level of awareness and empathy that encourages moral behaviors in a non-judgemental way

Title Power—the authority/influence a person has based on a specific title or role in an organization

Understudy performer—an actor hired to learn the part(s) of another actor in a production, so that they can replace them on short notice if necessary

Note

1 https://dictionary.apa.org/closure

Appendix F

A partial list of pertinent resources

Communication

    Annie E. Casey Foundation's terms & definitions   www.aecf.org/blog/lgbtq-definitions

    Disability Language Style Guide   www.ncdj.org/style-guide/

    Gay & Lesbian Alliance Against Defamation Media Reference Guide   www.glaad.org/reference/

    Human Rights Campaign's glossary of terms   www.hrc.org/resources/glossary-of-terms

    PFLAG's glossary of terms   www.pflag.org/glossary

Entertainment Services and Technology Association (ESTA) and the United States Institute for Theatre Technology's (USITT) guide to problematic terminology in theatre

www.usitt.org/news/esta-usitt-terminology-working-groups-launch-survey?fbclid=IwAR1XxavzHjgd2nYS-YsWa4yXC79Ul7d85i8E63xPWBiiF2QnX4Wk_54QlQk

Harassment and Reporting

    A Guide on Sexual Assault   www.florinroebig.com/sexual-assault-guide/

    Better Brave   www.betterbrave.org/

    League of Independent Theatres' toolkit   www.litny.org/antisexual-harassment-toolkit

    Love is Respect   www.loveisrespect.org/

    National Sexual Violence Resource Center   www.nsvrc.org/

National Alliance to End Sexual Violence	www.endsexualviolence.org/
National Online Resource Ctr on Violence Against Women	www.vawnet.org/
Rape, Abuse, & Incest National Network (RAINN)	www.rainn.org/
RAINN's National Sexual Assault Online Hotline	www.hotline.rainn.org/online
AC Online: Fighting Harassment at School and Work	www.affordablecollegesonline.org/college-resource-center/workplace-campus-harassment/
Workplace Guide for Transgender Individuals	www.learnhowtobecome.org/career-resource-center/workplace-guide-for-transgender-students/
Volunteer Lawyers for the Arts	www.vlany.org/

Human Rights & Individual Support

Actors Equity Association	www.actorsequity.org/
Art Equity	www.artequity.org/
Artists For Human Rights	www.artistsforhumanrights.org/
Artists Rights Society	www.arsny.com/
American Association of Community Theatre	www.aact.org/
American Association of Retired People	www.aarp.org/
American Association of University Women	www.aauw.org/
American Civil Liberties Union	www.aclu.org/
American Federation of Musicians	www.afm.org/
American Guild of Musical Artists	www.musicalartists.org/
American Guild of Variety Artists	www.agvausa.com/
American Society for Theatre Research	www.astr.org/
Americans for the Arts	www.americansforthearts.org/
Art 2 Action	www.art2action.org/
Association for Theatre in Higher Education	www.athe.org/

Black Theatre Coalition	www.blacktheatrecoalition.org/
Black Theatre Network	www.blacktheatrenetwork.org/
Black Theatre Commons	www.blacktheatrecommons.org/
Canadian Actors Equity	www.caea.com/
Consortium of Asian American Theatre & Artists	www.caata.net/
Directors Guild of America	www.dga.org/
Dramatists Guild of America	www.dramatistsguild.com/
Educational Theatre Association	www.schooltheatre.org/
Ella Baker Center for Human Rights	www.ellabakercenter.org/
Entertainment Services and Technology Association	www.esta.org/
Freelancers Union	www.freelancersunion.org/
Gay & Lesbian Alliance Against Defamation	www.glaad.org/
Guild of Italian American Actors	www.giaa.us/
Human Resources for the Arts	www.hrforthearts.org/
Human Rights Campaign	www.hrc.org/
Human Rights Foundation	www.hrf.org/
Human Rights Watch	www.hrw.org/
Indigenous Direction	www.indigenousdirection.com/
International Alliance of Theatrical Stage Employees	www.iatse.net/
International Theatre Institute	www.iti-worldwide.org/
Institute for Women's Policy Research	www.iwpr.org/
Job Accommodation Network	www.askjan.org/
League of Resident Theatres	www.lort.org/
NAACP	www.naacp.org/
National Assoc. Of Latino Arts and Culture	www.nalac.org/about/
National Conference of State Legislatures	www.ncsl.org/
National Dance Association	www.ndeo.org/
Off-Broadway League	www.offbroadway.org/
Production on Deck	www.productionondeck.com
SAG-AFTRA	www.sagaftra.org/

SAG-AFTRA Code of Conduct	www.sagaftra.org/sag-aftra-code-conduct
Stage Directors and Choreographers	www.sdcweb.org/
Stage Managers Association	www.stagemanagers.org/
The Actors Fund	www.actorsfund.org/
The Broadway League	www.broadwayleague.com/
The Craft Institute	www.thecraftinstitute.org/
The Movement for Black Lives	www.m4bl.org/
The Okra Project	www.theokraproject.com/
The Playwrights' Center	www.pwcenter.org/
Theatre Communications Group	www.circle.tcg.org/resources/edi
Times Up	www.timesupnow.org/
Title VI of the Civil Rights Act of 1964	www.justice.gov/crt/fcs/TitleVI
Title VII of the Civil Rights Act of 1964	www.eeoc.gov/statutes/title-vii-civil-rights-act-1964
Title IX of the Education Amendments Act	www2.ed.gov/about/offices/list/ocr/docs/tix_dis.html
United Nations Human Rights	www.ohchr.org/EN/pages/home.aspx
U.S. Equal Employment Opp. Commission	www2.ed.gov/about/offices/list/ocr/index.html
United States Institute for Theatre Technology	www.usitt.org/
University Resident Theatre Association	www.urta.com/
We See You W.A.T.	www.weseeyouwat.com/
WomenArts	www.womenarts.org/

Mental Health & First Aid

Actors Fund of Canada Mental Health Training	www.afchelps.ca/mhfa/
American Foundation for Suicide Prevention	www.afsp.org/
American Heart Association	www.heart.org/en
American Red Cross	www.redcross.org/
American Safety & Health Institute	www.emergencycare.hsi.com/

Appendix F

Behind the Scenes Mental Health training	www.wp.behindthescenescharity.org/mental-health-and-suicide-prevention-initiative/mental-health-first-aid-training/
Black Virtual Wellness Directory	www.wellness.beam.community/
Crisis Text Line, text "HOME" to 741741	www.crisistextline.org/
Hotline search engine	www.4help.org/
Inclusive Therapists	www.inclusivetherapists.com/
Lantinx Therapy	www.latinxtherapy.com/
Melanin and Mental Health	www.melaninandmentalhealth.com/
Mental Health First Aid	www.mentalhealthfirstaid.org/
Model First Aid Safety Training	www.modelfirstaid.com/
National Alliance on Mental Illness 1-800-950-6264	www.nami.org/help
National Safety Council	www.nsc.org/
National Suicide Prevention 1-800-273-TALK (8255)	www.suicidepreventionlifeline.org/
National Queer & Trans Therapists of Color Network	www.nqttcn.com/en/
NYC Well online service	www.nycwell.cityofnewyork.us/en/
Substance Abuse and Mental Health Services Administration 1-800-662-HELP	www.samhsa.gov/find-help/national-helpline
Taking Care —a series on mental health from Opera America	www.operaamerica.org/programs/events/conference-webinars/webinars/taking-care-a-series-on-mental-health-for-opera-professionals/?fbclid=IwAR2goO4kKUfSMeQt-AuJORxLIX4ZyxA9yUmVTlBux06gx3HVbKxYv5DNzjI
The Loveland Therapy Fund	www.thelovelandfoundation.org/loveland-therapy-fund/
The Trevor Project 1-866-488-7386	www.thetrevorproject.org/
Therapy for Black Girls	www.providers.therapyforblackgirls.com/
Therapy for Black Men	www.therapyforblackmen.org/
Veterans Crisis Line 1-800-273-8255	www.veteranscrisisline.net/
ZenCare - online therapist search	www.zencare.co/mental-health

Self-care

45 Simple Self-Care Practices, by Ellen Bard	www.tinybuddha.com/blog/45-simple-self-care-practices-for-a-healthy-mind-body-and-soul/
International Suicide Prevention Directory	www.suicideprevention.wikia.org/wiki/International_Suicide_Prevention_Directory
Mental Health America self-care	www.mhanational.org/taking-good-care-yourself#care
National Institute of Mental Health—self-care and mental health	www.nimh.nih.gov/health/topics/caring-for-your-mental-health/
TEDTalks on self-care	www.ted.com/playlists/299/the_importance_of_self_care
University at Buffalo's Self-Care Starter Kit	www.socialwork.buffalo.edu/resources/self-care-starter-kit.html

Index

Note: Page numbers in *italics* refer to figures.

accessories: and safety equipment, 124–125; tech and dress rehearsals, 194
accommodations: accessories, 194; costumes, 195–196; placeholders, 193–194; quick changes and crew, 195–196; touring, 218–221
accountability, 153–154
acknowledgement forms, 97, 107; educational situations, 115–116; questions/concerns, 116–117; staged intimacy, 117; storytelling, flexibility in, 117–118
Acrobat of the Heart (Growtowksi), 10
Actors Equity Association (AEA), 75, 81, 121, 143
Actors Fund, The, 79
advocacy, intimacy professionals, 39–48; actor, 47; artistic license, 46–47; definition, 40; designer, 48; director, 47; established practice, 44–46; fight choreographer, 47; money/funding, 41–42; rehearsal time, 43–44
AEA *see* Actors Equity Association
American Psychological Association, 30
American Red Cross's First Aid & CPR training, 37
American Theatre, 67
anchor points, 139, 148–149
anti-Black racism, 17–18
anti-harassment coalition, 21
anti-retaliation practices, 79
archival video taping, 123, 218

artistic: director, 73, 112; growth, 34, 35, *35*, *45*, 213; license, 46–47; research, 7
ASM *see* assistant stage manager
assistant stage manager (ASM), 214
Astrew, A., 84
audience content notice, 208–211, 220
audio cues, 158, 159, 178, 184
audition and callbacks, 105; acknowledgment forms, 115–118; auditioners, 106; context, forms, 116; director's vision, 106; failure, communication, 118–119; film and TV standards, 112–113; intimacy moment lists, 114–115; notices, 106–114; recasting, 119; students future agency, 118
audition disclosures, 63
audition notices, intentional phrasing, 111–112

backstage access, 190–191
backstage communication, 223
Bakkhai, 20
Bardwich, J.M., 44
Bellinger, B., 229, 230
Bennet, D., 74
Bentley-Quinn, K., 108
BIPOC *see* Black, Indigenous, and People of Color
Black, A., 3–5, 111, 112, 230, 246
Black, Indigenous, and People of Color (BIPOC), 23
Black intimacy, 49–50

Black Lives Matter (BLM) movement, 17–18
BLM *see* Black Lives Matter
Boal, A., 56
Bolender, C., 5
Bonnick, J., 192, 193
boundaries, 3, 10, 18, 19, 21, 26, 29, 32, 33, 34, 36, 38, 40, 46, 51, 71, 72, 77, 82, 85, 88, 106, 114, 116, 118, 119, 139, 141, 144, 145, 149–152, 154, 156, 173, 175, 176, 180, 200, 211, 213, 215–217
boundary checks, 148; agreement, not explain reasons, 151; blessings, 151–152; community-wide agreements, touch, 150; duration of time, 152–153; exercises, physical touch, 151; green, yellow, and red zones, 151; no-go zones, 150; opportunities, adjustment, 151; self-analysis, 150; verbalization and confirmation, 150; verbalizing yes zones, 151; verbal *vs.* physical, 152
breaks, 147–148
breath, character, 159–160, 160
Bridgerton, 24
Broadhurst Theatre, 188–189
Broadway productions, 22, 220
Broadway Stage Management Symposium 2020, 192–193
Broadway theaters, 229
Burgoyne, S., 31
Burke, T., 16–17

calling in, 84, 92
calling out, 83–84
camera use and visibility, 191–192
casting directors, 107, 110, 120, 121
check-in process, 135, 211–212
checklists, staging intimacy: after opening night, 244; in auditions, 240; condensed, 241; personal hygiene, 244–245; pre-production, 240, 242; before previews/opening, 244; in rehearsals, 240–241; running rehearsals, 243; before signing, 241; technical rehearsals, 243; things to discuss, 242–243
check-out process, 211–212
Chicago Reader, 19
Chicago Theatre Standards, 113, 157

child artists, 127–129
choreographic process, intimacy director: additional breaks, 147–148; anchor points, 148–149; approaches, 171–172; boundary check, 148; communication practices, supporting boundaries, 149–153; communication tips, boundary breaches, 153–158; desexualized language, 146; elements, staged intimacy rehearsal, 145–149; exit strategies, 147; fight choreographer and intimacy, 173; guideposts, 174–175; improvisation, 175; mapping, 158–170; masking, 149; multiple options, 176; pause word, 147; placeholders, 146; private *vs.* privacy, 146–147; stylistic differences, 174; tapping in and out, 148; time, scope, and collaboration, 173–174; written agreements/contracts, 176
Clair de Lune, 188–189
Clark, A., 68
closure practices, 30–31, 33, 56, 207, 226–228
Coen, S., 46
collaboration and intimacy direction, 55–56
communication: accountability, 153–154; awareness, location, 132–133; boundary breaches, 153–158; calling in, 84; calling out, 83–84; community accountability, 84; consistency, 192–193; and crew, 189–193; four-point script, 154–157; harassment, 82–85; healthful, 85; identity and inclusion, 130–131; metacommunication, 131–132; oops and ouch method, 157–158; pause words, 134; resolution in the moment, 82–83; styles, 130; supporting boundaries, 149–153; triumvirate of consent, 133–136
community-wide agreements, touch, 150
confidence *vs.* comfort, 34–35
consent, 26–28, 30, 32, 33, 38, 46, 48, 49, 56, 98; *see also* culture of consent; check-ins, 186–187, 196, 203; triumvirate, 103–105, 133; workshop, 142–144, 216
content notices, 63, 119, 188, 244; audience, 208, 209–211; intimacy, 97; and show advances, 219–220
context the W's of a show, 26, 27

contracts and riders, 97, 121–124; ability to amend, 123; acknowledged accommodations, 122–123; acknowledged dates, 122; actor contracts, 121; AEA, 121; archival video taping, 123; artists, 122, 123; communication, 123; employment agreement, 122; negotiations, 124; production company, 122; SAG-AFTRA, expectations, 121–122; signature page, 123; staging expectations, 122
Coriolanus, 10
costumes, 195–196
Cox, D., 19, 68
Crenshaw, K., 69
crew: orientation, 189–190; quick changes, 195–196
Cullors, P., 17
cultural competency, 48–49, 55, 56, 86, 101
cultural consultant, 39, 48, 56, 100, 101, 114, 229
culture of consent, 5, 7, 28, 48, 63, 98, 101, 103, 104, 106, 112, 130, 132, 204, 228, 235; communication techniques, 82–85; disclosures, 63, 113; harassment, 64, 73–79; institutional structure, 65, 66; mandatory reporter, 64; mental and emotional health, 85–86; power, types of, 68–73; power dynamics, 64, 66–68; questions, production, 86–88; reporting harassment, 79–82; sexual harassment and creating policy, 73–79; thoughtful leadership, 64–65

Dart, R., 19–20, 78
Daugherty, E.D., 195, 196
Death of a Salesman, 24
desexualized language, 98, 146, 190; abdomen area, 239; head and neck area, 238; lower extremities, 239; thorax area, 238; upper extremities, 239
Detroit Free Press, 68
Deuce, The, 21
Devised Theatre and Intimacy Checklist, 114, 240–241
directors, 120–121
disability justice and intimacy, 51
disclosures, 63, 113
discomfort scale, 34–36, 45, 151
distance between actors, *161*, 161–162, *162*

Dor, Y., 24
dramaturgy, 135–136
Drescher, F., 25
duration, actors movement, 163–164, *164*
Dynevor, P., 24

Education in Theatrical Intimacy as Ethical Practice for University Theatre (Shawyer and Shively), 38
EEOC *see* Equal Employment Opportunity Commission
ELLE magazine, 23
emotional audio cues, 159
emotional resilience and self-care, 224–225
Equal Employment Opportunity Commission (EEOC), 75
exit strategies, 140, 141, 147
expert power, 72, 103
extreme stage physicality, 158
Extreme Stage Physicality, 17

fat bodies and intimacy, 52
fight choreographer, 3, 10, 17, 47, 171, 173, 236–237
Fight Master, The, 10, 17
first rehearsal and orientation: consent workshop, 143–144; harassment policies, 143; introductions, 142–143
Fisher, L.T., 18
foundational vocabulary, staged intimacy, 31–34
four-point script, 154–157
Frankie and Johnny in the Clair de Lune, 22
Frederick, C., 23
French, J.R.P., 71

Garza, A., 17
gaze, actor, *166*, 166–167, *167*
Goldfeder, L., 159, 188, 189
Granke, D., 246
Growtowksi, J., 10
guideposts, 140, 174–175, 178

Haas, I., 120
harassment, 64; definition, 75–76; impact *vs.* intent, 76–77; #metoo movement, 74; organizational policy, 74–75; and

physical work, 74; policy, creation of, 78; RAINN, 76; reporting methods for, 79–82; retaliation, reporting process, 78–79; staging intimacy, 73, 74
Heartland Intimacy Design & Training, 18
Hennekam, S., 74
Herbsman, M., 51
Hertzberg, D., 195, 196
Hollywood, 12, 16, 20, 21, 23, 54, 66, 67
Hude, K.M., 124
Huffpost, 37
Humble Warrior Movement Arts, 40
hyper-sexualization, 23

ICOC *see* Intimacy Coordinators of Color
ID *see* intimacy director
IDC *see* Intimacy Directors and Coordinators
IDI *see* Intimacy Directors International
Impact of Acting on Student Actors: Boundary Blurring, Growth, and Emotional Distress, The, 31
impact *vs.* intent, 76–77, 91–92
informational power, 72
initiations, 162–163, *163*
institutional culture, 229–230
intensity, moment of intimacy, 168, *168*
intentional scheduling, 125
intersectionality: group dynamics, 70; multiple identities, human figure, 69, *70*; privilege and oppression, 69, *69*
intimacy; *see also* staged intimacy: consultant, 10, 33, 88; container, 140; content notices, 97; mapping (*see* mapping); moments list, 97, 107, 114–115; movement calls, 187, 201–204
intimacy captain, 187; candidates, 199–201; industry, 201; responsibilities, 199
Intimacy Captain Certificate workshop, 199
intimacy coordinator, 16, 32–33, 50, 113, 183; Black, 23–24; *Deuce, The*, 21–22; membership, 25; SAG-AFTRA, 24–25; training programs, 25
Intimacy Coordinators of Color (ICOC), 9, 18, 199
intimacy direction, 1, 4, 8, 10, 15, 16, 17, 26, 31, 32, 37, 40, 51, 52, 73, 75, 84, 116, 144, 145, 146, 149, 151, 159, 172, 173, 182, 192, 234; Broadway productions, 22; and collaboration, 55–56; consent, 33; goal, 36; license, 46; *New York Times, The*, 20; rates, 41; West End Theatres, 24
Intimacy Direction: A New Role in Contemporary Theatre Making (Steinrock), 15
intimacy director (ID), 5, 10, 19, 28, 41, 42, 45, 46, 49, 50, 52, 55, 97, 99, 101, 103–104, 105, 111, 113, 117, 120, 126, 127, 128, 133, 134, 136, 139, 140, 141, 142, 154, 171, 176, 177, 180, 181, 199, 200, 212, 217, 235; consent practices workshop, 143–144; definition, 32; maintaining intimacy, 145–149; mental health resources, 37; Oregon Shakespeare Festival, 22; West End Theatres, 24
Intimacy Directors and Coordinators (IDC), 5, 9, 10, 14, 15, 18, 22, 28, 34, 39, 70, 72, 89, 113, 134, 151, 158, 176, 246
Intimacy Directors International (IDI), 18, 19, 21, 26, 30, 33, 113, 120
intimacy organizations, 9; international companies, 234; practitioners, EDI work, 234; SAG-AFTRA industry protocols, 233; screen and film, 233; stage, 233
Intimacy Professionals Association (IPA), 18
intimacy specialists/directors (IS/Ds), 38
Intimate Encounters: Staging Intimacy and Sensuality, 17
IPA *see* Intimacy Professionals Association

James, A.C., 199
John Golden Theatre, 192
Johnson, T.D., 23, 50, 53
Journal of Consent-Based Performance, The, 16
Judd, A., 20

Kaplan, R., 69, *70*
Keller, H., 128
Killer Joe, 19
Kizer, M., 66
Kucan, D., 10

Latinidad and intimacy, 54–55
League of Independent Theater, 78
League of Resident Theatres (LORT), 74, 152

Lehmann, S.M., 74
Leong, D., 159
Let Us Work initiative, 19–20, 67, 78
Liem, C., 120
lighting designers, 197
Lincoln Center, 74
location, placement of hands and arms, 169, *169*
LORT *see* League of Resident Theatres
Lozoff, S., 5, 22, 172, 176

mandatory reporter, 64
mapping: audio cues, 159; breath, 159–160, *160*; distance, *161*, 161–162, *162*; duration, 163–164, *164*; gaze, *166*, 166–167, *167*; initiation, 162–163, *163*; intensity, 168, *168*; intimacy, 158; location, 169, *169*; shape, 170, *170*; tempo, 165, *165*
Martin, T., 17
masking, 117, 141, 149, 191, 197, 217
May I language, 141
MCARI *see* Minnesota Collaborative Anti-Racism Initiative
McDonald, A., 22
Meade, E., 21
Mendez, R., 173
mental and emotional health: Mental Health First Aid, 85; protocols, process, 85–86; resources, 85–86; theatrical productions, 37–39
Mental Health First Aid training, 37, 38
metacommunication, 131–132
#metoo movement, 16–17, 67, 74
Michael Chekhov method, 171
Michigan State University, 4, 10, 246
Mingus, M., 153
Minnesota Collaborative Anti-Racism Initiative (MCARI), 68
Miracle Worker, The, 128
Miramax, 20
modesty garments, 97, 125, 197
money/funding, 41–42
movement calls, 187, 201; cuing/production, 202; emotional content, 204; inconsistency, 202; performer confidence, 202; physicality, 202; practices, captains and stage management, 202–203

moving into theater: Broadhurst Theatre, 188–189; company information, 188; technical rehearsals, 187–188
Myers, L., 18

National Bureau of Economic Research, 73
National Council for Mental Wellbeing, 37
Newhauser, T.M., 2–5, 223, 230, 246
New York Times, The, 20, 22
Noble, A., 17, 151–152, 158
no-go zones, 150
notation, 140, 176–182; character name/symbol, 177, 178; clinical language, 177; director's intention, 177; privacy concerns, 181; style of, 179–180; tips, 178, *179*
notices, 106–108; acknowledgement forms, 107, 115–118; audition, 108–109, 111–112; casting, 107, 108–109, 111–112; casting notice, expanded details, 110–111; creatives, casting, 106; devised work and, 113–114; expanding intimacy, 109–110; film and TV standards, 112–113; intentional phrasing, 111–112; intimacy, 109–110; intimacy moments list, 107, 114–115; sample content, 108; vocabulary, 108; *Wendy and the Neckbeards*, 110–111
Not In Our House, 18
nudity, 21, 23, 25, 29, 30, 32, 36, 39, 42, 87, 96, 100, 106, 108, 110, 113, 117, 120, 122, 123, 146, 174, 176, 188, 190, 191, 197, 198, 218, 219, 221, 235, 237

Occupational Safety and Health Administration (OSHA), 87
Odcikin, E., 22
offering blessings, 151–152
O'Hara, R., 142
oops and ouch method, 157–158
open questioning, 141
Oregon Shakespeare Festival, 5, 22, 176
organizational structure, 65, 66
OSHA *see* Occupational Safety and Health Administration

Pace, C., 6, 10, 23, 46
pause word, 134, 141, 147
Penn, L., 22
Percy, M.C., 203, 204

permission, 33
personal barriers, 98, 125
pertinent resources, 253–258
pillars of intimacy, 19; change, 31; choreography, 29–30; closure, 30–31; communication, 28–29; consent, 26, 28; context, 26; terms and definitions, 27
placeholders: rehearsals, 146; removal date, 98, 146; technical elements, 193–194
PoD *see* Production on Deck
power: dynamics, hierarchy, 64, 66–68, 89–90; expert, 72; informational, 72; intersectionality, 69–70; punitive, 71; referent, 72; reward, 71; social, 70–73; systemic, 68; title, 71
Practical Approaches for Dealing with Extreme Stage Physicality, 17
practice scenarios, 230; artistic director, designer, production manager, 236; assistant SM, SM, fight choreographer, 236–237; crew heads and run crew, 237; director, ID, SM and lighting designer, 237; director, intimacy director and SM, 235; stage manager/assistant director, 235–236
pre-production process: accessories and safety equipment, 124–125; acknowledgment forms, 97, 107, 115–118; auditions and callbacks, practices for, 105–121; closed rehearsal protocols, 126–129; communication, creative team, 130–133; contracts and riders, 97, 121–124; desexualized language, 98, 146, 190; intimacy content notices, 97; intimacy moment list, 97, 107, 114–115; modesty garments, 97, 125, 197; personal barriers, 98, 125; placeholder, 98, 146, 193–194; rehearsal schedules, 125–126; script analysis, 98–105
President's Committee to Prevent Harassment, 75, 81
private *vs*. privacy, 146–147
Production on Deck (PoD), 65, 229
production pillars, intimacy: change, 31; choreography, 29–30; closure, 30–31; communication, 28–29; consent, 26, 28; context, 26; terms and definitions, 27
Profiles Theatre, Chicago, 19, 87

Proof that Positive Work Cultures are More Productive, 31
punitive power, 71

queer identity and intimacy, 52–53

RAINN *see* Rape, Abuse & Incest National Network
Ramos, C., 5, 40, 136
Rape, Abuse & Incest National Network (RAINN), 76
Rauscher, R., 220, 221
Raven, B., 71
recasting, 119
recommended practices *vs*. best practices, 11–12
Redman, S., 19
red zones, 141, 151
referent power, 72
rehearsals; *see also* technical and dress rehearsals: accommodations, performers, 181–182; anchor points, 139, 148–149; boundary checks, 140, 148, 150–153; choreographic process, intimacy director, 145–176; container, 140; exit strategy, 140, 147; first rehearsal and orientation, 142–144; guideposts, 140, 174–175; mapping, 140, 158–170; masking, 141, 149; notation, 140, 176–182; open questioning, 141; pause words, 141, 147; protocols, 126–129; red zones, 141, 151; responsible partnering, 144–145; riders, 182; schedules, 125–126; supporting change, process, 141–142; tapping in/out, 141; time, 43–44
replacements: emergency, 217–218; planned, 217
reporting harassment: availability, structure, 81; inclusivity, 81; TCG, 82; web-like structure, theatrical reporting, 79, 80, 80
resolution in the moment technique, 82–83
retaliation, reporting process, 78–79
reward power, 71
Rhimes, S., 24
Richardson, S., 19, 40, 46
Rodis, A., 19, 21, 113, 246

Roxborough, S., 66
RudduR Dance, 176

SAG-AFTRA *see* Screen Actors Guild and the American Federation of Television and Radio Artists
Saturday Night Live, 24
scenic design, 196–197
Screen Actors Guild and the American Federation of Television and Radio Artists (SAG-AFTRA): casting guidelines page, 113; improvements, nudity and simulated sex, 122; intimacy coordination accreditation program, 24–25; intimacy coordinator resources website, 113; membership, intimacy coordinators, 25; training programs, 25
script analysis, 98; directors and intimacy professionals, 103; stage manager, 99–102; triumvirate of consent, 103–105
SDC *see* Stage Directors and Choreographers
self-analysis, 150
self-care, 30
Sexual Content/Nudity (SC/N), 18
sexual harassment: communication, 82–85; definition, 75–76; impact *vs.* intent, 76–77; #metoo movement, 74; organizational policy, 74–75; and physical work, 74; policy, creation/modification, 78; RAINN, 76; reporting methods for, 79–82; retaliation, reporting process, 78–79; staging intimacy, 73, 74
Sexual Harassment in the Creative Industries: Tolerance, Culture and the Need for Change, 74
sexual violence, 3, 16, 18, 23, 32, 36, 76, 85, 100, 113, 121, 122, 188, 194, 218, 220
Shannon, M., 22
Shawyer, S., 38
Shively, K., 38
show, running of: accommodations, touring, 218–221; advance, 208; archival video taping, 218; audience content notice, 208–211; checking in and out, 211–212; closure practice, 226–228; emotional resilience and self-care, 224–225; maintaining performance, 212–215; replacement performer, 208; replacements, 217–218; technical rider, 208; transference energy and responsible communication, 222–224; understudies, 215–217; understudy performer, 208
Simon, D., 21
Sina, T., 10, 17, 19, 20, 120, 121, 246
Slave Play, 22, 142, 192
Smith, S., 23, 24
social power, 67; bases of, 71; expert power, 72; informational power, 72; punitive power, 71; referent power, 72; reward power, 71; team members, 72–73; title power, 71
sound: department and mic packs, 198; design, 197–198
Stage, The, 24
staged intimacy: advocating methods, intimacy professionals, 39–48; Black intimacy, 49–50; collaboration and direction, 55–56; cultural competency, 48–49; definition, 32, 100; and disability justice, 51; discomfort scale, 34–36; events surrounding, 15–25; fat bodies, 52; foundational vocabulary, 31–34; Latinidad, 54–55; mental health, theatrical productions, 37–39; necessary team, 49; production pillars, 26–31; queer identity, 52–53; specializations, 48–57
Stage Directors and Choreographers (SDC), 22
stage management, 2–3, 5, 10, 14, 30, 37, 81, 85, 92, 99, 101, 125, 126, 135, 143, 148, 168, 177, 179, 181, 182, 190, 192, 197–200, 202, 204, 213, 220, 235, 246
stage manager: consultants, finding of, 100–101; implied moments, 99–100; inspection, written dialogues, 99; tracking sheet, 101, *102*
Stage Managing Intimacy for Intimacy Directors and Coordinators, 103
Staging Sex: Best Practices, Tools, and Techniques for Theatrical Intimacy (Pace, C.), 6, 10, 23
Dr. Steinrock, J., 28, 34–35, 227, 228
Stern, M.A., 192, 193

Stratford Festival, the, 20
Sullivan, A., 128
systemic power, 66, 68, 71

tagging in and out, 148
Talbot, L., 24
tapping in and out, 148
TCG *see* Theatre Communications Group
technical and dress rehearsals: accommodation, actors, 193–198; communication and crew, 189–193; consent check-ins, 186–187; intimacy captains, 187, 199–201; intimacy movement calls, 187, 201–204; moving into theater, 187–189
tempo, actor, 165, *165*
Theatre Communications Group (TCG), 82
theatre creatives, 5–6
Theatre Hierarchy Chart, 65, 66
Theatre of the Oppressed, 56
Theatrical Intimacy Education (TIE), 18, 23, 46, 158
The Impact of Acting on Student Actors: Boundary Blurring, Growth, and Emotional Distress, 31
thoughtful leadership, 64–65
TIE *see* Theatrical Intimacy Education
Time's Up foundation, 21
title power, 71
Tometi, O., 17

Tran, D., 67
transference energy, 222–224
triumvirate of consent: director, 103, 104; intimacy director, 103, 104; members, 103; overlapping relationship, *104*; script analysis, 105; stage manager, 103, 104

understudies, 215–217

Vaughn, S., 10
VICE magazine, 120
Virginia Commonwealth University, 17

Wagner, D., 195, 196
Warden, C., 22, 37, 142, 154, 157, 200, 246
Waugh, R., 24
Weinstein, H., 16, 18, 20
Weinstein Company, the, 20
Wendy and the Neckbeards, 108; casting notice, expanded details, 110–111; intimacy moments list, 115
We See You movement, 23, 67
White American Theatre collective, 67
Wilcher, C., 5, 52
Wilson, B., 127, 129
written agreements/contracts, 176
W's of a show, 26, *27*

yellow zones, 151

Zimmerman, G., 17

For Product Safety Concerns and Information please contact our EU representative GPSR@taylorandfrancis.com
Taylor & Francis Verlag GmbH, Kaufingerstraße 24, 80331 München, Germany

www.ingramcontent.com/pod-product-compliance
Lightning Source LLC
Chambersburg PA
CBHW070556300426
44113CB00010B/1276